"This is Jim Rockford. . ."

THE
ROCKFORD
FILES

"This is Jim Rockford..."

THE
ROCKFORD
FILES

ED ROBERTSON

POMEGRANATE PRESS, LTD.
Los Angeles   London

This is a Pomegranate Press, Ltd. book.

"This is Jim Rockford..."
THE ROCKFORD FILES

All episode summaries included in this text
were written by the author, with the exception of
"A Blessing in Disguise," which was provided by Ren-Mar Studios.

Library of Congress Catalog Card Number: 95-068878
Tradepaper Edition ISBN: 0938817-36-1

First Printing: 1995
10 9 8 7 6 5 4 3 2

For Pomegranate Press, Ltd.:

Publisher/Editor: Kathryn Leigh Scott
Creative Director/Book design: Benjamin R. Martin
Cover design: Heidi Frieder
Cover photographs: Gene Trindl

Printed and bound in the United States of America
by
McNaughton & Gunn, Inc.
Saline, Michigan

POMEGRANATE PRESS, LTD.
Post Office Box 17217
Beverly Hills, CA 90209-3217

For Tony Maddox — Best of luck in Chicago

Acknowledgments

Part of the romance associated with being a private eye (at least, as seen in novels and in films) is the idea that you get to work alone. Certainly, Jim Rockford liked that aspect of his job — but he'd also be the first to admit that it never quite works out that way. There was always somebody who helped him when he needed it most, whether it was Beth Davenport or his dad Rocky bailing him out of jail, or Dennis Becker providing him with a crucial tip.

Of course, writing a book isn't quite as dramatic as some of the tasks that Rockford took on, although it is formidable in its own way — and it's certainly impossible to do without the help of a great many people. I hope I haven't overlooked anyone.

For their time, patience and professionalism in granting interviews, I thank Frank Price, Luis Delgado, Howard Browne, Jack Garner, Jack Wilson, Gretchen Corbett, and Jo Swerling Jr.

I am particularly indebted to James Garner, Juanita Bartlett, Charles Floyd Johnson, and Stephen J. Cannell, all of whom took time from the making of the new *Rockford Files* movies to take part in this project; and to Roy Huggins and Adele Mara, for not only answering dozens and dozens of questions, but for granting me access to their personal files regarding the series.

This book could not have been completed without the help of Francis Cavanaugh, Director of Photography, CBS-TV; Grace Curcio and Christine Trepczyk of the Cannell Studios; Kathy Ezso, Sally Scovel, and MaryAnn Rea of Ren-Mar Studios; Colleen Lightfoot of Mike Post Productions; Kimberly Koonen of Price Entertainment; Jennifer Allen; Dave Charmatz and Judith Currin of A&E; Ella Wells and Ann Gaines of MAD Magazine; Bobbi Delgado; Gene Trindl; Photofest of New York; Dennis Bertsch of Movieland Productions and David Martindale.

I also thank JoAnn and Selby Collins; Barry Gruber; Frank Free; Rusty Pollard; David Miller; Bob Charger; Stuart Shostak; Mary DeBoom and Jon Strauss; and Bob Rubin.

A big Thank You to the various members of the following organizations who provided assistance and/or information along the way: San Francisco Public Library; University of Southern California Reference Library; Certification Section, Civil Processing Division, Los Angeles County Records Center (special thanks to Dante for service above and beyond the call of duty); Screen Actors Guild; Directors Guild of America; National Academy of Television Arts and Sciences; ASCAP; Susan Chicone of Nielsen Media Research; and Sherry Ceiling of DeForest Research, Inc.

Special thanks to:

Burk Delventhal, Mariam Morley, Scott Emblidge, Mary Jane Sylvia, and Ron Baxter;

At Pomegranate Press: Kathryn Leigh Scott and Ben Martin;

Geoff Miller, for all your warmth and hospitality;

Michael Wright; my mother Josephine Robertson; my family; my friends;

and

Cathy McCarthy, with much love.

AUTHOR'S NOTE

As Count Galeazzo Ciano observed in his *Diary* of 1942 (and which was echoed by President John F. Kennedy after the Bay of Pigs incident two decades later): "As always, Victory finds 100 fathers — but Defeat is an orphan."

There are two "fathers" to *The Rockford Files*, Roy Huggins and Stephen J. Cannell; not surprisingly, each has his own version of how the series came to be. According to Cannell, *Rockford* was borne out of an emergency situation brought on by the Writers Guild strike of 1973. Whereas script preparation of television series scheduled to premiere in the fall usually commenced sometime in the spring, because the writers' strike did not settle until mid-summer, the production schedules for many series (including *Toma*, a police drama on which Cannell worked as a writer/producer) were thrown out of whack. Cannell recalls Roy Huggins, the executive producer of *Toma*, determining that the series was going to have trouble meeting its airdates (and, specifically, that the fifth episode of the show was still going to be in the lab the week it was scheduled to go on the air); in order to buy themselves some time, Huggins decided to shoot two episodes of *Toma* simultaneously. Huggins gave Cannell a story [which introduced a private investigator named Tom Rockford] and told him to turn it into a teleplay as soon as possible, so that they could begin filming. Five days later, Cannell delivered the pilot script.

Huggins' account of the origin, however, is considerably less dramatic — once he learned of James Garner's desire to return to television, he decided to reincarnate *Maverick* as a contemporary private eye series. However, while Huggins' and Cannell's versions are distinctly different, they are not entirely opposite. Huggins had originally intended to produce the *Rockford* pilot as an episode of *Toma*, although those plans were almost immediately abandoned. And there was a breakdown in *Toma*'s production schedule (series star Tony Musante injured his leg in November 1973) that had an adverse impact on the show's ability to have the episodes that were scheduled for broadcast in December filmed, processed and delivered to the network on time. Both Huggins and Frank Price, who was at the time the President of Television at Universal Studios (where *Toma* was produced) recall these circumstances; however, neither remember this or any other emergency having any bearing on the creation of *The Rockford Files*.

Cannell, in fact, did not actually enter the picture until several weeks after Huggins had developed the idea of *The Rockford Files* and presented it to Price for approval. However, it is without question that once Cannell did become involved, he made several significant contributions to the creation of *The Rockford Files*. According to Huggins, Cannell is largely responsible for the style of the pilot episode, which in turn provided the basis for the style of the series. In addition to enhancing Huggins' original concept of the Rockford character (such as originating Rockford's peculiar preference to live and work out of a trailer), Cannell created two of *Rockford*'s regular characters — Angel and Rocky. Cannell also suggested that Mike Post and Pete Carpenter compose the music for the series.

The problem with trying to conform various accounts of a given story is that regardless of how hard you try, the details will never quite mesh perfectly. However, as I reviewed the transcripts of my interviews and pored over the various documents and accounts regarding *The Rockford Files* that I collected over the course of my research, it became clear to me that the creation of the series was indeed a collaboration. Therefore, a true picture of the events pertaining to its origin can be gleaned from both Huggins' and Cannell's accounts of the story. This, ultimately, is what this book attempts to provide.

Table of Contents

Introduction

He looked like Steve McGarrett. He dressed like Joe Mannix. But he acted like no other private detective prime time television had ever seen. When he threw a punch, Jim Rockford (James Garner) was more likely to hurt his own hand than his opponent. He rarely carried a gun (he didn't have a permit), and on those occasions when he did, he was more likely to point the weapon than fire it. Rockford hated trouble, wouldn't hesitate to quit in the middle of a case if things got too rough, and had no qualms about telling you why ("You're damned right I'm afraid!"). And he never forgot the bottom line — he charged $200 a day ("*plus* expenses") for his services, although he usually found that his clients stiffed him more often than paid him.

Most private eyes (at least, the ones who are portrayed on television) have a police contact. But because Rockford was an ex-con (he was unjustly convicted of armed robbery and served five years in prison before receiving a full pardon), he didn't always trust the police. For that matter, nearly everyone in the Los Angeles Police Department despised Rockford because he had a penchant for solving cases that the cops had either closed or considered unsolvable. (In fact, every time the P.I. showed up at headquarters with a broken nose or a bloody lip, morale in the department automatically went up ten percent.) The one exception was the overworked and grossly underappreciated Sergeant Dennis Becker (Joe Santos), who genuinely liked Rockford even though he was occasionally embarrassed by their relationship (particularly whenever it interfered with his police duties).

Rockford had a lot of other characteristics that TV audiences could identify with. He had a paunch (he had a weakness for Oreo cookies). He also liked to drink beer and eat fast food (in one episode, Becker calls him "the taco king"). He preferred watching baseball and basketball games over the theater or opera. He didn't like to exert himself (if he could, he'd spend all day fishing on the beach). He didn't like going to the dentist (he once put off a root canal appointment three times). He'd go to any lengths (even asking for a note from his doctor) to avoid jury duty.

Rockford could be a rascal — he was once considered one of the finest grafters in the business. But he also had a sweetness that particularly came across in his relationship with his father, Joseph "Rocky" Rockford (Noah Beery) — a retired truck driver who doesn't quite understand what his son does for a living. Rockford had a big heart (sometimes, despite himself), which explains why he occasionally worked *pro bono* for his friend and attorney Beth Davenport (Gretchen Corbett). But he also had a limited amount of patience, which was often exhausted by the exasperating antics of his former cellmate Angel Martin (Stuart Margolin).

Fueled by excellent writing, memorable characters, and the star power of James Garner, *The Rockford Files* enjoyed a solid five-and-a-half-season run on NBC (1974-1980), and remains one of the most popular television programs of all time. Reruns of the 118 original episodes have played continuously in syndication and on national cable TV over the past 15 years. The Emmy Award-winning series returned to prime time in 1994 as a series of two-hour movies on CBS — the first of which, "I Still Love L.A.," was the highest-rated TV-movie of the 1994-95 season.

The enduring popularity of *The Rockford Files* is remarkable, considering that (with the exception of one season) the show was only marginally successful in the ratings. After its first year, when it finished in the Top 20, *Rockford* lost nearly 20% of its total audience in its second season. Although the series would never recover the viewers it had lost, it held onto the majority of the viewers it still had, registering solid if not spectacular audience figures during its final four seasons on NBC. (Ironically, the series was panned by a number of TV critics during its first season, when it was a ratings smash; yet it proceeded to win five

Emmys — including the Best Dramatic Actor award for Garner in 1977, and the Best Dramatic Series award in 1978 — during the years when its audience numbers were considerably lower.)

The Rockford Files was one of the first shows to add a whimsical sense of humor to the TV detective genre — just as *Maverick* was the first to infuse humor in the Western genre nearly 20 years before. Not coincidentally, both series were conceived and produced by Roy Huggins. *Rockford* was also the show that thrust Stephen J. Cannell into the upper tier of television producers — Cannell collaborated with Huggins on the creation of the series, and took over the reins of the show after Huggins' departure at the end of the first season. It was under Cannell's direction that *Rockford* won the Emmy for Best Dramatic Series in 1978. *Rockford* also provided a launching pad for writer/producers Juanita Bartlett (*Scarecrow and Mrs. King, In the Heat of the Night*), David Chase (*Northern Exposure*), Jo Swerling (*The Commish*) and Charles Floyd Johnson (*Magnum, P.I.*). The series also brought into prominence the innovative music duo of Mike Post and Pete Carpenter.

The Rockford Files has stood out in the public consciousness for reasons ranging from the singular characterizations portrayed on the show, to the wacky phone messages that began each episode, to the tremendous appeal of James Garner himself. I became particularly reminded of this as I conducted research for this book. Whenever I was on the phone seeking information from libraries, newspapers, and other media outlets, once I mentioned the subject of my book, the person on the other line would inevitably bubble, "You know, that has always been my favorite show!" *"This is Jim Rockford..."* examines what made *The Rockford Files* appealing, as well as how the series demographics gradually changed from its initial, older core audience to encompass viewers of all ages.

The Rockford Files has also survived despite a number of controversies that plagued the series behind the scenes. NBC was initially reluctant to finance the pilot because of its previous experience with Garner (an ill-fated Western series called *Nichols*); even after it eventually ordered *Rockford*, the network still didn't understand the show's sophisticated sense of humor. A conflict between Garner, Huggins and executive producer Meta Rosenberg led to the departure of Huggins after the first season. Problems fomented by a different approach to the show's humor during the second season first led to an angry confrontation between Garner and Universal Television president Frank Price, then ultimately resulted in the significant loss in audience mentioned above. A power play between Universal Studios and Garner's production company resulted in the loss of one of the show's most popular characters. Finally, the abrupt end of *The Rockford Files* (brought on by Garner's illness), coming on the heels of a startling report indicating that the series was $9 million in the red, precipitated a bitter legal battle between the actor and the studio that would last nearly ten years. We'll explore these aspects of the show's history in detail.

I also discovered, as I conducted interviews for this book, that the people who made *Rockford* also remember the series with affection. Ask anyone who has ever worked on the staff or crew of a James Garner production, and they will all characterize their experience in one word — family. You'll get a sense of what that environment was like through the recollections of many members of the Garner family — Juanita Bartlett, Jo Swerling, Luis Delgado, Gretchen Corbett, Charles Floyd Johnson, Jack Wilson, and Jack Garner. In addition, Roy Huggins, Stephen J. Cannell and Frank Price will walk us through the events leading to the premiere of the series. Plus, you'll hear from James Garner himself — the actor, the director, the employer, and the man.

"This is Jim Rockford..." This is the history of *The Rockford Files*.

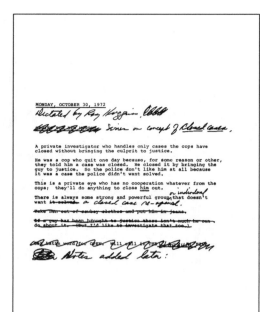

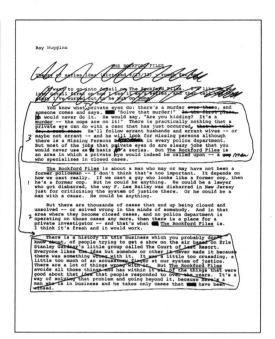

Above, left to right: Two early drafts of Roy Huggins' concept of *The Rockford Files*, both of which were transcribed from tape recordings made during one of his "story drives." Note that, according to the 1972 document, Huggins had apparently given thought to casting Ben Murphy (one of his stars on *Alias Smith and Jones*) as the "private investigator who handles cases the cops have closed."

From the personal file of Roy Huggins, and reprinted with his permission.

Part 1:

Thank You, Jane Musante
(or)
"I Guess We'll Have to Do This One"

The roots of *The Rockford Files* date back to October 1972, when Roy Huggins first gave thought to a television series concerning "closed cases." The protagonist would be "a private investigator who handles only cases the cops have closed without bringing the culprit to justice," Huggins wrote at the time. "He was a cop who quit [the force] one day because, for some reason or other, they told him a case was closed. He [finally] closed the case by bringing the guy to justice, so the police don't like him at all because it was a case the police didn't want solved." Huggins believed a series of this kind would be open to many dramatic possibilities, given the nature of closed cases: "There is always some strong and powerful group or individual that doesn't want a closed case re-opened." Huggins initially called the project *The Clausum Files*, after the Latin word for "closed."

However, Huggins couldn't develop that idea right away because he was busy with another project — the pilot for a series based on the exploits of New Jersey undercover police detective David Toma. The fact that Huggins was producing a straight police drama was somewhat unusual, considering that most of the writer/producer's other series were the antithesis of traditional law-and-order shows. *Maverick*'s protagonist was a con artist; *The Fugitive* centered around a man escaping from an unjust murder conviction (and an obsessed police lieutenant); *The Outsider* was about an underprivileged, underpaid P.I. whose chief antagonist was the Police Department; the attorneys on *The Bold Ones* were always getting their clients out of jail (after they'd been put there by less-than-honest police officers); *Alias Smith and Jones* concerned two career outlaws who were seeking amnesty (while trying to avoid the numerous bounty hunters determined to turn them in); and *Cool Million* was about a detective who charged his clients one million dollars per case.

But after meeting David Toma, Huggins discovered that the detective had more in common with his television characters that he'd first imagined. The real Toma was a maverick, insofar as he was frequently in conflict with his colleagues in the police department. He was also, by his own admission, a consummate con artist who often used disguises in his work. And, like the lawyers in *The Bold Ones*, Toma had infinite compassion for those who suffered arrest and trial — he once had to seek medical treatment because the prospect of testifying against persons he would like to have seen released made him physically ill.

What really made *Toma* peculiar, however, was the situation facing Universal Studios with regard to star Tony Musante. Prior to agreeing to do the series, the talented but intense performer had made it clear to the studio, and to Huggins, that regardless of how popular *Toma* might become (or how lucrative making the series might prove to be), he would star in the series for no more than one year.

Although Huggins believed Musante was serious when he first stated his position, he did not actually think the actor would carry it out. "I told the people at the Black Tower [the building housing the executive offices of MCA, Universal's parent company] that I didn't believe we should take Tony's statement seriously," he said. "I figured that if the show was a hit — even if he *hadn't* said that business about only doing it one year — he would come to us and ask for a new contract. I wanted the people in the Tower to know what Tony had said, even though I didn't believe there would ever be a problem."

Neither did the studio. In fact, according to Frank Price, regardless of what Musante may have said, the actor was contractually bound for a second season of *Toma* — provided that ABC renewed the series. "At the time we'd made the *Toma* pilot, I had made a deal with Tony Musante, whereby after the first season, he would have been obligated to do only 13 shows a year [as opposed to a full season of 22 shows], each additional year that *Toma* was on, up to another four years," Price said. "I made that deal because I couldn't get Tony to commit to doing every show [other than in the first year]."

In the meantime, Huggins, who was apparently unaware of these negotiations, did everything he could to accommodate Musante in order to keep him interested in doing the series. For instance, Huggins, who personally developed most of the stories for *Toma* (as was his practice on all his other television series), began meeting regularly with his star and soliciting his input on the stories that were planned for the show. On one such occasion during the summer of 1973, Huggins invited Musante and his wife Jane to his Bel Air home to discuss a story he had written about a woman who hires a derelict to "stand in" for her wealthy fiancé (who had died only hours before their wedding) so that she can "stage the marriage" and inherit the dead man's fortune.

Although the Musantes liked the story, they weren't convinced it was the right kind of story for *Toma*. "In fact, Jane Musante suggested that it might work better as a private eye story," Huggins said. "I thought about it, and I agreed with her. So I laid that story aside, thinking that I might come back to it later, and we continued discussing other stories for *Toma*." In hindsight, that was one of the best things that ever happened to Huggins. "And I thank Jane Musante at least once a month for giving me another series," he chuckled.

A short while later, Huggins received a telephone call from his brother-in-law Luis Delgado, whose personal friendship and professional association with James Garner spans nearly 40 years. Delgado informed Huggins that Garner was interested in doing another television series. "Luie, that's very good news," Huggins told Delgado. "I'll come up with something for Jim."

Huggins thought back to the story he'd first developed for *Toma* (the one that Jane Musante suggested had the makings of a private detective story) and decided to rework it as a possible vehicle for Garner. So he took to the road — literally — as was part of the routine he practiced while developing stories for all his television series and movies. Huggins would embark on a three-or-four-thousand mile drive, and dictate stories into a tape-recorder while he drove; four or five days later, he'd return to the studio with several tapes' worth of stories that included not only a detailed plot, but notes pertaining to characterizations, the nature of the relationships in the story, and actual dialogue. By the time they were transcribed, Huggins' stories were often longer than the script for which they would be written.

Huggins not only reshaped his murder mystery into a private eye story, but incorporated the character he had first sketched nearly a year earlier. By the time he was finished, Huggins had developed the "private investigator who only handled closed cases" into a character that bore a striking resemblance to his greatest television creation. "I wanted to develop the story as a pilot for Jim," Huggins recalled, "and then I decided that I ought to do *Maverick* as a private eye series."

Maverick (ABC, 1957-1962) was the revolutionary Western that not only made James Garner a star, but launched Huggins into the upper echelon of television producers. In an era in which prime time television was saturated with Westerns featuring traditional altruistic heroes who never hesitated to involve themselves in the plight of others, *Maverick* depicted a man who *did* think twice — and whose first thought was usually "What's in it for me?" He was a man who avoided trouble, but who would tackle it head on if left with no choice; who relied on his wits more often than on his gun; and who unabashedly never lost sight of his own self-interest. Maverick's attitudes may have been socially unacceptable, but television audiences loved him — the series was a Top Ten hit during its first two years on the air.

Maverick was developed at a time when both Huggins and Garner were under contract at Warner Bros. Around the time when Huggins first conceived the idea for the series, he discovered that Garner had an instinct for playing the kind of humor that made *Maverick* work — a subtle, wry, understated humor that was based on a total understanding of the character's thoughts and motivations. "I don't think there's ever been anyone like Jim Garner playing that kind of character," said Huggins. "That is a traditional role — the sly con man with a twinkle in his eye, who is willing to change his opinion *in a second*. It is the country bumpkin who is really *very* smart, who surprises you by being smarter than the city slickers — but who also is modest, and wry, and underplayed. And also, of course, a man who tries *never* to appear to be stalwart and brave.

"Some lines, like punch lines or joke lines, are almost always funny, no matter how they are read. But humor that genuinely works is the kind that comes out of character — it's funny only if the actor knows what the character is thinking as he is saying those lines. That's what Jim does so well. And to this day, I have no idea why that particular character was so clear to Jim — I'm not even sure if Jim knows. But there's no question that he was the perfect vehicle for *Maverick*."

Huggins figured that what worked once before, could work again. "I had great faith in Jim Garner," he reasoned. "I figured that if I did a private eye series in which Jim played Maverick, it would be a tremendous success." So Huggins developed a modern-day private eye who was the spit and image of Bret Maverick — a character who would argue with a woman client over whether she would pay for his lunch; who is more likely to get hurt whenever he's in a fight, so he has to think his way out of trouble; and who absolutely does not want to be a hero. Huggins christened his new creation "Tom Rockford." "I thought it had the right sound," he said. "It was a rugged-sounding name for a character who was anything but rugged."

Because Huggins was busy producing *Toma*, he originally designed *The Rockford Files* (as he now called the pilot) as an episode of *Toma*. Huggins' original story called for a scene at the outset of the episode establishing that Detective Toma had been probing the circumstances surrounding the death of the derelict on behalf of the old man's daughter. Although Toma believed there was something strange about the case, his initial investigation led him nowhere; as a result, his superior officer Spooner (played by Simon Oakland) ordered him to put the case aside. But the conscientious Toma wouldn't let the matter rest, and so he advised the girl to bring the case to his friend Tom Rockford, a private investigator who only handled closed cases.

In mid-September 1973, Huggins presented *The Rockford Files* to Frank Price. Price was very familiar with Huggins — they had worked together years before on *The Virginian* (NBC, 1962-1970), and they were also related to each other (Price is Huggins' son-in-law). Price liked the concept and gave Huggins the go-ahead to develop *Rockford* as an episode of *Toma*. In October 1973, Huggins gave the task of writing his story as a teleplay to Stephen J. Cannell, the immensely talented individual who was also a producer on *Toma*.

Cannell not only completely understood Huggins' concept, he added nuances of his own, so that by the time the script was finished, private eye Rockford and the world in which he lived were the collaborative efforts of two great talents. The inspiration for one such embellishment came out of Cannell's reactions to an episode of *Mannix*, the long-running CBS private eye series starring Mike Connors. "The day before I started writing," Cannell began, "I'd seen this episode in which a little black girl who had lost her mother comes to Mannix and says, 'Mr. Mannix, my mother's missing, and I don't know where she is. My little brother and I are alone at home. We can't find her. You're a private investigator, can you help me?' Mannix says to the little girl, 'Why, yes. I absolutely would.' The girl then asks, 'How

Stephen J. Cannell   **Roy Huggins**

much do you cost?' And Mannix says, 'How much have you got?' So the little girl reaches into her pockets, pulls out some lollipops and quarters, and dumps them on Mannix's desk. Mannix looks at the girl and says, 'That's just the right amount.'

"As soon as I saw that, I thought, Bingo! If that same little girl went up to Rockford, he'd say, 'What, are you kidding me? I've got expenses!' That locked me into that whole idea of how Rockford was this kind of guy that never did anything for free, because he had to pay his bills — in fact, that sequence [at the beginning of the pilot] where he ran the credit check on Lindsay Wagner came right from that *Mannix* episode."

The longer Cannell wrote, the quirkier Rockford became — and the more Cannell became delighted with the character. "I was having so much fun writing it," he continued. "Every time Rockford was threatened, he'd quit. It was so much fun to write something that you'd never been able to write before — where if somebody threw a gun down on him, he'd say, 'Look, I've been giving this some more thought, and I just don't think that there's much more that I can really do.' And then I would have him present Lindsay Wagner with itemized lists of his expenses: 'Now, I didn't charge you for the gas, or for the time I peeled rubber, but it's x-number of cents a mile,' and so forth and so on. And she'd look at him and say, 'What is it with you and these lists?'"

Rockford's reluctance and unceasing self-interest, of course, were characteristics that were present in Huggins' original concept — just they had been, years before, on *Maverick*. But Cannell, without question, understood the concept, almost as well as Huggins himself did. And Cannell added several facets to Huggins' story, including the creation of two of *Rockford*'s most memorable characters.

"I had originally written a very commonplace character — a semi-heavy who I had not considered to be very important," Huggins said. "Steve took that character and came up with Angel, which I thought was an absolute stroke of genius."

Just as Rockford is a modern-day version of Bret Maverick, Angel Martin is reminiscent of Dandy Jim Buckley, the character Roy Huggins had designed as a contrast to Maverick —

both are grafters, but only Maverick has something of a conscience. Similarly, while Rockford is somewhat mercenary, he does have his principles — he'd turn down a case if he thought it would be a waste of the client's money. Angel, on the other hand, would do just about anything for a buck (including advertising himself as a hit man just to collect the front money).

Whereas Mannix had a posh downtown office, Cannell had Rockford operating out of a house trailer ("It's cheap, tax-deductible, earthquake-proof, and when I get a job out of town, I take it with me"). In Cannell's first draft, the trailer was located in a vacant downtown lot; however, by the final draft, the trailer had been relocated to the beach. While Mannix had a dedicated secretary, Rockford's "support staff" consisted of a telephone answering machine.

Cannell then made one other important change. "I'd always been amused by the fact that no character in private-eye history, that I could recall, ever had a family," he recalled. "They were always such iconoclastic, lone characters. It's like the Greek gods never had families. So I thought, 'I'm going to give this guy a family. I'm going to give him a dad.'"

Cannell decided to pattern Rockford's relationship with his father after his relationship with his own dad. "I named him after my father, Joseph Cannell," he said. "My father had an interior design business in Los Angeles [where Cannell was born and raised] which he wanted me to inherit. And when I became a writer, my dad thought I was the stupidest guy on the planet! Now, he's my best friend, but he just couldn't understand why I would want to be a writer — he would just say to me, 'Why would you want to do that, when you've got this business waiting for you?'

"So I decided that I was going to write Rockford's dad like he was my dad — because my father was very embarrassed that I'd passed up the family business. His friends would ask, 'Hey, what's Steve up to these days?' And my dad would have to say, 'Well, he's walked away from my company, and he's scratching around out there with all those guys with gold chains around their necks.' He was very embarrassed."

So Rockford was going to have a father—Joseph Rockford (affectionately known as "Rocky"), who drove a truck and who had no idea of what his son did for a living. In fact, in one episode also written by Cannell ("The Four Pound Brick"), Rocky stretched the truth by telling a friend that his son "is really a truck driver who only does private investigation on the side."

"Look at it my way," Rocky explains to Rockford later in the episode. "If I tell folks that my son's in trucking, right away they know what I'm talking about. But if I tell them my kid's in the private eye business — they just don't understand."

Because Rocky doesn't understand what his son does any better than his friends do, Rockford tries to explain his work from time to time. But it isn't always easy to do. "When you're driving a rig, you know that Lancaster is ten miles down the road," he tells his dad. "But when I'm on a case, a lot of times I don't know what's down the road."

In the meantime, at some point between the time Cannell began writing the script in mid-October 1973 and the time it was completely drafted in early November 1973, a decision had been made regarding *The Rockford Files*. Instead of being developed as a spinoff of *Toma*, the pilot was now being planned as a possible 90-minute made-for-TV movie.

Huggins read the script and thought it was "beautiful." Cannell had perfectly reincarnated Bret Maverick — interestingly enough, without having any knowledge of who Huggins had in mind to play Rockford. Cannell had figured that the role would go to an actor like James Wainwright, a "leading man" type who was under contract to the studio, and therefore easily accessible. (In fact, Wainwright had recently starred in a private detective series for Universal —*Jigsaw*, in 1972-1973.)

In truth, Price and Huggins had begun exploring other possibilities in the event that Garner either didn't like the pilot or was somehow unavailable to do it. "I had discussed casting with Roy, and one of the things I had discussed was the idea of Robert Blake playing Rockford as a 'short' detective—because you're always looking for something that makes your show a little different," recalled Price. "I had seen *Electra Glide in Blue* (1973), a feature starring Robert Blake, and I was very amused by it, because the makers of that film took advantage of the fact that Blake was short. I particularly thought the humor that was involved in *The Rockford Files* would work if Rockford was a short detective. There's that scene in the pilot, for example, where the big guy (William Smith) is following Rockford, and Rockford has to go into the men's room, where he puts the soap on the floor. That scene would go over very well if you had a little guy playing Rockford."

In fact, when the word spread that Price had been considering a "not too tall" lead to play Rockford, a casting executive at the studio sent Price a memo recommending character actor Terry Kiser (*Weekend at Bernie's*) for the role.

Today, it may sound sacrilegious to think of anyone other than James Garner playing Rockford. But you have to keep two factors in mind. First, not only did Price consider other actors in case Universal couldn't get Garner, but Huggins himself already had an auxiliary plan in the making. "If I had ever done *Rockford* without Jim Garner, I might not have used the 'Maverick character,'" Huggins said. "I might have made Rockford more like the character I used in *The Outsider* — a loner who was a little put-upon, and somewhat rough around the edges."

In fact, in the notes for his September 1973 presentation to Frank Price, Huggins wrote that *The Rockford Files* "is about a man who may or may not have been a former policeman — I don't think that's too important. It depends on how we cast, really. If we cast a guy who looks like a former cop, then he's a former cop. He could be a lawyer who got disbarred, or he could be a man with a cause. He could be anything." Think of Rockford in those terms, and the idea of another actor playing hi—be it Robert Blake, James Wainwright, or even Darren McGavin (who starred in *The Outsider*)—is not incongruous.

The second factor to consider is that Universal had reservations about working with Garner that stemmed from the fallout surrounding the actor and NBC over Garner's previous television venture, a short-lived series called *Nichols*. "There was a general feeling, which I believe emanated from NBC, that Garner and Meta Rosenberg [Garner's agent and business partner] could be difficult to work with," Price recalled. "NBC had worked with Jim and Meta on *Nichols*, and that proved to be a very negative experience."

An offbeat, turn-of-the-century Western, *Nichols* attracted a lot of attention when it premiered on NBC in September 1971. The series marked Garner's return to weekly television after a ten-year motion picture career, and it was also produced by Garner's Cherokee Productions company for Warner Bros. (the studio that Garner had defeated in court in a 1960 breach-of-contract dispute). *Nichols* featured an immensely talented cast and crew, including Stuart Margolin, Margot Kidder, John Beck, Neva Patterson, producer-director Frank Pierson (*Cat Ballou*, *Cool Hand Luke*, *Presumed Innocent*), and future *Rockford* writer-producer Juanita Bartlett.

Garner played a career cavalryman named Nichols who returns to the eponymous Arizona town founded by his grandfather and soon finds himself coerced into becoming sheriff by the Ketchams, the corrupt family who runs the town; however, Nichols, who's a bit rascally himself, spends more time upending the Ketchams (and pursuing his own self-interest) than he does upholding the law. The series apparently aimed for the unconventional, character-driven humor that Garner had honed on *Maverick* (and in such pictures as *Support Your Local Sheriff* and *Skin Game*) — Nichols didn't carry a gun unless he had to, and wouldn't hesitate avoiding trouble by sneaking out the back door. However, the humor in *Nichols* was both inconsistent (sometimes dry, sometimes broad) and erratic (sometimes it worked, sometimes it didn't) — not to mention hampered by excruciatingly slow pacing.

After a few weeks on the air, *Nichols* was in serious ratings trouble. NBC gave it a new time slot during midseason, and even retitled the show *James Garner as Nichols* in the hopes that Garner's name would attract more viewers. Garner even tried to retool the series by killing off the main character in the final episode and replacing him with a twin brother (also played by Garner), a more traditional, itinerant Western character who avenged the death and took over as sheriff (and as the focal point of the show). But nothing worked. Television audiences never accepted *Nichols*, and NBC cancelled the series at the end of the season.

Garner took the failure of *Nichols* very hard — for many years, he railed at NBC for not supporting the show, which he proclaimed "the best TV series he'd ever done." Universal, which had a close relationship with NBC (it supplied many hours of television for the network), was very much aware of the problems with *Nichols* — which would account for their own qualms about working with Garner.

However, Universal did not dismiss the notion. After all, Garner was still a widely recognizable personality, so the studio knew that it could market a television series around him — particularly a series produced by Huggins, who knew Garner's strengths intimately and who could bring them out like few others can.

In truth, Universal had more concerns over a promise Garner had made to Rosenberg after *Nichols*: if he ever returned to television, he would make her the executive producer of whatever series he appeared in. Rosenberg had made her reputation as a tough-negotiating agent (her other clients included Robert Redford, Alan Arkin, Richard Benjamin, William Devane) before becoming Garner's partner in Cherokee Productions in 1964. Rosenberg had experience in television — she had packaged shows such as *Hogan's Heroes* and *Ben Casey*; i.e., she sold the ideas for these series, helped her clients put together the series, and assisted the network in finding sponsors. However, her track record as a producer was not very good (Rosenberg was the executive producer of *Nichols*).

"I think we explored whether it was possible to get Jim without Meta," Price recalled. "But then Roy called me, and he said he felt he could work with both Meta and Jim."

In November 1973, Garner notified Huggins that he wanted to do *The Rockford Files*. There was still the matter of the promise Garner had made to Rosenberg, but as far as Huggins was concerned, that wasn't a problem. Although Huggins wrote most of the shows he produced, he often removed his name from those credits because he didn't like seeing it flashed onscreen more than once (if at all); if he didn't give the credit entirely to someone else, he would take it under a pseudonym (such as "John Thomas James").

Huggins informed Garner that Rosenberg could have the "executive producer" title on *The Rockford Files* — on one condition. "I told Jim that she wouldn't actually be the executive producer," he said. "I said that I would be running the show. Jim said, 'That'll be all right, as long as I can give Meta executive producer credit.'"

Garner also asked Huggins to make one small change in the script. "I had originally named the character 'Tom Rockford,' after one of my sons," Huggins said. "Jim asked me to change his first name to 'Jim,' and so we did." Garner's reasoning: since most people on the set (like the director) tend to talk to the star as if he were the character, Garner figured he would feel more comfortable if they did so using his own name ("Okay, when Jim does this in this next scene..."). At any rate, Huggins was happy to oblige (he also happens to have a son named Jim).

Apparently Garner had been considering another television series offer, but changed his mind once he read *The Rockford Files*. "I believe there was something at MGM that I was thinking about doing, but *Rockford* was much more attractive because of that character," Garner recalled. "Steve Cannell wrote a wonderful script. I don't know whether he had me in mind when he wrote it, but he might have, because when I first read it, the character was all there."

In the meantime, Frank Price saw *The Rockford Files* as a way of resolving the uncertainty hanging over *Toma* regarding the future of Tony Musante. "I had two ways to go about that," he said. "One, I had hoped to talk Tony into changing that provision [whereby he'd only have to do 13 shows a year if *Toma* was renewed] — and I believed, if he was happy with the show, there was a good chance of that happening.

"My backup plan was to do a 'wheel,' like what we had done with *The NBC Mystery Movie* [whereby two or three shows rotate with each other every week in the same time slot]. I was ready to offer *The Rockford Files* to ABC and pair it with *Toma*, and those two shows would alternate in *Toma*'s time period."

Price's scheme covered all the bases: it would have sold one more series (*Rockford*) to ABC; and it probably would have kept *Toma* on the air (with Musante intact). There was only one problem: ABC passed on *The Rockford Files*. "They didn't like the script," Price said. "And they weren't interested in doing *Toma* as part of a 'wheel.' They sneered at that idea."

Given the cloudy situation regarding Musante, perhaps ABC may have rejected *Rockford* simply because it was down on *Toma*. That may also have been the reason why ABC ultimately cancelled *Toma* at the end of the 1973-1974 season — despite the fact that the series had drawn decent audience figures throughout the year. Instead of getting two shows for the price of one pilot, ABC lost any chance of keeping Musante, while *The Rockford Files* eventually became a monster hit for another network. (However, Universal Television did not give up on *Toma*. After persuading ABC to reconsider its decision, Price and Huggins replaced Musante with Robert Blake and retooled the entire series. In January 1975, *Toma* went back on the air — only now under the title *Baretta*.)

Meanwhile, Price began offering *The Rockford Files* to the other networks. "I called John McMahon, who was NBC's head of the West Coast at the time," he recalled. "I sent him the pilot script, and I told him that we had interest from Garner in doing the pilot. I also told him that I felt that we wouldn't have the problems with *Rockford Files* that existed on *Nichols*, because Roy would be connected to it, and he felt he could have a good working relationship with Meta and Jim."

"Selling a series to a network is a special problem," added Roy Huggins. "You have an idea for a series, and then you have a way of selling that idea to a network — and the two may not have any connection." If *The Rockford Files* was going to sell, NBC had to be convinced that it was unlike any detective series that had ever been done. Because prime time television was inundated with detective shows at the time, Huggins knew that the network was unlikely to purchase another private eye series unless it had something that made it stand out. That something could be expressed in terms of locale (*Hawaii Five-O*, *The Streets of San Francisco*, which were both filmed entirely in those respective cities), a visible characteristic (*Cannon* was fat, *Barnaby Jones* old, *Kojak* bald, *Ironside* wheelchair-bound) or some other idiosyncrasy (*Columbo* was a slob, *Harry O* rode the buses).

Even though the concept of *Rockford* (*Maverick* as a private eye) had already addressed that matter, Huggins decided the best way to sell the series was to play off its title. "In some cases, you could say something like 'I want to do Jim Garner as a private eye,' and the network will buy the series," Huggins continued. "But in the case of NBC and *The Rockford Files*, that wouldn't have worked, because NBC had just done *Nichols*, which was a costly failure. So I decided to sell *The Rockford Files* as a series with Jim Garner about a private eye who only handles closed cases. That would make it sound different. This has happened time and time again—*Mannix*, as an example, started as a detective who works in an agency that bases its procedures on computers; that sold the series, but that concept was quickly forgotten."

Huggins admits that "he only handles closed cases" was nothing more than smoke and mirrors. "No homicide case is ever closed," he said. "The case that Rockford took on in the pilot was never closed — the police considered it inactive and unsolvable, but they never closed it. And I knew that. But I used it as a gimmick to help sell the series. So, *The Rockford Files* were 'closed files.'" (The "closed cases" story point was also incorporated in many of the early episodes for the benefit of those viewers who may have been watching the show for the first time. However, once *Rockford* had established itself as an enormous hit, it became less of a need to remind the viewers of that particular story point.)

By this time, it was December 1973. If Price wanted to market *Rockford* as a potential Fall 1974 series, the pilot had to be completed and ready for broadcast in the Spring, which meant that production of the pilot had to begin no later than February — which in turn meant that the pre-production planning had to get underway no later than the first of January. In order to get the ball rolling, Price needed to close the deal quickly. So he imposed an artificial deadline on NBC — the network had 24 hours to make up its mind on *The Rockford Files*.

"Sometimes it helps generate enthusiasm if you tell the network, 'Hurry! Get it now, or it won't be there,'" he explained. "That's the way we did business at Universal — we often, in general, financed our own development. That meant that the networks couldn't just sit on a script — if they turned it down, we could offer the project to someone else. However, when the network finances the development, it's a different story. You can't just pull it away in 24 hours — you can only act on it when they give you permission."

Price's strategy worked. McMahon called the next day and told him that NBC would finance the pilot. In late December 1973, Garner and the studio agreed to terms on a one-year contract with five consecutive one-year options. Filming on the pilot began in February 1974.

Although NBC had commissioned the pilot of *The Rockford Files*, enough members of the brass had their doubts about its prospects as a series — assuming that the pilot tested well. (The memories of the *Nichols* fiasco were still fresh in their minds.) As per standard practice in the television industry, the network arranged for an advance screening of the pilot through ASI, a market research company based in Burbank that previews television commercials and programs before live audiences, who then record their responses to the programs via use of a dial. Oftentimes, the ASI results are the deciding factor in swaying the networks (as well as potential sponsors) into purchasing new shows. The case of NBC and *The Rockford Files* was no exception.

At this time, Don Durgin was the president of the NBC television network. Although his offices were based in New York, Durgin was in Los Angeles on business at the time *Rockford* was scheduled for screening. Durgin attended the ASI session, along with Price, Huggins, Cannell, and Jo Swerling Jr. (Huggins' executive assistant). The screening took place on March 22, 1974.

ASI, as a rule, considers a series pilot or commercial to be successful if it appeals to 70% of the test audience. *Rockford* scored an 85. "We blew the needle off the ASI," recalled Cannell. "We had the highest rating of any pilot ASI had ever tested up through that time. In fact, it was so high, NBC couldn't believe the score, so they re-tested it — and it scored even higher on the second test." The second screening took place on March 27, 1974 — the same date the pilot was scheduled to air on NBC.

In fact, one scene in particular was so popular, the arrow measuring the audience's approval nearly went off the chart. "During that scene in which Rockford pours soap on the bathroom floor and he hits the guy with the roll of nickels, that needle went way into the 90s," said Cannell. "I'd never seen that needle go that high. But you could just hear the audience howling through the glass wall of the booth where we were all sitting."

NBC president Durgin was astonished. "When the screening was over," Huggins added, "and the results were in, Don Durgin just shook his head, and he said, 'Well, Roy, after *Nichols*, we never thought we'd ever do another show with Jim Garner. But I guess we're going to have to do this one.'"

NBC aired *The Rockford Files* as part of a *World Premiere Double Feature* on March 27, 1974, then announced a few weeks later that *Rockford* would be part of its Fall lineup. Production of the series began in earnest in June 1974.

Lindsay Wagner and James Garner

JAMES GARNER
in
THE ROCKFORD FILES

An NBC World Premiere Movie
Production Number: 81796
Original Airdate: March 27, 1974

Additional Cast: Lindsay Wagner (Sara Butler), William Smith (Jerry Grimes), Nita Talbot (Mildred Elias), Joe Santos (Sergeant Dennis Becker), Stuart Margolin (Angel Martin), Robert Donley (Joseph "Rocky" Rockford), Bill Mumy (Nick Butler), Pat Renella (Morrie Talbot), Michael Lerner (Dr. Reuben Seelman), Ted Gehring (Norm Mitchell), Joshua Bryant (Captain Harry Dell), Bill Quinn (Harvey Butler), Robert B. Williams (Arnold Demura), Claude Johnson (Officer), Mike Steele (Danford Baker), Jack Garner (Bar Patron), Luis Delgado (Groom)

Executive Producer: Meta Rosenberg	**Assistant Director:** Howard G. Kasanjian
Associate Exec. Producer: Jo Swerling Jr.	**Unit Manager:** William W. Gray
Produced by: Stephen J. Cannell	**Film Editor:** John Dumas
Director of Photography: Lamar Boren	**Sound:** John Kean
Teleplay by: Stephen J. Cannell	**Color by:** Technicolor
Story by: John Thomas James	**Titles and Optical Effects:** Universal Title
Directed by: Richard T. Heffron	**Editorial Supervision:** Richard Belding
Art Director: Robert Luthardt	**Music Supervision:** Howard Mooney
Set Decorations: Don Sullivan	**Costume Designer:** Charles Waldo

Billings, L.A.P.D. You know, Thursday is Chapman's 20th year, and we're giving a little surprise party at the Captain's. I think you should come. By the way, we need five bucks for the present.

Synopsis. *Rockford reluctantly agrees to investigate the death of Harvey Butler, an elderly derelict whose body was found beneath the Santa Monica pier two months ago. (Although the police consider the case unsolvable, Butler was in fact strangled to death by a man named Jerry Grimes, a karate expert with a mean streak.) Butler's daughter Sara thinks there's a connection between her father's death and socialite Mildred Elias, who has been putting Nick Butler (Sara's brother) through medical school. Although his initial investigation leads him nowhere, Rockford becomes curious when he discovers Grimes tailing him shortly after the private eye interrogates Mildred Elias.*

The sequence in which Rockford literally upends Jerry Grimes (William Smith) not only demonstrates how Rockford will often use elemental means to work his way out of trouble, but also showcases the character's droll sense of humor. It's an important scene that encapsulates what *The Rockford Files* is all about. As is the case with many of the other staples of the series, the development of that sequence was the development of that sequence was the collaborative effort of Roy Huggins and Stephen J. Cannell.

Cannell, who had been a fan of Huggins since *Maverick*, had worked closely with Huggins on *Toma*, so he had become familiar with many of his boss' idiosyncrasies. "Roy always had this thing about how heavies or private eyes in the movies are always following people around in bright red cars, just because they're cinematic — whereas nothing like that ever happens in real life," said Cannell. "So I put this guy in a bright red Cadillac with a white interior, and I had him following Rockford. And I had Rockford basically saying and thinking what Roy would always say: 'What kind of an idiot tries to follow you in a frigging red Cadillac?'"

In the pilot, of course, Grimes follows Rockford into a nightclub. However, in Huggins' original story, the confrontation took place in a dark alley — Grimes peers down the alley; when he isn't looking, Rockford emerges from the shadows and pounds him in the stomach. While Grimes was initially as vain and dimwitted as we ultimately see him in the pilot (Huggins' story describes him as being "so conceited, he's slow-witted; he's so attracted to women that he stopped thinking when he was about 19 — he found out he didn't have to think"), he was also originally oafish, and not exactly a formidable opponent. Cannell changed that by making Grimes a strongman who was also expert in karate. Rockford's only chance against this man is through trickery — first he distracts Grimes, then he nails him with a sucker punch. This sets up one of the classic lines of the series: "You know what's wrong with karate, Jerry? It's based on the ridiculous assumption that both people will fight fair." (Rockford had hidden a roll of nickels inside his fist.)

After reading and discussing the first draft with Cannell, Huggins suggested relocating the Rockford-Grimes confrontation to the men's room of a nightclub. "There's a man in there, and Rockford pretends to be an obnoxious drunk, to get the man out," according to Huggins' notes dated January 7, 1974. "The man leaves. Rockford unscrews the liquid soap container and douses half of the floor with it. Now Rockford can also use the roll of nickels, because he's really rigged it."

But Rockford still has to get Grimes to walk into the trap. This is where Cannell made the next contribution: "I have Rockford standing across the room saying, 'Well, I think there's a problem with big, overdeveloped guys like you.' And Bill Smith says, 'Meaning?' And Rockford says, 'You know — queer!' We'd already established that Smith was a martial arts guy, and so he plants his foot to make his kick — and of course, he goes down. Rockford steps over and whacks him with the roll of nickels — nothing but sucker punches. He'd never get into a fight with this guy, because *I* wouldn't get into a fight with this guy. And that was my whole idea with Rockford — I wrote him as if he were me."

Cannell and Huggins had determined that after Rockford stunned Grimes, he would strap Grimes' feet to the top of a bathroom stall, then slap the upside down Grimes with his own wallet. Huggins then suggested that while Rockford interrogates Grimes, he is interrupted by a bar patron who walks into the bathroom. Huggins originally had the man immediately turning around and walking out — only Cannell changed that. "Rockford and the man go into a kind of Alphonse and Gaston banter," Cannell continued, alluding to the characters from Beckett's *Waiting for Godot*. "The guy walks in and says, 'Oh, I didn't know the room was being used!' Then Rockford says, 'It's okay, we'll be through in a minute.' And the guy says, 'No, no, no. I can come back.' And then Rockford says, 'No, no, no. It's okay.'"

The bar patron is played by Jack Garner (James Garner's older brother). "That was a fun time," he recalled. "But I also remember that, the next time I did something on the show, the big joke around the set was 'Well, Jack, you finally got out of the bathroom!'"

* * *

Near the end of the pilot episode, Rockford fires his pistol into the engine of a plane flying several thousand feet above him — and somehow manages to hit it. But that wasn't how the scene was supposed to play. The script called for the plane to fly no higher than 15 feet above the ground, so that when it flew directly over Rockford, he would have a clear shot at the belly of the engine — and a good chance of causing some damage.

As the scene stands, however, it is the one moment of incredulity in an otherwise excellent film. (In fact, it was the subject of the one overwhelmingly negative finding in ASI's Program Test Report.) Huggins knew it, too — in fact, he became so concerned over that scene that he offered to put up his own money in order to reshoot it. "I made a proposition to the Black Tower: 'Let me reshoot that, and if the pilot sells, you pay for it; but if it doesn't sell, I'll pay for it,'" he said. "Because a scene like that could be the difference between the show selling and the show not selling. If we reshot it, and the pilot sold, it would have been worth the extra expense. And if I was wrong — if I reshot it, and the pilot still didn't sell — I was willing to pay for it myself."

The studio declined Huggins' offer — the scene stayed in — and, of course, NBC purchased *The Rockford Files*, anyway. But that gives you an idea of Huggins' approach to television producing. It is a given in television that if you have a popular show, the majority of your audience (say, 80%) will tune in every week. Put another way, even if an episode one week is not up to par, you know that most viewers will still come back the next week. So, if you're a producer, there are two ways you can go about planning your series — you can aim for the mass core audience, or you can strive to reach the minority of viewers that might be a little more discriminating.

Roy Huggins went by the latter approach. "I had always tried to cater my shows to that 20% that might not come back the next week," he said. "If I thought there was something in the script or in the film that I knew would insult the intelligence of the upper tier of the audience, or be otherwise unacceptable to them, I would remove it. And I have always tried to follow that rule throughout my television career."

* * *

Stephen J. Cannell originated the idea for what has become one of *Rockford*'s signature elements — the decidedly offbeat telephone messages that we hear at the beginning of every episode. The messages were almost exclusively written independent of the script, and often do not pertain to the episode, although there are some exceptions — such as the tag in "Chicken Little is a Little Chicken," whereby Beth asks Rockford to babysit her cats (which we actually see him doing later in that episode).

For the most part, writing those one-liners was a collaborative effort on the part of the writers and producers. "I've got to tell you," said Juanita Bartlett, "toward the end of our run, we were getting 'messaged out.' I'm not kidding. We had everybody doing them. I remember that Jackie Cooper and Lou Antonio [two of our directors] would often come up with ideas for the phone messages — which we would immediately pounce on! Sometimes it was a matter of 'If you have any ideas, come see us, please.'" In some episodes (such as "Beamer's Last Case," "Rosendahl and Gilda Stern are Dead," and "Guilt"), Rockford plays back the messages on his phone machine as part of the story; those shows posed an extra challenge, because they would require the writers to come up with two or three messages in addition to the eight-second tag at the beginning of the show.

The person who was responsible for making sure that each episode included the phone message tag was usually Charles Floyd Johnson. "And that wasn't always easy," he said. "The writers would be busy with writing and preparing the episodes, and I would be busy taking care of other things. The picture would be dubbed, and ready to go — but it would still need to have a phone message added before we could deliver it to the network. I would say, 'Hey, guys, we need to add a tag,' and they would sometimes groan or put a 'hex' on me. Sometimes out of self-defense, I would write out four or five and present them to Steve or Juanita or David Chaseand say, 'Okay, choose the one you like, because we need one.' So it was very much a collaborative effort, and we all had fun writing them."

NOTE: The phone messages for each episode are included in the episode guide. The messages appear between the guest cast listings and the plot synopsis of each show.

* * *

Executive producer Meta Rosenberg was particularly involved with the casting of secondary characters and guest stars. Rosenberg had always wanted Noah Beery Jr. to play Joseph Rockford, but Beery was unable to film the pilot (he had been starring in a series with James Franciscus called *Doc Elliot*). By the time *The Rockford Files* was ordered as a series, *Doc Elliot* had been cancelled — which meant that Beery was now available.

"Noah Beery was a great choice," said Roy Huggins. "After all, he and Jim do kind of look like father and son." But Huggins thought that the casting of Beery brought another kind of verisimilitude to the series. "It's always bothered me that in the movies, the father is always bigger than the son," he said. "That's crazy — in the world we live in, the son is always bigger than the father. So I think the fact that Meta selected an actor who was shorter than Jim Garner added an element of realism to the series."

Rosenberg also made an excellent choice in casting Stuart Margolin as Angel Martin, Rockford's permanent cross to bear. (In addition to co-starring with Garner on *Nichols*, Margolin had played a character named Benny the Squealer in *Cops*, a pilot Rosenberg had produced in 1973.) It's hard to picture anyone else in the role — Margolin's expressive eyes say everything even when he isn't actually saying anything. It's not easy to take a character who has little (if any) redeeming qualities and portray it with conviction, yet that's exactly Margolin managed to do with Angel.

"There really wasn't anybody else in consideration for Angel," said Juanita Bartlett. "Jim Garner loves working with Stuart. From the moment they worked on *Nichols*, Jim said of Stuart, 'He gives you more than almost any other actor I can think of.' There's a wonderful thing that happens between Jim and Stuart. They just work so beautifully together."

Joe Santos has credited Stephen J. Cannell for casting him as Dennis Becker. Cannell had remembered Santos' work as a Mafia hit man in the first episode of *Toma*, as well as his co-starring role in the 1973 miniseries *The Blue Knight* with William Holden. Years later, Santos would work for Cannell again — he played Lieutenant Harper in Cannell's *Hardcastle and McCormick* series.

Rockford Facts. The 90-minute pilot was re-edited into a two-part episode (entitled "Backlash of the Hunter") and is included in the rerun package that airs on the A&E cable network and on independent television stations. The two-part version includes a phone call from Officer Billings (Luis Delgado) that appears at the top of the show; that phone call was actually lifted from a sixth season episode ("The Hawaiian Headache") and edited into the pilot. However, Delgado appears in the pilot — as himself. He's the groom whose back is to the camera during the wedding sequence near the end of the film; as the scene ends, the minister addresses him as "Luis Delgado."

* * *

In the pilot, Rockford tells Sara that he was wrongly convicted of armed robbery and served five years in San Quentin before he received a pardon from the Governor of California. In his original story, Roy Huggins provided some additional background explaining how Rockford was eventually cleared of the charges, as well as why he became a private investigator. "[Rockford] kept writing letters to people, and he finally found this old retired lawyer who became interested in his case [and] found the answer — literally found the guy who was guilty," Huggins wrote in October 1973. "When Rockford got out, he went to the old man and asked what he could do to repay him. The old man said Rockford could work with him. The old man died a couple of years ago, and Rockford stayed in the investigating business.... Rockford feels strongly about closed cases because he was the victim of one."

Huggins had considered dramatizing these aspects of Rockford's past in the first season (in an episode aptly called "Flashback"). Although that particular segment was never made, the series frequently referred to Rockford's prison background, either by introducing a character who served time with Rockford (such as Gandolf Fitch), or by having Jim tell a story about some lesson he learned while doing time (as he does in the pilot, as well as in "To Protect and Serve"). Interestingly enough, the fourth-year episode "The House on Willis Avenue" features the man who was Rockford's mentor — only the character was changed from a retired lawyer to a veteran P.I.

* * *

Although Huggins had come up with the *Rockford Files* title when he first conceived the idea for the pilot, he also submitted several alternate titles (*Rockford*, *Rockford's Files*, *The Rockford Style*) for NBC's consideration shortly before production of the pilot got underway. The underlying assumption would be that the title would somehow incorporate the name "Rockford" — a point about which series star James Garner felt very strong.

According to the pilot script, Angel's given name is "Al Martin." However, the character was only identified as "Angel" throughout the pilot film. Later in the series (the episode "Chicken Little is a Little Chicken"), we're told that Angel's first name is "Evelyn."

William Smith appeared as one of the riverboat gamblers in the 1994 feature film version of *Maverick* starring James Garner.

EDITORS: For release in weekend editions of Aug. 24-25

SHOWTIME

the colorful world of entertainment

"The Rockford Files" airs Fridays this fall, NBC, with James Garner as Jim Rockford. Noah Beery plays Rockford's father. Not just another "investigator" tale — the show is said to have a Raymond Chandler-like flavor.

Promotional material such as this originally appeared in trade papers during the fall of 1974. (From the collection of the author.)

Part 2: The Episodes

First Season: 1974-1975

Because of the apparent effortlessness that he brings to his performances, it's often said that James Garner doesn't so much act as merely play himself. The fact that Garner really does work hard is often overlooked. "Jim is a very, very intelligent actor who hasn't gotten the credit that he deserves because he makes it look so easy," said writer/producer Juanita Bartlett. "When you see him on *Rockford Files*, he isn't playing himself — he is playing a character. But he makes it look so real that you think you're looking at Jim Garner."

It isn't easy to make yourself look natural and easy — nor is it easy for Garner to explain exactly why he excels at his craft. "I don't know what I bring to my roles — if I bring anything at all," he said. "And I don't really 'create' — at least, as far as I know. I read the script, and if I understand the character, I do it. I don't try to 'do things' with it.

"In the case of *Rockford*, I understood the humor, and what the writers were trying to do, just by reading the script. I just went with what the writers wrote — in fact, you'd have to ask the writers [what I bring], because, to me, it's all in the writing. And if the words aren't on the paper, I ain't gonna make 'em any better."

According to Roy Huggins, the key to Garner's success with Rockford (and with Maverick before that) lies in the actor's absolute understanding of the character's thoughts and motivations. "That was a very important part of Jim's great success with that Maverick/Rockford character," he said. "In the case of those two shows, the dialogue is never as important as understanding what the character has in mind. I know Jim would not have done those shows as well as he has if he didn't have great insight into how that character thinks and what motivates him."

During a 1986 interview on ABC-TV's *20/20*, Garner said that one of the most important skills an actor can learn is how to listen. "That was one of the first things I learned in this business," he said. "By listening, you put yourself in it. You know what's going on. You're reacting to it. I never learned dialogue — I learned thoughts."

That brings to mind something else that Garner brings to the package. He is one of the finest reactors the film industry has ever known, rightly compared with the likes of Cary Grant, Jack Benny, and Bob Newhart. Oftentimes, you'll know exactly what his character is thinking simply from watching the look on Garner's face. *The Rockford Files* exploited Garner's skills as a reactor by constantly placing Rockford in situations with characters who were decidedly off the wall.

For example, Stephen J. Cannell's "White on White and Nearly Perfect" pairs Rockford with Lance White (Tom Selleck of *Magnum, P.I.*), an intrepid gumshoe who behaves as if he's a character in a pulp fiction story. Rockford and Lance investigate a kidnapping, but the trail soon runs cold. Lance, who lives a very providential life, suggests returning to his office, where he believes a clue will be waiting for them. Rockford can't believe what he's hearing: "There's not going to be a clue waiting for us in the office — it just doesn't work out that way!" "Oh, yes, it does," Lance insists. "You go back to the office, and you sit down and you wait, and somebody will come in and tell you what you need." Rockford and Lance proceed to Lance's office, where, incredibly enough, a statuesque beauty named Belle Labelle is not only waiting for them, but brings them a clue that leads to a break in the case.

Watch Garner's reactions throughout that sequence, and you'll see a man who is thinking to himself, "I can't believe I'm in the same room with these people." Knowing what Rockford is thinking makes the few lines he has in the scene ("Would you mind if I run out and get some popcorn?") that much more funny.

"Rockford is an island in a world where people can be pretty bizarre," said Bartlett. "He is a very reasonable, very sane man who recognizes the insanity — and you can see that in his eyes, and in his face and his expression. Rockford recognizes the insanity, and he accepts it, although he certainly can do without it."

James Garner provides the impetus for *Rockford*'s sophisticated sense of humor. Situations or lines of dialogue that ordinarily may not be funny suddenly are funny because of Rockford's character and Garner's impeccable understanding of how to play it. "Jim can take a ordinary line and hand it back to you gift-wrapped, because he'll know how to deliver it," said Bartlett.

Yet, even after it had purchased *The Rockford Files*, NBC apparently didn't understand what made the series work. "The programming department had a big problem with the first script," recalled Frank Price. "They didn't like it because they weren't getting the humor."

Price met with NBC's West Coast programming executives to try to straighten out the problem. "They didn't see the script as funny," he said. "I kept telling them, 'It *is* funny,' and they kept saying, 'No, it's not.' I finally decided to read the script aloud to them, which helped them understand the humor — they'd laugh a little, or at least smile, at some of Rockford's lines. I'd then say, 'These lines will be funnier when Jim Garner is saying them!'"

Take, as an example, this sequence from that first episode, "The Kirkoff Case" (also written by Cannell), in which Rockford tries to clear a man accused of murdering his parents. A band of thugs kidnap Rockford and transport him to an abandoned warehouse, where they proceed to pummel him severely. After Rockford is worked over, the ringleader (a creep named Muzzy Vinette) advises the P.I. to drop out of the case.

```
    Muzzy:    You're a private detective, and I know you gotta work for
a living. I understand that. But your client is guilty of murder. You
know, murder. Yeah, and I know it to be a fact, the D.A. knows it, and
the cops and every newspaper editor knows it. So how come you're trying
to prove it otherwise?

    Rockford:    Why, that was this morning. I just stopped working for
him. I never really liked him very much.

    Muzzy:    It ain't that I really care that much about Larry Kirkoff.
No. I think the kid's a creep for killing his mom and dad. But that's
not the reason why I want you to quit fooling around with this.

    Rockford:    You're right — I understand.

    Muzzy:    No, you don't understand.

    Rockford:    No, I don't.
```

In the interest of fairness, NBC wasn't the only one that failed to understand the humor in "The Kirkoff Case." Both *The San Francisco Chronicle* and *Weekly Variety* cited the above scene as a "violence-for-violence's sake beating that contributed nothing to the story." And it's true that a situation in which someone is being beaten is not ostensibly funny.

But if you found yourself in Rockford's position, there's a good chance you might also do whatever it takes, without hesitation — be it dropping your client, or contradicting yourself — simply to get Muzzy Vinette to leave you alone. Once Muzzy goes away, Rockford's free to resume his investigation, which is exactly what he does. That's what makes this scene funny. The humor in this situation works because it's humor based on a character — the kind of character that James Garner understands masterfully.

"That was one of the greatest readings I ever heard Jim do," added Huggins. "Only Jim Garner can say those lines ['You're right, I understand.' 'No, you don't understand.' 'No, I don't.'] in a way that makes the audience laugh like crazy. Nobody else can do that."

Perhaps Cleveland Amory said it best when he reviewed *The Rockford Files* for *TV Guide* in December 1974: "A lot of what Mr. Garner does in this show is funny. It's not *fast* funny, mind you — everything Mr. Garner does, including think, is done slowly. But the fact remains that he is — in a kind of instant-replay, double-take way — slow funny. In other words, he grows on you." Even *Variety*, despite its criticism of the first episode, recognized Garner's style ("sardonic, and sometimes a little whimsical") as one of the show's strengths. The trade paper also predicted that *The Rockford Files* would benefit from "a good audience rollover" following its lead-ins on NBC's Friday schedule, *Sanford and Son* and *Chico and the Man*.

A look at the ratings figures for the season bear that out. *Rockford* finished in the Top 30 during each of its first five weeks of the season. As *Variety* noted, *Rockford* had a tremendous advantage heading into the season — its 8:00-9:00 p.m. lead-in was anchored by *Sanford and Son*, the No. 3 show on television in 1974 (and No. 1 on Friday nights), averaging nearly 50% of the total television-watching audience every week. *Rockford* held onto the majority of this enormous built-in audience, with an average share of 37.8%.

But, more importantly, *Rockford* won its own time slot on a consistent basis throughout

its first season. The series cracked the Top 20 in its fourth week (the episode "Exit Prentiss Carr," which finished No. 14), then made its way into the Top Ten after Week 13 ("Caledonia, It's Worth a Fortune!," which ranked No. 10). *Rockford*'s audience grew over the course of the season — in fact, ABC changed its Friday 9:00-10:00 p.m. lineup three times over the course of the season, to no avail. Over the course of the final six weeks of the campaign, *Rockford* was averaging nearly 28% of all television households (and 43% of all televisions in use). *The Rockford Files* finished the year in the Top 20 (it ranked No. 12), with an overall average rating of 23.8.

The ratings figure refers to the estimated percentage of all U.S. "television households" — i.e., households that own at least one TV set — who watched *Rockford Files*. The share, or "HUT number," refers to the percentage of all "households using television" — i.e., households whose TV sets were actually in use at the time of the broadcast. In other words, of the total number of people watching television from 9:00-10:00 p.m. on Fridays during the 1974-1975 season, nearly 40% of that audience, on the average, watched *Rockford Files*.

Rockford's average audience share in 1974-1975 becomes even more impressive once you consider that it was a Friday night show. The television industry traditionally considers Friday and Saturday to be low HUT nights because, as a rule, the majority of the "TV-watching universe" (those viewers aged 21-49) are not at home. Not surprisingly, *Rockford*'s demographics consisted primarily of older viewers (ages 50 and up), an audience that likely recognized in *Rockford* the sophisticated character-driven humor they remembered from *Maverick*. (Ironically, according to newspaper reports, NBC had considered scheduling *Rockford* for Sundays at 10:00 p.m. — a time period during which as many as 70% of the "TV-watching universe" are at home watching television.)

The Rockford Files succeeded not only because it had a star with proven audience appeal in James Garner — it also told stories featuring a character with proven audience appeal. The strength of the Maverick/Rockford character is that he is not only unorthodox, but that he is ultimately smarter than anybody else. This is worth pointing out because it explains why *Rockford* stumbled in its second season — the series suffered a huge loss in audience during the period of time when the series featured stories that went against the character's strength.

The success of a film or television series often depends on the lead actor — and not just in terms of performance. The principal sets the tone of the entire production by his or her demeanor. James Garner's contributions in this regard cannot be overstated. Not only was he the star of the show, he was the owner of the company that made it, which meant that he was ultimately responsible for the makeup of the crew. "Jim Garner is perhaps the all-around best series lead that I've ever encountered," said Jo Swerling. "He really was a leader on the set. He set a tone on the set. And this is terribly important to having an efficient operation, and also one that does good work. He protected the crew — now, if he saw somebody that wasn't pulling their weight on the crew, he would speak up and we would make a change. That didn't happen very often, though — because there was such an atmosphere of family on the set that he created, and he was responsible for, changes didn't happen very often, because everybody did try very hard to live up to their responsibilities. The morale on the set was always high no matter how many hours they had to work. And that is all attributable to Jim."

In many respects, Garner is a practical person; this is particularly illustrated in his approach to hiring people. "I want people who want to go to work every day, and put in a full day's work, so that they can walk up to the pay window proudly and say, 'I got my check,'" he said. "I like people who are proud of their work. And I have a crew that's wonderful. Every one of them is like that."

Garner knows that the key to maintaining a happy work environment requires both taking care of little things (such as providing the members of his crew with the best coffee and food available), as well as providing the people he hires with the room they need to do their best. As an executive, he remains aware of every aspect of the operation without being obtrusive. "I like to let people do whatever they do," he said. "I think you get better work that way. They know that they won't have somebody looking over their shoulder all the time. Now, I know what everybody's doing on the show, and they realize that, but they also don't feel as if I'm looking over their shoulder."

In particular, Garner has always placed total confidence in the people who write for him — a quality that has never been lost on Juanita Bartlett. "I was on the set one day while they were filming an episode [of *Nichols*] I had written," she recalled. "I was standing over to the side when Jim came in to do a scene. Jim crossed over to me, and he said, 'Juanita, is it all right if I changed a line from so-and-so to so-and-so?' I said, 'No.' And he said, 'Oh, okay,' and he turned around and walked away. Jim took another look at the script, and they filmed the scene. He did it exactly as it was written.

"After the scene had been shot, I went over to him and I said, 'Jim, there was a reason I didn't want you to change that line.' Jim looked at me and said, 'I assumed there was.' He didn't care what the reason was — if it was okay to change it, fine; but if I said, 'No,' he figured, 'Well, she must have a reason.'

"I went back to the office, and I told [*Nichols* producer] Frank Pierson what had happened. Frank looked at me and he began to laugh uncontrollably. I didn't understand what he thought was so funny. And Frank said, 'You told not just the star, but *the owner of the series*, that he couldn't change one of your lines?' And I said, 'But, Frank, if he changed it, it would have changed the whole meaning of the scene.' Frank couldn't believe it — he just came unglued.

"But that's the way Jim is. He said to me once that he let people do what they did. And if we used a director that was a bad director, Jim would say, 'We may not use him again, but first, I'm going to give him a chance to do his thing. And if a writer can't write for me, we don't use that writer again. But let the writer write, let the director direct, and I'll do what I'm supposed to be doing.' And, believe me, that is refreshing, and rare, beyond belief.

"Jim Garner is such a joy to work for, because he truly is a rare one."

Many of the members of the Rockford crew have been with Garner so long, it's as if they were a family. Luis Delgado, assistant director Cliff Coleman and stunt coordinator Roydon Clark have known and worked with Garner since before the days of *Maverick*. Executive producer Meta Rosenberg was Garner's agent for over 20 years, and she remained a part of Cherokee Productions until 1982. Lamar Boren was the cinematographer on *Nichols*; when Boren left *The Rockford Files* after two seasons, he was replaced by Andrew Jackson, whom Garner met on *The Castaway Cowboy*. And Bartlett had been Rosenberg's secretary for several years before she made her first break as a writer on *Nichols*.

"Jim is so loyal to his staff and crew," said Bartlett. "It really is his family, and he wants to kept it together. There are people working on these *Rockford* movies for CBS that I first met on *Nichols*, and who have been with him all that time. Whenever Jim works, if they're available, they're with him."

"Jim had a lot to do with hiring the right kind of people," added Luis Delgado. "In fact, you'd be surprised at the number of people that are in line waiting to work with Jim on *Rockford Files*, or on anything he makes — because they know that he'll see to their needs, and that he treats his crew as if they were a family."

Familiar guest stars in *Rockford*'s first season include Joseph Cotten, James Woods, Jill Clayburgh, Julie Sommars, Roger Davis, Dick Gautier, Linden Chiles, Lara Parker, George DiCenzo, Thayer David, James McEachin, Sharon Gless, Suzanne Somers, Paul Michael Glaser, Linda Kelsey, Shelley Fabares, Ramon Bieri, Greg Mullavey, Bill Mumy, Diana Muldaur, Neva Patterson, Gordon Jump, Lindsay Wagner, and Tony Musante.

The many faces of Jim Rockford.

The Theme to The Rockford Files

The role of the music composer in film or television is to create music that reflects the particular goals and attitudes of the writer and/or producer of the film or series. Series co-creator Stephen J. Cannell wanted music that captured *Rockford*'s sophisticated yet sassy brand of humor, but he also wanted the show to have a fresh sound. He turned to his friend Mike Post, who (along with his collaborator Pete Carpenter) had revolutionized the art of film and television scoring a few years earlier by infusing it with contemporary music.

Most film composers through the early 1970s were either classically-based or big-band jazz-based. Post brought a rock and folk background to television (he was music director on *The Andy Williams Show* from 1969-1971); Carpenter had worked with Earle Hagen in scoring such series as *The Danny Thomas Show*, *That Girl* and *I Spy*. "Nobody had done rock 'n' roll music on dramatic television prior to the time when Pete and I began [in 1972]," said Post. "Nobody before us knew how, because nobody had a background in rock 'n' roll who could also fit music precisely to film."

Post and Carpenter broke ground in film scoring by taking the approach originated by the great Henry Mancini and applying it to contemporary music. "Before Mancini, everyone scored film and television in a style that had been derived from the silent movies — taking music that was classically based and trying to fit it to film," Post explained. "Then, as the art of film scoring became more perfected, and the art of fitting music to picture became more precise, a lot of composers became (as we say in the music industry), very 'queuey.' In other words, practically every time the camera moved, or every time someone said a line of dialogue, the music changed.

"Mancini saw that it wasn't necessary to change the music so many times within a given score. All you needed to do was come up with a tune for a scene, and play the tune from Point A to Point B; unless there was a big shift in the locale, or the feeling, or the timbre of the scene, there was no need to change the music. And so, in a two-or-three-minute queue, Mancini may have made only two or three changes — whereas before him, you might have heard as many as 25 changes in the mood of the music for that one scene. Pete and I took Mancini's template and applied it to what was [at the time] more contemporary music."

While Carpenter came from a more traditional music background, he also had a feel for contemporary music. "We had kind of a strange orchestra, in that it was half-legit, half-rock 'n' roll," said Post. "We were the first to use volume pedals [for spooky scenes]; the first to use breakup guitar [for action scenes]; and the first to use the harmonica as a blues instrument — prior to us, the harmonica had only been used in Westerns."

Post and Carpenter were also the first duo to use the Dobro guitar, which had previously been considered strictly a bluegrass instrument, on an action-adventure series. "That's why the music on *Rockford* sounds, if not country, then country rock," said Post. "It could also sound Midwestern, which is exactly what James Garner is (he's from Oklahoma)."

Post credits Cannell with providing the musicians with the necessary impetus to translate *Rockford* into music. "I can't say enough about how much it means to sit down and talk to a guy like Cannell," said Post. "He's the real guide. He's really good at telling me what I need to know in order to get inspired."

Cannell provided Post with a vivid description of *Rockford*'s attitudes. "We talked about the kind of guy Rockford was — how he was more interested in collecting his $200-a-day plus expenses than in catching bad guys," Post said. "And that he was kind of quirky — how, because he'd been to the joint, he had a 'Kiss my ass' attitude toward the police (despite his friendship with Becker); how he was friends with Angel, even though he knew Angel would steal him blind if he could; and how he also had a wryness and sweetness about him, which you could see in his relationship with Rocky."

Duly inspired, Post and Carpenter went to work. "We tried to write music that has humor," said Post. "We wanted to create music that was 'tongue in cheek,' but at the same time, with your fist on your hip — as if you're saying 'Hey, kiss my ass!'"

"It's catchy," said James Garner in a 1974 press interview. "I think viewers will like the theme music by Mike Post. It's a driving beat with a harmonica backed up by a big band."

In fact, if there's one instrument in the entire composition that truly captures the flavor of *The Rockford Files* onto music, it's the harmonica. "I've always thought the harmonica sounded kind of sassy," said Post.

During the Spring of 1975, Post added a bridge to the series theme, re-recorded the theme, and released the music as a single. "The Theme of *The Rockford Files*" ranked as high as Number 10 on the Billboard charts ("I'd always thought it would make a good record," he said). The lengthened version of the theme was so popular that it was ultimately included into the opening sequence of the series, beginning with the second season.

Over the past 20 years, Post and Carpenter have created the music for numerous series, including *L.A. Law*, *Hill Street Blues*, *Magnum, P.I.*, *The A Team*, and *NYPD Blue*.

1. THE KIRKOFF CASE

Production Number: 41401

Original Airdate: September 13, 1974

Teleplay by: *Stephen J. Cannell*
Story by: *John Thomas James*
Directed by: *Lou Antonio*

Guest Cast: Julie Sommars (Tawnia Baker), Roger Davis (Travis Buckman), James Woods (Larry Kirkoff), Philip Keneally (Muzzy Vinette), Milt Kogan (Marsh), Abe Vigoda (Al Dancer), Sandy DeBruin (Hostess), Dino Seragusa (Maitre D'), Dennis McCarthy (Calvin Carras), Fred Lerner (Parking Attendant), Melissa Mahoney (Carhop)

Jim, it's Norma at the market. It bounced — you want us to tear it up, send it back or put it with the others?

Synopsis. *Larry Kirkoff was indicted for the double murder of his parents, but he was never convicted because the prosecution couldn't place him at the scene of the crime, and the police never found the murder weapon. Larry hires Rockford to find evidence that would clear him of both crimes. Although Rockford believes Kirkoff is guilty, he can't quite resist the potential payoff (a $20,000 fee if he cracks the case). Jim discovers that the Kirkoff murders may be linked to a real estate fraud, but he also finds that his investigation could have fatal ramifications after mobsters work him over and warn him to drop the case.*

A filmed story is told three times: first by the writer; then by the actors and the director, who interpret the writing; and finally, in the post-production process, which includes editing, the most crucial part of post-production. Film editing requires not just a mastery of technical skills [such as splicing footage and dubbing sound]; it also requires an understanding of the craft of telling stories. In fact, many "cutters" (as they're known in the industry) who are particularly gifted storytellers often graduate to other fields of the film industry. Frequent *Rockford* director William Wiard and writer/producer Gordon Dawson, to name just two, began their film careers in the cutting room.

If an editor is not in sync with what the writer or producer has in mind, then the cut of the film may include (or exclude) footage that could affect the complexion of the entire story. For that reason, Roy Huggins, who originated the stories for nearly every series episode or TV-film he ever made, paid close attention to the editing of all his projects — and often served as an auxiliary editor. "Roy was incredible in the cutting room, in terms of what he could do with film," said Jo Swerling. "If he saw some footage that he thought might detract from the story, Roy would try to change it — he'd flip it around, blow it up, run it backwards, put wild lines on it, or do whatever it took to make the film work."

As an example, once while watching dailies [the footage of scenes filmed the previous day], Huggins decided that a scene depicting a holdup would be more effective if the actor playing the gunman fired a shot (which he hadn't done in the original footage). Rather than reshoot the entire sequence to include the gun shot, Huggins "manufactured" the gun shot just by working with the footage he had — first by instructing his editor to scratch the film at the point where the actor is seen holding the gun for approximately ten frames; then by asking the sound effects technician to dub a gunshot effect onto the film.

"Roy used to say that editing a film was like peeling the layers of an onion," said Swerling. "Each time you take a pass at the picture, you peel a layer off the onion, until you finally get it down to where the thing is lean and hard. Sometimes, after you're finished cutting, you end up short on footage; if that happens, you have to selectively build the film up back to where it's on footage. That was Roy's technique, and it's the technique that Steve Cannell and I still use today." *NOTE: "Footage" refers to both the material contained within the film, as well as its total running time. In series television, the final cut of an one-hour episode must run approximately 48 minutes. (The network sells the remaining portion of the program's air time to potential sponsors.)*

Huggins firmly believed that the quality of what went on the air was reflected by the amount of time spent in post-production — after all, it was always his philosophy to cater his shows to the "minority" (the 20% of the audience that might not tune in next week). Huggins' philosophy didn't always sit well with Universal, whose Business Department often complained that Huggins' shows cost one-third more than any other show produced at the studio. The extra expenditures were always tied to post-production. But it was hard to argue with the results. The quality of Huggins' shows was usually reflected by high audience figures and, in some cases, recognized by professional associations within the industry. *The Rockford Files*, for example, was recognized by the Motion Picture Sound Editors Association as the Best Sound Edited Television Series of 1974.

Rockford Facts. Huggins had originally designed "The Kirkoff Case" for *Toma* (as an episode entitled "How to Get Away with Murder"). Because that segment was never produced, Huggins took his story and reworked it as a *Rockford* story.

This episode is available through MCA/Universal Home Video as part of its Rockford Files collection.

2. THE DARK AND BLOODY GROUND

Production Number: 41402

Original Airdate: September 20, 1974

Teleplay by: *Juanita Bartlett*
Story by: *John Thomas James*
Directed by: *Michael Schultz*

Guest Cast: Linden Chiles (Elliot Malcolm), Nancy Malone (Elizabeth Gorman), Patricia Smith (Ann Calhoun), Walter Brooke (Clyde Russell), Tom Bower (Officer Hensley), Mark Alaimo (Farber)

Gretchen Corbett.

Hey, Jim, this is Louie down at the Fish Market — you gonna pick up these halibut or what?

Synopsis. *This episode introduces Gretchen Corbett as Rockford's attorney Beth Davenport, who (as Becker puts it) "collects lost causes like they were rare coins." Beth's client Ann Calhoun has been accused of the murder of her husband, poet Kevin Calhoun. Jim would rather pass on the case, since the evidence linking Ann to the crime seems insurmountable (not to mention the fact Ann has no money), and he becomes less inclined to pursue the matter after two attempts are made on his life. But the case takes an interesting turn after Rockford uncovers a connection between the murder victim and the legal rights to the novel The Dark and Bloody Ground.*

Gretchen Corbett recalls having a hunch at the time she filmed this episode that the role of Beth Davenport might ultimately prove to be very important for her. "I had recently signed a television contract with Universal, and had appeared in several of their shows — *Kojak, Columbo, Marcus Welby*," she said. "And I believe it was during my first year as a contract player that I auditioned for a guest role on *The Rockford Files*. There was something about the character Beth that I knew — it 'spoke' to me, because I'm a reasonably intelligent woman, and they didn't write such roles at the time. That is, there weren't as many 'strong, smart' female characters on television as there are today; back then, women were usually limited to playing the wife, or the girlfriend.

"I was treated with such gentle hands by Monique James, the woman who ran the contract system at Universal, that I didn't have the feeling that there was ever any heavy-duty competition for the role — and I'm not sure that there ever was. It was a guest shot. And so, I think, Monique said to Meta Rosenberg, 'I've got your gal,' and I came in and met with Meta and the folks, and I got the job.

"And it was in the shooting of that show that I had a gut feeling that it was a terribly important time for me, and I really needed to do it 'good.'"

That, she did. Beth became a recurring character which Corbett would play in a total of 30 episodes throughout the first four seasons of the series. "They liked the character, and I think they also liked the rapport I had with Jim," she said.

"Gretchen was perfect for that part," added Roy Huggins. "She was a very bright actress to begin with, and it wasn't difficult for me to imagine her playing a lawyer."

"The Dark and Bloody Ground" establishes that there was once a romantic relationship between Rockford and Beth. Given the age difference between Corbett and James Garner (she is 20 years younger), that made Beth a particularly challenging role for Corbett to play. "In that show, the producers pushed me to look and behave a little older than I appeared, because they didn't want to make Rockford look like he was disgusting," she said. "Jim was very sensitive about that kind of stuff. Every now and then, there would be a hint about their past — in fact, there was one show ['A Portrait of Elizabeth'] with a scene where it was the morning after, and Rockford was in my apartment. But there was never anything explicit between those two characters."

Because of the mature and intelligent manner in which Corbett played Beth, the notion of a past relationship between Rockford and her is believable, regardless of the age difference. "I think that's what the producers were going for," iterated Corbett. "They wanted to make sure that relationship came across 'okay.'"

Rockford Facts. Sometimes it takes a while to find the right vehicle for a story. Roy Huggins first wrote "The Victim Who Never Was" (the story on which "The Dark and Bloody Ground" is based) in July 1972. Over the course of the next two years, he developed the story on three separate occasions (first as a two-hour TV-movie, then as a one-hour series pilot, and later as an episode of *Toma*); although each of these projects was scrapped for various reasons, Huggins eventually produced "The Victim Who Never Was" as a segment of *The Rockford Files*. Perhaps Huggins kept returning to the story because of its terrific plot twist — 17 U.S.C. § 24, the peculiar loophole in U.S. copyright law which stipulated that if a publisher purchased a book, but the author died before the copyright is renewed, all rights to the book reverted to the author's surviving spouse. (This statute was revised in 1976.)

Interestingly enough, The Rockford Files had an in-house expert on copyright law — Charles Floyd Johnson, an attorney who served as an advisor in the U.S. Copyright Office in Washington D.C. from 1967-1970 before he moved into television. Johnson worked as a production coordinator for many series at Universal (including Toma); he was Rockford's production coordinator on the pilot and early in the first year before eventually becoming the show's associate producer (and, later, one of its producers). In 1967, Johnson had published a pamphlet entitled Copyright and Developing Countries. "I remember I was asked a lot of questions when they made that episode because of my experience in that area," he said.

3. THE COUNTESS

(a.k.a. "Call Girl Countess")

Production Number: 41410

Original Airdate: September 27, 1974

Teleplay by: *Stephen J. Cannell*
Story by: *John Thomas James*
Directed by: *Russ Mayberry*

Guest Cast: Susan Strasberg (Deborah Ryder), Art Lund (Mike Ryder), Dick Gautier (Carl Brego), Harold J. Stone (Sorrell), Todd Martin (Policeman), James Cromwell (Terry), Florence Link (Old Woman), Jeanne Le-Bouvier (Woman), Mel Allen (Cab Driver)

Hey, Rockford! Very funny. I ain't laughing — you're gonna get yours.

Synopsis. *Socialite Deborah Ryder hires Rockford to stop an extortionist named Carl Brego, who knows that Deborah was once linked to a numbers racket in Chicago. As part of his* *surveillance, Rockford videotapes a meeting between Deborah and Carl; then, while pretending to be another blackmailer who wants a piece of the action, he confronts Carl and threatens to turn the tape over to the police unless Carl cuts him in. But Rockford's ploy backfires. A mysterious assailant shoots Carl dead — and when an elderly couple who witnessed Rockford at the scene of the crime notifies the police, the P.I. becomes the prime suspect in the killing.*

In this episode, Sergeant Becker makes a brief reference to his wife Nancy. However, either Becker remarried, or his wife's name was changed, because when Pat Finley (*The Bob Newhart Show*) began playing Mrs. Dennis Becker (starting with the second season episode, "The Farnsworth Stratagem"), the character was known as Peggy.

According to this episode, Rockford's address is 2354 Pacific Coast Highway in Los Angeles. Later in the series, it will be changed to 29 Cove Road in Malibu.

Rockford Facts. The basic storyline of "The Countess" is similar to that of "Lovely Lady, Pity Me," a novel written by Roy Huggins that was published in *The Saturday Evening Post* in the 1940s.

4. EXIT PRENTISS CARR

Production Number: 41405

Original Airdate: October 4, 1974

Teleplay by: *Juanita Bartlett*
Story by: *John Thomas James*
Directed by: *Alex Grasshoff*

Guest Cast: Corinne Comancho Michaels (Janet Carr), Warren Kemmerling (Lieutenant Furlong), Mills Watson (Sergeant Larsen), Stephen McNally (Chief Bailey), William Jordan (Terry Warde), Wallace Rooney (Eric Saunders), Hank Rolike (Eddie), Thomas Rubin (Delivery Boy), Roberta Collins (Nancy Helmond), Heath Jobes (Jack Clark)

It's Morrie. Got a call from Davis at the IRS. You were right — they bounced your return. Call me.

Synopsis. *Rockford's old flame Janet Carr hires him to tail her philandering husband Prentiss. Rockford locates Prentiss at the Bay City Motel, but he finds the man dead — an apparent murder victim. Without actually telling them that he's already investigated the scene of the crime (and thus possibly implicate himself and Janet to Prentiss's death), Rockford manipulates police officers Furlong and Larsen into investigating the motel room. When the officers report* *that Prentiss apparently committed suicide, Rockford accuses them of tampering with the evidence. After he's thrown out of town, Rockford surreptitiously continues to probe — and discovers a link between Prentiss' death and an embezzlement scheme at the insurance company where Prentiss worked.*

Although Roy Huggins wrote nearly all the stories for every television series he produced (and then assigned to another writer to compose the teleplay), his name rarely appeared among the writing credits for his shows — as a rule, he gave the credit to whomever wrote the teleplay. However, beginning in the 1960s and continuing through the 1970s, Huggins' name did appear in the story credits — as "John Thomas James," a pseudonym named after three of Roy's sons.

Supervising producer Jo Swerling Jr. recalled that "John Thomas James" was once very much in demand by other studios.

"We used to get calls from agents and from other producers who would ask, 'You know, that John Thomas James is pretty prolific. Who's his agent?'" he said. "Depending on what they wanted, we'd either make up a story or level with them. Universal even had the name on a separate parking space, which meant that Roy had two parking spaces on the lot. So a lot of people thought that 'John Thomas James' was an actual guy."

"John Thomas James" received individual writing contracts from the studio, as well as separate correspondence from the networks. In one instance, ABC wanted to include footage from a *Toma* episode written by "John Thomas James" in a montage of TV detectives it was preparing as a segment to be featured on the Emmy Awards telecast in 1974. The network needed the author to sign a release form, and in fact had the form addressed to "John Thomas James." Huggins signed the form on James' behalf.

5. TALL WOMAN IN RED WAGON

Production Number: 41415

Original Airdate: October 11, 1974

Teleplay by: *Stephen J. Cannell*
Story by: *John Thomas James*
Directed by: *Jerry London*

Guest Cast: Sian Barbara Allen (Sandra Turkel), George DiCenzo (Stoner), John Crawford (Dr. Kennilworth), Susan Damante (Charlotte Duskey), Angus Duncan (Joe Baron Jr.), Ryan MacDonald (Motel Manager), Dave Morick (James Darrow), Rudy Diaz (Maddey), Robert Raymond Sutton (Morrie), James Murtaugh (Steve McWilliams), Jack Stamberger (Station Manager)

Jim, it's Jack — I'm at the airport. I'm going to Tokyo and I want to pay you the $500 I owe you. Catch you next year when I get back...

Synopsis. *The "tall woman in red wagon" is one Charlotte Duskey, a newspaper city editor (and former gangland moll) who suddenly vanished — along with the $1.2 million she inherited from her late paramour, gangster Joe Baron. Sandra Turkel, a co-worker of Charlotte's who is unaware of her friend's checkered past, hires Rockford to investigate the disappearance.*

The secret of a good confidence game," Rockford explains to Sandra in this episode, "is the right props. You can waste a lot of time on people if you don't have the right props." In "Tall Woman in Red Wagon," we're introduced to one of Rockford's most valuable (and most memorable) "props" — the portable printing press that he keeps in the back seat of his car.

Rockford Familiar Faces. John Crawford, who plays Dr. Kennilworth in this episode, previously appeared with James Garner in 1964's *The Americanization of Emily*.

6. THIS CASE IS CLOSED
(90-minute episode)

Production Numbers: 47595/47596

Original Airdate: October 18, 1974

Teleplay by: *Stephen J. Cannell*
Story by: *John Thomas James*
Directed by: *Bernard L. Kowalski*

Guest Cast: Joseph Cotten (Warner Jameson), Sharon Gless (Susan Jameson), James McEachin (David Shore), Fred Sadoff (Howard Kasanjian), Joseph DellaSorte (Torrance Beck), Norman Bartold (Hollis Cotton), Eddie Fontaine (Lieutenant Larry Pierson), Del Monroe (Vic), Jude Farese (Harry), Stu Nisbet (Bartender), Geoffrey Land (Mark Chalmers)

You really want Issue in the 7th? Come on, that nag couldn't go a mile in the back of a pick-up truck! Call me.

Synopsis. *Warner Jameson believes that Mark Chalmers, the jetsetting Ivy Leaguer engaged to his daughter Sue, is not all that he appears to be, so he hires Rockford to check into Mark's past. Rockford's investigation takes him to Newark, New Jersey, where he is hounded by local police and federal agents. The matter becomes worse for Rockford when he returns to L.A. — first, he's tailed by another private investigator, then he's kidnapped (and almost killed) by mobster Torrance Beck and his goons. Federal agents rescue Rockford from Beck, but then they interrogate him for reasons they won't make clear. Rockford becomes so fed up that he not only quits the case, he drops out of the P.I. business all together. Meanwhile, when Mark Chalmers* *discovers that Jameson is having him investigated, he abruptly calls off the engagement. A stunned Sue Jameson asks Rockford to investigate why Mark mysteriously changed his mind, but Jim can't help her (even if he wanted to) without compromising his professional relationship with her father. But Rockford becomes drawn back into the case anyway once he discovers Mark has been murdered.*

James Garner competed against himself on the night this episode was first broadcast (October 18, 1974). "This Case is Closed" went head-to-head with *They Only Kill Their Masters*, a 1972 Garner feature that aired on *The CBS Friday Night Movie*. *Rockford* bested *The CBS Friday Night Movie* in that night's Nielsen ratings. (Incidentally, *They Only Kill Their Masters* was written by Lane Slate, who briefly served as producer of *The Rockford Files* during the 1975-1976 season.)

"This Case is Closed" features noted screen actor Joseph Cotten (*Citizen Kane*), who reportedly agreed to do the guest shot because of his long friendship with executive producer Meta Rosenberg.

Rockford Facts. The character "Howard Kasanjian" was named after the assistant director with the same name who worked on the *Rockford Files* pilot.

This episode airs as a two-parter in syndication.

7. THE BIG RIPOFF

Production Number: 41416

Original Airdate: October 25, 1974

Teleplay by: *Robert Hamner and Jo Swerling Jr.*
Story by: *John Thomas James*
Directed by: *Vincent McEveety*

Guest Cast: Jill Clayburgh (Marilyn Polanski), Normann Burton (Melvyn Moss), Fred Beir (Steve Nelson), Bruce Kirby (Carl LeMay), Nedra Dean (Nancy Frazier), Warren Vanders (Earl Pitt), Kelly Thordsen (Sheriff Neal), Suzanne Somers (Ginny Nelson), Christine Dixon (Stewardess), Jenny Maybrook (Ticket Clerk)

It's Audra — remember last summer at Pat's? I've got a 12-hour layover before I go to Chicago. How 'bout it?

Synopsis. *Nancy Frazier hires Rockford to investigate the death of her lover Steve Nelson, who allegedly perished in a plane crash. Nancy believes that Steve's wife Virginia arranged for the accident, but Rockford suspects that Steve is alive — and that he and Virginia faked the accident as part of a scheme to bilk their insurance company out of $400,000. Jim also thinks* *that Nancy's in on the scam, because she skipped town almost immediately after Rockford reported back to her. Rockford persuades the insurance company to hire him in order to find Steve Nelson and recover the money.*

"The Big Ripoff" features another *Maverick* touch. After the two operatives beat up Rockford and leave him to die along the side of a lonely road, model Marilyn Polanski rescues Rockford (she'd been following Rockford in his own car). Marilyn nurses Jim back to health, and advises him to take it easy, but Rockford is determined to press on. "Is there anything you won't do for money?" asks Marilyn. "I won't kill for it, and I won't marry for it," replies Rockford. "Other than that, I'm open to just about anything."

Rockford Facts. "The Big Ripoff" is a retooled version of "The $20,000 Carrot," a private eye story which Roy Huggins had written for *The Outsider* in 1968.

This episode is available through MCA/Universal Home Video as part of its Rockford Files collection.

8. FIND ME IF YOU CAN

Production Number: 41412

Original Airdate: November 1, 1974

Teleplay by: *Juanita Bartlett*
Story by: *John Thomas James*
Directed by: *Lawrence Doheny*

Guest Cast: Joan Van Ark (Barbara Kelbaker), Paul Michael Glaser (Ralph Correll), Richard Drout Miller (Sergeant Doane), Joseph Stern (Morgan Tallman), James Lydon (Wyatt), Adrian Ricard (Miss Connor)

This is the Blood Bank. If you don't have malaria, hepatitis or TB, we'd like to have a pint of your blood.

Synopsis. Barbara Kelbaker approaches Rockford with an unusual request — she wants to hire him to find out if she can be "found." But Barbara refuses to explain why (and, in fact, she doesn't even give Rockford her real name) because she's frightened for her life. Barbara witnessed her boyfriend, Denver crime lord Ralph Correll, murder another man. Barbara believes that Correll is after her, and she figures that if Rockford could find her, so could Correll.

The storyline of "Find Me If You Can" is very similar to that of "Girl on the Run," a Roy Huggins short story which Huggins later adapted in 1956 as the basis of the pilot of the TV series *77 Sunset Strip*. Although Huggins acknowledges the similarities between the two stories, he recalls that he'd been thinking along a different line when he first came up with "Find Me If You Can." "That story began simply with that idea — somebody comes up to Rockford and says, 'I want to know if I can be found. I won't tell you a thing about me, but I want to know whether I can be found,'" said Huggins. "Although I now can see that the background story is very much like 'Girl on the Run,' I don't recall deliberately using that story as a *Rockford*, but it may have been done unconsciously."

Rockford Funnies. Rockford sustains a nasty-looking gash near his left eye after he's been grazed by a bullet. Although his father is understandably concerned ("Look at that gash — two inches to the right, and you'd have been missing that eye!"), Jim remains remarkably optimistic. "Look at it this way," he tells Rocky. "Two inches to the left, and he would've missed me completely."

9. IN PURSUIT OF CAROL THORNE

Production Number: 41406

Original Airdate: November 8, 1974

Teleplay by: *Stephen J. Cannell*
Story by: *John Thomas James*
Directed by: *Charles S. Dubin*

Guest Cast: Lynette Mettey (Carol Thorne), Robert Symonds (Miles Keeley), Jim Antonio (Cliff Hoad), Bill Fletcher (Nate Spinella), Irene Tedrow (Dixie), Sandy Ward (Detective Boris Sausman), Vince Howard (Patrolman)

This is the Message Phone company. I see you're using our unit — now how 'bout paying for it?

Synopsis. *Rockford is hired to tail Carol Thorne, a recently paroled convict, by an elderly couple who claim to be the parents of Cliff Hoad, Carol's boyfriend. Rockford doesn't realize that he's been played for a mark — his "client" is really a master con artist named Miles Keeley, who, along with Cliff and two other men, robbed a Marine Corps payroll of $1.2 million three years earlier. Because of a snafu, Cliff alone ended up with all the money (although Miles and the others managed to escape). Miles wants Carol to lead him to Cliff — and to where Cliff stashed the money.*

Like all other aspects of film production, planning the look of a show requires a total understanding of what the writer and producer want to accomplish. Because *Rockford* was primarily written "in house," the writers were usually available for

James Garner, Meta Rosenberg and Stephen J. Cannell on the studio lot.

consultation in the planning of the look of the show. This is particularly helpful if you encountered an element of the script that may pose a practical difficulty. "Say you have a two-page scene that was written to take place outside a gas station in Santa Monica," said supervising producer Jo Swerling. "During the prep time, we might find a location in Santa Monica that's perfect for that scene. Only there's one problem — there's nothing else around that location that could be used for that script. That means that scene would require a major company move across town just to shoot two pages.

"Now, normally, you try to shoot anywhere from 8-10 pages a day. By going out of your way just to shoot that one scene, by the time you're finished loading the trucks, moving everything across town, unloading, setting everything up, shooting the scene, breaking for lunch, wrapping everything up, loading up the truck again, and then heading off to the next location (or back to the studio), you will have burned off at least one-third of your shooting time. In the meantime, you still to have to shoot eight pages in whatever is left of the day. And you really don't want to make two moves in one day, because you're not grinding out film when you're moving — you're spending your shooting time inside a truck.

"So we would say to whoever wrote the script, 'You know, there's a diner nearby the location where we're shooting several other scenes. Would you mind if we play this scene in a diner instead of a gas station, because that would save us an additional company move.' Now, of course, the gas station can't be critical to the scene — and in many cases, it isn't. The writer is simply picking a location that works for him or her, whereas another location might work equally as well."

10. THE DEXTER CRISIS

(a.k.a. "Cherchéz la Femme," or "Find the Woman")

Production Number: 41408

Original Airdate: November 15, 1974

Written by: *Gloryette Clark*
Directed by: *Alex Grasshoff*
Guest Cast: Lee Purcell (Susan Parsons), Linda Kelsey (Louise Adams), Ron Soble (Kermit Higby), Tim O'Connor (Charles Dexter), Joyce Jameson (Marge White), Burke Byrnes (Deputy), Bing Russell (Lieutenant)

I staked out that guy, only it didn't work out like you said. Please call me — Room 234, County Hospital.

Synopsis. *Wealthy entrepreneur Charles Dexter hires Rockford to locate his mistress, Susan Parsons, but doesn't disclose his true motives until much later (Susan ran off with over $250,000 of Dexter's money). Rockford joins forces with Susan's roommate, law student Louise*

Adams, who thinks there's a connection between Susan's disappearance and the driver of a car which had been following Susan for several days. Rockford and Louise travel to Reno, where they not only find Susan, but come across the man who'd been tailing her — Kermit Higby, a private investigator with whom Rockford has clashed in the past.

Because Jim Rockford is essentially Bret Maverick in modern dress, it seems only fitting that Rockford is as much an expert in games of chance as his TV Western alter ego. Like Maverick, Rockford knows that playing roulette, like playing poker, is a game you can only win if you're patient. "No roulette wheel is ever in perfect balance," he explains in "The Dexter Crisis." "All you have to do is figure out the bias, and keep playing until they catch onto what you're doing. That gives you a 6-7% advantage. If you can keep them from figuring your action, you can rip 'em good." (Rockford then adds that he once hit one of the Grand Hotels on the Vegas Strip for over $50,000.)

11. CALEDONIA —
IT'S WORTH A FORTUNE!

(a.k.a. "No Stone Unturned")

Production Number: 41414

Original Airdate: December 6, 1974

Teleplay by: *Juanita Bartlett*
Story by: *John Thomas James*
Directed by: *Stuart Margolin*

Guest Cast: Shelley Fabares (Jolene Hyland), Ramon Bieri (Sheriff Prouty), Richard Schaal (Leonard Blair), William Traylor (Wilson), Sid Haig (B.J.), Rudy Challenger (Dr. Watkins), Don Eichner (Gerald Hyland), Robert Ginty (Gib Moore), Robert Ellenstein (Motel Manager)

It's Doc Jones. What'd you do to the hand, son? Three fractured knuckles.... You hit somebody?

Synopsis. *Gerald Hyland, who was convicted of embezzling over $4 million several years ago, is brutally beaten by two prison inmates. Shortly before slipping into a coma, Hyland leaves his wife Jolene a cryptic clue to where he had supposedly buried nearly $750,000 in rare stamps which Hyland had purchased with the stolen money shortly before his arrest. However, in order to recover the stamps, Jolene must team up with Jerry's former cellmate Leonard Blair — with whom, unbeknownst to her husband, she once had an affair. The conniving Len has the map* *leading to the stash, but the map is useless without Jolene's directions. Because she knows Len will doublecross her at the first opportunity, Jolene hires Rockford to protect her interest.*

One reason why *The Rockford Files* has endured is its timelessness — with few exceptions, the series has very little in the way of topical humor or subject matter that would specifically date it to the time period in which it was made (the mid-to-late 1970s). Interestingly enough, some of the women's fashions seen on the series (such as platform shoes and miniskirts) have come back "in vogue" in recent years.

However, there are some behaviors seen on the series that may have been acceptable 20 years ago, but which are now considered "politically incorrect" (and, in some cases, illegal). For example, many of the characters (including Rockford) smoke cigarettes — and nobody seems to mind. Also, as we see in several instances throughout this episode, passengers in motor vehicles do not always wear their seat belts (the mandatory law had not yet gone into effect). However, NBC's Standards and Practices department, which monitored the content every series episode and TV-movie for accuracy and/or questionable material, *did* mind about that one, and stated its displeasure in a memo regarding this episode: "There is no reason why [seat belts] should not have been in use. Please inform all concerned that this is a serious matter which will continue to be reviewed. We hope it will not become necessary to edit future scenes because they do not properly support our concern regarding the use of safety belts and harnesses." (Although Roy Huggins usually strove to eliminate anything that might offend the upper tier of his viewership, he apparently overlooked that particular detail; however, he did make a big notation in red ink on his copy of the memo: "PLEASE NOTE.")

Rockford Facts. "Caledonia — It's Worth a Fortune!" recycles a line that Huggins had first used in "Point Blank," the pilot episode of *Maverick* which Huggins had written in 1956. At the end of "Point Blank," the sheriff orders Maverick "to get out of town in ten minutes," to which Maverick replies, "Sheriff, I've gotten out of towns this size in *five* minutes." Similarly, in the first act of "Caledonia — It's Worth a Fortune!," Sheriff Prouty, who has taken an immediate dislike to Rockford, asks how long would it take Rockford to leave town. "About fifteen minutes," says Rockford. "Why don't you make it ten?" cracks Prouty.

Incidentally, the sheriff is played by Ramon Bieri, who later co-starred with James Garner in Bret Maverick.

12./13. PROFIT AND LOSS
(Two-parter)

(a.k.a. "Fiscal Dynamics, Inc.")

Production Numbers: 41417/41418
Original Airdates: December 20 and 27, 1974

Teleplay by: *Stephen J. Cannell*
Story by: *John Thomas James*
Directed by: *Lawrence Doheny*

Guest Cast: Ned Beatty (Leon Fielder), Sharon Spelman (Doris Parker), Paul Jenkins (Stan Gorrick), Val Bisoglio (Carl Bovino), Albert Paulsen (Kurt), Michael Lerner (Arnold Love), Priscilla Pointer (Helen Morris), John Carter (Alec Morris), Ray Girardin (Ted), Donald Billett (Don Shavelson), Joe E. Tata (Solly Marshall), Jay J. Saunders (Computer Programmer), Tracy Bogart (Teresa), Tom Rosqui (Norm Mitchell), Al Stephenson (L.J.), Barry Cahill (Sergeant)

Hey, Jimmy — this here's Teeter Skerritt. Remember me? From the Army. I'm stuck here in town — how 'bout I come over and bunk with you, buddy?

This is Mrs. Bosley at the Library. We billed you for your overdue book, Karate Made Easy. We abuse our Library if we don't get our cards renewed...

Synopsis. Computer programmer Alec Morris comes to Rockford for protection upon discovering that his employer, the powerful corporation Fiscal Dynamics, Inc., has been forging information on its annual report in order to carry off plans to purchase another corporate giant. Rockford witnesses two men abduct Morris, but after reporting the matter to the police, he not only finds Morris safe and sound, but faces a false report charge when Morris denies that anything ever happened. In addition, CEO Leon Fielder threatens to sue Rockford for $10 million unless he stays out of FDI's affairs. Rockford's about to drop out of the matter when he is hired by Doris Parker, who has long suspected FDI of murdering her husband (who also worked as a computer programmer for the company). Upon reading that the man who printed FDI's annual report was found dead in his shop, Jim deduces that both Doris' husband and the printer were killed after they, like Morris, discovered the forgery scheme. With the help of Doris (and his father), Rockford sets out to prove it.

Early in the first act of Part One, after he is beaten up by the two men who kidnap Alec Morris, Rockford calls the police and asks for "Lieutenant Becker." Either this was an oversight, or Becker must've gotten into big trouble with the department, because by the time we see him again (in the episode "Sleight of Hand"), he's been bounced back to sergeant. Of course, Becker was promoted to lieutenant for good in the fifth season episode "Kill the Messenger."

14. AURA LEE, FAREWELL

Production Number: 41413

Original Airdate: January 3, 1975

Teleplay by: *Edward J. Lakso*
Story by: *John Thomas James*
Directed by: *Jackie Cooper*

Guest Cast: Lindsay Wagner (Sara Butler), Robert Webber (Senator Evan Murdock), Greg Mullavey (Dirk Shaefer), Kelly Lange (Commentator), Bill Mumy (Trask), Melissa Greene (Aura Lee Benton), Henry Slate (Oscar), Tom Scott (Motel Clerk), Linda Dano (Ellen Murdock), Ed Crick (Campaigner)

Mr. Rockford, you don't know me, but I'd like to hire you. Could you call me at — My name is, uh — Never mind. Forget it.

Synopsis. *Once again, Rockford teams up with Sara Butler (the woman who hired him in the pilot episode to solve the murder of her father). Sara wants Jim to prove that the apparent suicide of her girlfriend and employee Aura Lee Benton was really a murder. Aura Lee died of a heroin overdose, but Sara suspects foul play because she knows Aura Lee did not take drugs. After some probing, Rockford and Sara discover that a high-profile state senator, a drug pusher, a fatal hit-and-run accident, over $2,600 in hush money, and a blackmail scheme are all linked to Aura Lee's death.*

Like Maverick, Rockford is capable of having a romantic relationship with a woman — without ever losing sight of his own self-interest. At the end of the episode, Rockford wants to know how Sara plans to pay him. Sara had planned to pay Jim with the cash she found in Aura Lee's apartment, but she can't because the police have confiscated the money. Sara offers to pay Rockford on the installment plan ("like we did before"), then leans forward and kisses Rockford. Although Rockford enjoys the kiss, he doesn't lose sight of the bottom line. When they finish smooching, Rockford smiles at Sara and says, "I want the pink slip to your car."

Lindsay Wagner (*The Bionic Woman*) reprises the role of Sara Butler. Bill Mumy (*Lost in Space*), who had played Sara's brother in the pilot, also guest stars in "Aura Lee, Farewell," albeit in a completely different role. Mumy plays an artist named Trask, who sells his paintings on the streets of Venice in the funniest scene of this episode. Rockford asks if Trask needs a permit to sell his paintings. "I told you, I paint what I feel," Trask replies. Upon glancing at one of the paintings, Rockford cracks, "You must not feel well."

15. SLEIGHT OF HAND

(a.k.a. "Nightmare")

Production Number: 41423

Original Airdate: January 17, 1975

Teleplay by: *Stephen J. Cannell and Jo Swerling*
Based on the Novel *Thin Air* **by** *Howard Browne*
Directed by: *William Wiard*

Guest Cast: Lara Parker (Diana Lewis), Pat Delany (Karen Mills), Allan Miller (Michael Cordeen), John Steadman (Morrie Blauner), Gerald McRaney (Irv), Howard Curtis (Vince Minette), Wayne Wynne (Detective Olson)

Rockford, this is Mr. Dow. If you think I'm gonna pay to have your car repainted, you're nuts — you can take your expense bill and stuff it!

Synopsis. *Rockford makes an exception to his own rule of never interfering with an open police case when he investigates the disappearance of his girlfriend Karen Mills, who mysteriously vanished in front of her home moments after returning from a trip to San Francisco with Rockford and her daughter Julie. While the police link Karen's disappearance with the brutal murder of her next door neighbor, Rockford's probe eventually uncovers a connection between his girlfriend, a mysterious woman named Diana Lewis, and a fugitive underworld kingpin.*

In January 1973, Roy Huggins and Jo Swerling Jr. took over the reins of *Jigsaw*, a low-rated police drama starring James Wainwright as an investigator for the California State Bureau of Missing Persons. In an effort to save the series, Huggins and Swerling reworked the premise of the series and made Wainwright's character a private eye. In order to generate attention for "the new, improved *Jigsaw*," Universal Studios put forth a major publicity campaign that resulted in the series getting a·second review in all the major newspapers and trade journals, including *Variety*. Although Huggins' first episode of *Jigsaw* — an adaptation of the Howard Browne mystery novel *Thin Air* — was critically acclaimed, the ratings for the series did not improve. *Jigsaw* was cancelled in the Spring of 1973.

Huggins had always liked *Thin Air*, and so he decided to adapt it once again — this time, as a story for *The Rockford Files*. "It's tough to come up with good stories, week after week after week," he confessed. "I liked *Thin Air* — it was a story that I'd always thought had a great opening; and it happened to be written by an old and dear friend of mine, Howard Browne [whose friendship with Huggins covers nearly 40 years].

"I knew that I had done a *Thin Air* story only a couple of years before [on *Jigsaw*]. But I also remembered that *Jigsaw* never had high audience numbers. And so, I figured, 'Here's a story that was on a show that nobody watched, so I'm going to adapt it again. I'll make changes in it — with Jim Garner, it will look completely different.' That was pretty much what was going on in my mind at the time."

However, Huggins did catch some flak from *Variety*, whose reviewer accused the producer of "cribbing from himself" after recognizing "Sleight of Hand" as a remake of the *Jigsaw* episode of 1973. "Well, that shows you that *Variety* had a very good reviewer," replied Huggins. "He was showing that he was on his toes. And I'll tell you — two years is a little soon to bring something back. If you're going to do that, you ought to wait at least seven." (Or, in the case of *Maverick* as *The Rockford Files*, maybe as long as twenty.)

Ironically, while *Variety* may have been astute in recognizing the recycled plotline of "Sleight of Hand," the trade journal neglected to mention that the episode itself is excellent. Swerling and Stephen J. Cannell create a faithful adaptation of Browne's classic whodunit, while James Garner delivers one of his finest performances in the entire series.

Rockford Funnies. Helen Alexander, who was Jo Swerling's assistant at the time, volunteered her beige handbag as one of the props for the *Jigsaw* adaptation of *Thin Air*. When Alexander learned that Huggins was going to remake that episode on *The Rockford Files*, she wrote a witty memo — which she signed "Helen Alexander's handbag" — asking Huggins if she could "play" the same part.

I am Helen Alexander's handbag. I have recently been informed that the Jigsaw episode in which I starred — well, had a featured lead — well, I did have a big zoom closeup — and for which I was personally selected by Roy Huggins, is being remade as an episode of Rockford Files. Naturally, I'd like to play the part again.

In case you may be worried that I have aged in the meantime, I'd like you to know that I have since had my face lifted. In addition, although my figure is still the same, I have a varied wardrobe, so that I am available in black, tan, and navy, in addition to the beige outfit in which I previously played the role.

Please keep me in mind when you start casting. Somehow or other, I missed being nominated for an Emmy, but I'm sure that if you gave me another chance, that honor will be in the bag.

P.S. Although I do not belong to SAG, I do belong to BAG.

Although Alexander's white handbag was used in the episode (it has a zoom closeup midway through the first act), it was once again overlooked in the Emmy Awards nominations for 1974-1975.

16. COUNTER GAMBIT

Production Number: 41420

Original Airdate: January 24, 1975

Written by: *Howard Berk and Juanita Bartlett*
Directed by: *Jackie Cooper*

Guest Cast: Mary Frann (Valerie Thomas), Eddie Fontaine (Moss Williams), Burr deBenning (Harry Crown), Ford Rainey (Manny Tolan), M. Emmet Walsh (Edgar Burch), Garry Walberg (Arnold Cutter), Eric Server (Daniel Kramer), Barbara Collentine (Miss Bolting)

It's Lori at the Trailer Park. A space opened up — do you want me to save it, or are the cops gonna let you stay where you are?

Synopsis. *Insurance agent Edgar Burch hires Rockford to recover a $250,000 pearl necklace that was apparently stolen by Moss Williams three years ago — shortly after Williams asked Jim to locate the woman who supposedly stashed the pearls. Rockford decides to play both sides of the fence, but instead gets burned.*

The "stolen" necklace was never stolen. Williams hired Burch to get Rockford to find the pearls — so that he can steal them and frame Jim for the theft. With the help of Valerie Thomas (the owner of the pearls), jewel appraiser Manny Tolan, and his old stir mate Angel Martin, Rockford sets out to clear himself.

Like Maverick, Rockford's not above committing a little larceny (so long as no one gets hurt). In this episode, Rockford takes advantage of Valerie's affections for him in order to get the combination of her apartment safe. Rockford asks Valerie to store a box, which allegedly contains valuable papers for another client, inside her safe while they're out on the town. Valerie doesn't realize that the box contains a sound-activated tape recorder, which began to play once Rockford spoke to Valerie and continued to record as Valerie locked the safe. After Rockford retrieves the box the next day, he rewinds the tape, plays it back, and determines the combination by counting the clicks. (Rockford knows that most safes are insulated from the outside, but not from the inside; once you figure how to get a tape recorder inside a safe, you can record the combination.)

17. CLAIRE

(a.k.a. "Lady on the Run")

Production Number: 41422

Original Airdate: January 31, 1975

Written by: *Edward J. Lakso and Stephen J. Cannell*
Directed by: *William Wiard*

Guest Cast: Linda Evans (Claire Prescott), W.L. LeGault (Stone), Jackie Cooper (Captain Highland), Lane Smith (Willett), M.P. Murphy (Carl), Douglas V. Fowley (Ted)

Mr. Rockford, this is the Thomas Crown School of Dance and Contemporary Etiquette. We aren't going to call again. Do you want these free lessons, or what?

Synopsis. *Rockford's former fiancé Claire Prescott asks him to find Charlie Manning, an undercover police detective who used Claire as an informant as part of an important narcotics investigation. When Manning is found dead, Claire becomes the prime suspect; meanwhile, she's also the target of the real killers. Rockford tries to smuggle Claire out of town. But the killers kidnap Rocky, and they threaten to kill him unless Rockford delivers Claire.*

Rockford Writeoffs. When we first see Rockford in this episode, he's helping his father do his taxes. Rocky is trying to claim a check for $260, which he said he loaned Jim to help pay for Jim's car. "That check bounced — you can't claim a check as a deduction if the check bounced," says Jim. "No wonder you have tax problems." Actually, Rocky should have declared his truck as a tax writeoff, because it's often used as part of Jim's business (as is the case in this episode).

18.SAY GOODBYE TO JENNIFER

(a.k.a. "The Witness Vanishes")

Production Number: 41407

Original Airdate: February 7, 1975

Teleplay by: *Juanita Bartlett and Rudolph Borchert*
Story by: *John Thomas James*
Directed by: *Jackie Cooper*

Guest Cast: Hector Elizondo (John Micelli), Pamela Hensley (Jennifer Ryburn), Ken Swofford (Floyd Ross), Kate Woodville (Marilyn Rae), Thayer David (Carl Birrell), Regis J. Cordic (Dr. Evan Stuart), Len Lesser (Colby), Clint Young (Harrison), Beverly Gill (Mary Ann), Vince Cannon (Ricky Pont)

This is Mrs. Landis. Three times this month I come to clean and it always looks like people've been fighting in there: furniture broken, things tipped over. I'm sorry, but I quit!

Synopsis. *Supermodel Jennifer Ryburn allegedly died in a fiery car accident that occurred shortly after the fatal shooting of her boyfriend Ricky Pont, a murder that the police (and the mob) believe she committed. But Jennifer's photographer and former lover John Micelli thinks she's alive and hiding in Seattle, and he wants Jim to find her and to prove her innocence. Rockford's reluctant to take the case — he believes Mitch is too distraught over Jennifer's death to think clearly, and he knows that his involvement could implicate Mitch, who was very jealous of Pont, in Pont's murder. Mitch and Rockford's lives becomes endangered when mobster Carl Birrell, who raised Pont like a son, learns about their investigation. Birrell wants Jennifer found and killed.*

Keep an eye out for two Hollywood landmarks (and a sly bit of humor) in Act I, during the scene in which Mitch meets Rockford downtown after returning from Seattle. Rockford and Mitch take a walk along Hollywood Boulevard, pass by the venerable Roosevelt Hotel (where the first Academy Awards were presented in 1929), and make their way up the famous Hollywood Walk of Fame. That particular scene begins with a closeup of the star of actor Robert Young, who in 1975 was one of the biggest names in television — Young was the star of the top-rated *Marcus Welby, M.D.*, which (like *The Rockford Files*) was produced at Universal. (Coincidentally, Pamela Hensley, who guest starred in this episode, would later join the cast of *Marcus Welby, M.D.* in the Fall of 1975.)

In real life, James Garner and Stephen J. Cannell each have a place on the Hollywood Walk of Fame. Garner's star is in front of the world-famous Mann's Chinese Theater (across the street from the Roosevelt Hotel), while Cannell's star is actually located in front of the Roosevelt. Also, the West Coast headquarters of the Cannell Studios are located in the Lareina Building on Hollywood Boulevard, one block away from the hotel.

Rockford Fashion. This episode features a rarely seen aspect of Rockford's sartorial personality — for the first and only time in the series, he wears a lot of turtleneck sweaters (his choice of fashion while in Seattle).

19. CHARLIE HARRIS AT LARGE

(a.k.a. "Crime Without Witness")

Production Number: 41409

Original Airdate: February 14, 1975

Teleplay by: *Zekial Marko*
Story by: *John Thomas James*
Directed by: *Russ Mayberry*

Guest Cast: Tony Musante (Charlie Harris), David Spielberg (Sergeant Tom Garvey), Warner Anderson (Alfred Bannister), Diana Muldaur (Linda Bannister), Eddie Firestone (Haines), Mel Stewart (Police Lieutenant), Zekial Marko (Dr. Gabriel)

Hey, Jim, it's me — Suzie Lewis, from the laundromat. You said you were going to call, and it's been two weeks. What's wrong — you lose my number?

James Garner and Tony Musante.

Synopsis. *Charlie Harris, a "high society hustler" who was Rockford's cellmate for two years at San Quentin, is the leading suspect in the murder of a socialite whom he recently married. Charlie is innocent, and he even has an alibi (a woman he knows only as "Cassandra"), only she's disappeared, so he needs Rockford to help him find Cassandra and clear his name. Rockford soon discovers that Charlie's mystery woman is married to Alfred Bannister, a powerful business magnate who wants to suppress any knowledge of his wife's involvement with Charlie. Bannister threatens to have Rockford killed unless he drops the case.*

This episode features Tony Musante, who starred as *Toma*, the series produced by Roy Huggins and Stephen J. Cannell, and the vehicle for which the Jim Rockford character was originally created. "Tony is a very focused actor with a great sense of his craft," recalled Huggins. "We once did a story on *Toma* about someone who was deaf. I ran into Tony one day while we were shooting that episode, and I noticed he was carrying some books. He showed them to me — they were books about the deaf. That shows you the kind of conscientious, serious actor that Tony is."

Rockford Fun. Listen carefully to the baseball game that Rocky is watching on television during Act IV — you'll catch the names of *Rockford*'s executive producer ("Last time up, Rosenberg really shelled him"), associate producer ("Here comes Johnson, with the hook"), co-creator ("Now Cannell's coming in") and executive story consultant ("Here comes Bartlett from the bullpen"). Also: Zekial Marko, who wrote the teleplay for this episode, appears briefly as police doctor Gabriel.

20. THE FOUR POUND BRICK

Production Number: 41421

Original Airdate: February 21, 1975

Teleplay by: *Leigh Brackett and Juanita Bartlett*
Story by: *Leigh Brackett*
Directed by: *Lawrence Doheny*

Guest Cast: Edith Atwater (Kate Banning), William Watson (Ross), Jess Walton (Laura Smith), Paul Carr (Sergeant Andrew Wilson), John Quade (Tennen), Jack Knight (Officer Drexel), Bruce Tuthill (Waiter), Frank Campanella (Morrie), John Furlong (Minister)

This is Shirley, from the bank. The answers are No, No, and Yes: No, we won't loan you money; No, we won't accept any co-signors; and Yes, your account's overdrawn. I get off at 4:30...

Synopsis. Kate Banning, a longtime friend of Rocky's, always said that her son David, a rookie police officer, took better care of his car than himself, so she becomes suspicious when Dave is killed in an apparent traffic accident. Jim agrees to look into the matter, but he soon faces a dilemma. Rockford finds signs that point to foul play, but he also uncovers evidence that could implicate Dave in a crooked narcotics operation. If he probes further, not only could Rockford resolve the nature of Dave's death — he could also impugn Banning's good name.

Noah Beery had a great career, and he came from a really talented family of actors," said makeup artist Jack Wilson. "His dad was one of the great movie villains of the silent screen era, and his uncle, Wallace Beery, won an Oscar in 1932 for *The Champ*. I had worked with him quite a bit on *Rockford*, and he was truly wonderful to be around. It's kind of funny — back then, I hadn't really thought about what he had done, but lately, I've come to realize what a marvelous performer he was. On any given day, you could turn on the TV and catch him in some really great films — *Inherit the Wind, Sergeant York, Of Mice and Men, Red River*. He was in all kinds of great pictures. He was a fine actor whose career spanned a long time."

Rockford Facts. Rocky's speeches in the *Rockford Files* scripts were always headed "Joseph," because Stephen J. Cannell named the character after his father Joseph Cannell. In fact, while he was interviewed for this book, whenever Cannell mentioned Rockford's father, he always referred to the character as "Joseph."

21. JUST BY ACCIDENT

Production Number: 41427

Original Airdate: February 28, 1975

Written by: *Charles Sailor and Eric Kalder*
Directed by: *Jerry London*

Guest Cast: Neva Patterson (Louise Hartman), Steven Keats (Duane Bailey), David Spielberg (Sergeant Tom Garvey), Fred Sadoff (Matt Springfield), E.J. Peaker (Jeannie Szymczyk), Joey Aresco (Billy Jo Hartman), Oliver Clark (K. Julian Krubm), Alan Bergmann (The Doctor), Millie Slavin (Assistant Bank Manager), Beatrice Colen (Woman Bettor), Michael Fox (The Announcer), Gordon Jump (Freddie), Fritzi Burr (County Clerk), Sal Acquisto (Gas Station Attendant), Susan Keller (Vivian)

This is Thelma Sue Binkley. It's about the research I called you about — the family tree? Did you talk to your daddy? We may be kin!

Synopsis. *Demolition derby driver Billy Jo Hartman's plans to retire from the field and move onto dirt racing are cut short when his car is pushed off a cliff by a man named Duane Bailey. Although the police classify the death as accidental, Billy Jo's mother Louise hires her longtime friend Rockford to investigate. The matter becomes more intriguing when Louise discovers that her son had named her as the beneficiary on a $200,000 life insurance policy he'd taken out on himself — although Billy Jo was a champion driver, he didn't make enough money* to afford such an expensive policy. Louise doesn't realize that Billy Jo was involved in an elaborate life insurance scam orchestrated by Bailey and crooked salesman Matt Springfield, and that her son was killed because he wanted out. When Rockford discovers that Springfield and Bailey were behind Billy Jo's death, his own life becomes endangered.

Davids Spielberg reprises his role of Tom Garvey, whom we first saw in "Charlie Harris at Large." Garvey was an hard-nosed character at first — Roy Huggins' original story for "Charlie Harris" described him as having "an inhuman coldness, a distance quality, and a deadly politeness that is impolite as hell." However, the character was mellowed out, because Garvey's demeanor toward Rockford in "Just by Accident" is considerably more friendly.

Also appearing in this episode: Neva Patterson, who had co-starred with James Garner and Stuart Margolin on *Nichols*; and Gordon Jump, a few years away from becoming Mr. Carlson on *WKRP in Cincinnati*.

22. ROUNDABOUT

Production Number: 41424

Original Airdate: March 7, 1975

Teleplay by: *Mitchell Lindemann and Edward J. Lakso*
Story by: *Mitchell Lindemann*
Directed by: *Lou Antonio*

Guest Cast: Jesse Welles (Nancy Wade), Ron Rifkin (Tom Robertson), Mills Watson (Edward Moss), Frank Michael Liu (Kenneth Mamato), Virginia Gregg (Eleanor Wainwright), Joe E. Tata (Agent Hanzer), George Wyner (Strock), Robert Ward (The Hotel Clerk), Fred Lerner (Freeman), Chuck Hicks (Klaus)

This is Marilyn Reed. I want to talk to you — Is this a machine? I don't talk to machines! [Caller hangs up. Phone goes dead.]

Synopsis. *An insurance company hires Jim to deliver a $10,000 check to Nancy Wade, the sole beneficiary on her late mother's policy. Rockford travels to Las Vegas, where Nancy works as a lounge singer, and eventually discovers that she has been exploited by her manager, Tom Robertson, who has been using her money to fund business ventures owned and operated by the syndicate. After he is attacked and robbed of the check by some of Robertson's men, Rockford schemes to turn the tables on the slick operator. Aiding him in the cause is Japanese electronics executive Kenneth Mamato, another victim of Robertson's maneuvers.*

One of several *Rockford* episodes filmed on location in Las Vegas, "Roundabout" features one of the slowest chases in the history of prime time television (and quite possibly, in all of film). In Act IV, Rockford is wired for sound when he meets Robertson outside Hoover Dam — as soon as Rockford says the code word ("Geronimo!"), FBI Agent Hanzer and the rest of the police are supposed to converge on the scene. But Robertson panics and dashes inside, forcing Rockford to chase him on foot throughout the entire Hoover Dam building. Because Rockford, unlike "most private eyes," is a little out of shape, it doesn't take long for him to become winded. However, Robertson's not in great condition, either — in fact, both men are gasping and chugging by the time Rockford finally catches up to Robertson. As they both sit down and catch their breath, the camera pulls away — enabling the viewer to see that the two men have chased each other all the way to the bottom of the dam.

Interestingly enough, the foot chase was not in the original script. The scene called for a car chase. However, the script also included the following note with regard to the staging of this scene: "Sequence to be staged to accommodate location yet to be selected." Apparently, once the Hoover Dam location was chosen, it was decided to change the sequence from a car chase to a foot chase inside the building — which changed the dynamics of the entire scene.

Rockford Facts. This episode also features a sequence in which Rockford visits Nancy Wade at the Las Vegas lounge where she performs. As Rockford makes his way toward Nancy, he has to work his way through a bevy of showgirls, one of whom offers him "an appreciative look" as he passes by. After reviewing the script, NBC's Standards and Practices cautioned "Let's keep television propriety in mind concerning the costuming of the 'scantily-clad chorus girls,' avoiding such anatomical exposure as might make the scene unacceptable."

Although these remarks may seem prudish today, we have to bear in mind they were made 20 years ago, at a time when "propriety" in television was considerably more strict. The standards in television have certainly changed, although not always for the better; if staged today, this sequence would likely be filmed in slow motion, and would include gratuitous footage of cleavage and bare midrifts.

Still, these comments are interesting because they provide us with a window into what was considered acceptable and what wasn't. For instance, Standards and Practices frequently objected to the number of times the words "Damned" and "Hell" appeared in the *Rockford Files* scripts (whereas today, a script containing those two expletives, and none other, would be considered fairly tame). In fact, Roy Huggins recalled that S&P once asked him to remove the word "danged" from a script because "they [S&P] thought the audience might hear it as 'damned.'"

Second Season: 1975-1976

Exactly how executive producer Roy Huggins departed from *The Rockford Files* remains one of the cloudier episodes in the show's history—at least, based upon what was published at the time. In 1974, *TV Guide* reported that Huggins was banned from the *Rockford* set because he and James Garner couldn't get along. Another item in 1979 claims that Huggins left the show after a few episodes because he and Garner disagreed "over how the show should be done."

A closer look at these allegations, however, shows that there's more to them than meets the eye. First of all, Huggins rarely set foot on the set of any of his shows, unless he was directing an episode, or if an emergency came up that required his immediate attention. Huggins primarily concerned himself with only two areas of production — the development of stories and scripts, and the editing of the film. All other aspects of the show were left in the hands of Jo Swerling, Stephen J. Cannell, and others like them. (In fact, as mentioned earlier, Huggins was often out of town while the show was in production—he would be away tape-recording new stories during one of his patented "story drives.")

The matter of Garner and Huggins disagreeing over how *Rockford* should be made is also easy to disprove. It was not at the time (nor has it ever been) Garner's style to tell his producers, directors and writers how to do their jobs—he respected their capabilities and let them be.

However, relations between the actor and the producer have not always been smooth — and they became particularly strained as the result of an article published two weeks before *Rockford*'s premiere in September 1974.

Shortly before leaving for a five-week vacation in Europe, Huggins consented to a telephone interview with a reporter from *Daily Variety*. The conversation centered around a condition that was widely known throughout Hollywood: because production was at such a peak in the television industry (and the number of exceptional professionals was at a premium), it was extremely difficult for producers to find experienced personnel to fill jobs that had unexpectedly become vacant. For example, say you had a talented film editor who was suddenly hired for a directing job on another series. Finding a replacement who was as good as that editor would be a challenge — because none of the other "top level" editors are available (they would have already been hired by other production companies), you may have to choose an editor who has promise, but not as much experience.

However, Huggins went on to tell the reporter that this condition did not have an adverse impact on *The Rockford Files*, because the entire makeup of the crew was excellent. Huggins also noted that the series was fortunate enough to have top-quality directors — many of whom did not ordinarily do hour-long episodic television, but who agreed to do *Rockford* because of the unique qualities of the show, and because of their respect for James Garner.

The following morning, *Variety* published the article under the banner headline *TV SERIES TALENT SHORTAGE*. The tone of the article gave the impression that Huggins believed that *The Rockford Files* was plagued by a lack of talent, "not only in above-the-line, to actors, writers, and directors, but below-the-line, where [the article quotes Huggins as saying] 'we are using people who have had no experience whatever in film.'" By the time the paper came out, Huggins had already left for Europe, so he had no idea had badly he had been misquoted until after his return.

The item caused a stir throughout the film industry — and particularly incensed Garner and Meta Rosenberg, who were personally responsible for selecting many of the personnel who worked on the show. Supervising producer Jo Swerling Jr. interceded on Huggins' behalf by stating in a memo to Rosenberg that Huggins had indeed been misquoted. Rosenberg apparently didn't believe that (she contended that the reporter had a reputation for accuracy); however, Swerling countered that while the journalist in question may have been "accurate relative to other trade reporters," he was still prone to errors even after he'd been supplied with accurate information. To illustrate his point, Swerling recalled an instance in which the Publicity Department at Universal supplied that same reporter with a promotional flyer regarding the production of *Pretty Boy Floyd* which stated that the TV-movie was "written and directed by Clyde Ware for producer Jo Swerling Jr." The reporter wrote that the film was "written by Clyde Ware and directed by producer Jo Swerling Jr."

"Let me emphasize that this serious error was made even though the accurate information was clearly furnished in writing," Swerling wrote Rosenberg. "If [this reporter] can make that kind of error, he is certainly capable of making more serious errors when his article is based on a telephone conversation." Swerling's memo also noted that Huggins' assistant, Dorothy Bailey, was present in his office at the time of the interview; Bailey heard Huggins' comments during the conversation and also believed that the producer had been misquoted.

When he returned from vacation, Huggins clarified his comments in a rebuttal published in *Variety*. "The fact is that the *Rockford* crew is one of the best I have ever had, largely because of Jim Garner, who has a way of attracting good people and keeping them," he wrote. "We have been lucky on *Rockford* in getting some actors and directors who work for us because of Jim."

Apparently, however, that wasn't enough. A rift developed between the Huggins camp and the Garner/Rosenberg camp, which led to the kind of published remarks against Huggins that appeared in the likes of *TV Guide*. Huggins never retaliated, with the exception of one remark that encapsulizes the peculiar nature of his relationship with Garner. "Jim and I have a love/hate relationship," Huggins said on *60 Minutes* in 1980. "I love him, and he hates me." (The "feud" was never entirely resolved until several years after *The Rockford Files* left the air.)

Although Garner and Huggins are alike in many ways — both are introverted, both are personable, both are extraordinarily gifted in their respected crafts — they are also two fundamentally different people. For Garner, it is very important to create a sense of family in the working environment. Ask anyone who has ever worked with Garner, and they will inevitably use the word "family" when describing their experience with him. Garner thrives on surrounding himself with people that he trusts and cares for. Huggins, however, never became a part of that family circle — although, by his own admission, that was a matter of choice. Huggins, keep in mind, was preeminently a writer, which means that he was often reclusive by choice — he would often isolate himself for days at a time in order to concentrate on developing stories and rewriting scripts. "When I was producing television, I lived in a world of story development — telling the stories, reading them, rewriting them, and editing them," he explained. "That was predominantly my world — until the time I'd come home, when my family would become my world."

Also factoring in the equation: Garner's film career, which stumbled after a promising start. Although Garner had starred in some successful and acclaimed motion pictures in the 1960s (*The Wheeler Dealers, The Americanization of Emily, The Great Escape, Support Your Local Sheriff*), he never quite became a "big movie star." While that in part may have been attributed to bad choices, the fact that Garner had been so closely identified with *Maverick* didn't help him, either. Garner had created such a lasting impression with his portrayal of the silver-tongued grafter that for years he was perceived (by filmmakers and moviegoers alike) as an actor who could only play "tongue in cheek" characters. Only within the past 15 years has Garner been able to shake that perception completely, through his efforts in such TV films as *Heartsounds, Promise, Decoration Day*, and *My Name is Bill W.*, as well as his Oscar-nominated performance in *Murphy's Romance*.

Although he and Garner were never close friends, Roy Huggins has known Garner so long and so well that he believes he understands Garner like few people can. Huggins agrees that Garner was determined to shake the "tongue in cheek" label — but he also believes there's a little more to it than that.

"This is only my opinion — and I could be wrong," Huggins cautioned. "But I believe that when Jim first returned to television, it was very important to him that his new show should succeed. Now, as you know, *Nichols* failed, and that was a trauma, so much so that he gave a series of interviews over several years saying things like: 'This show was a great show; it was a show that was so good no one understood it, because it was ahead of its time.' And that allowed him to live with the suggestion that he couldn't do it alone — that if he wanted a success, he had to work with a strong producer. And in that first season on *Rockford*, Jim had to face it: he had succeeded with *Maverick*, failed with *Nichols*, and now he was succeeding with *Rockford* — which may be why he was so eager to get me off the show. My colleagues, however, are of the opinion that the close relationship of Garner and Rosenberg was at the heart of the move to have me taken off the show."

Be that as it may, this much is clear. Garner did come to Huggins at a pivotal point in his career — after the failure of *Nichols*, and at a point when his once-promising motion picture career was on the decline. The tremendous success of *The Rockford Files*, particularly during its first season, resuscitated Garner's career. Although the show struggled in the second season, this much is also clear: the show continued for four successful years after Huggins, during which time Garner won the Emmy Award for Best Dramatic Actor, and the series itself won the Emmy for Best Dramatic Series. That was important to Garner because it proved that he could succeed on his own.

As a rule, Huggins left all his series after one or two seasons because that was the point at which he felt he had exhausted all storytelling possibilities for a given series. In the case of *The Rockford Files*, he had decided to move on before Garner spoke up. But Huggins' decision was also based in part on the fact that his plate was full — by the end of the 1974-1975 season, Huggins had launched another series, *Baretta*, and had begun developing another private detective series (*City of Angels*). But since *The Rockford Files* was a big hit, Huggins wanted to ensure that the series would remain that way — his contract provided that once he lauched a show, he would be paid his production fee (which increased from season to season), regardless of whether he continued to be involved in the show or not. This particular provision had already been applied to several other shows that Huggins had either created or produced for Universal.

But Huggins knew that *Rockford* had someone who was perfectly capable of running the show in his place. "I had Steve Cannell, and I knew that he could do it," said Huggins. "And I honestly believed that was the only way the studio could avoid losing him. Steve was far too great a talent to be restricted to just writing and acting as a secondary producer."

Just as Huggins was about to break the news to Frank Price, Garner met with Price and asked to have Huggins removed from the show.

Price was reluctant to make any change. "One of the reasons that I wanted so strongly to keep Roy on *Rockford Files* is that I didn't know anybody who was better with a certain kind of sophisticated humor in that dramatic form than he was," he said. "*Maverick*'s been a good example of that, and certainly *Rockford*. In the case of both shows, there's a danger of getting carried away with the fact that the show was funny, and starting to turn it into a farce. And if it goes that way, it destroys the show — it's amusing for a while, but the credibility of the show just goes away. Roy was always good at making sure the show measured up in that regard."

Since Huggins had planned to step down anyway, the matter of his departure was a *fait accompli*. However, Huggins did convince Price to turn over the critical area of story and script supervision to Cannell. While Meta Rosenberg retained the title "executive producer," it was Cannell who ultimately ran the show after Huggins left *Rockford* at the end of the first season.

* * *

Meanwhile, after taking a beating by NBC's Friday night lineup all year long the previous season, CBS went for the jugular by moving *M*A*S*H* and *Hawaii Five-O* — both Top Ten shows in 1974-1975 — to Friday nights beginning in September 1975. The Eye Network scheduled *Hawaii Five-O* opposite *The Rockford Files* in the critical 9:00-10:00 p.m. time slot. The head-to-head competition between *Rockford* and *Five-O* was one of the most heavily anticipated events of the Fall, comparable to the hype surrounding another prime time showdown (*Home Improvement* vs. *Frasier*) which would take place nearly twenty years later.

Legend has it that NBC and Universal became so concerned over *Hawaii Five-O* that they exerted tremendous pressure on Stephen Cannell and Meta Rosenberg to "remove the humor" from *The Rockford Files* in order to make *Rockford* more like *Hawaii Five-O*. However, like most legends, that story really doesn't hold up when you take a closer look at it. In the first place, *Rockford* had everything going for it heading into its second year — it was a huge hit, having won its time slot throughout the previous year; and its huge audience continued to grow, particularly during the summer, when the reruns attracted many new viewers to the show. No network in its right mind would want to tamper with something that's already working. Secondly, the networks usually think in terms of "What makes this show different?" *Rockford*, by virtue of its irreverent attitude toward the private eye genre, already was different — it wouldn't make sense for NBC to insist on having the show conform to *Hawaii Five-O* by removing the humor. Finally, Universal Studios (and, in particular, its head of television Frank Price) loved the humor of *The Rockford Files* — it was Price who had to act out the scripts before the network programming executives who were befuddled by the show's sophisticated brand of humor.

However, late in the summer of 1975, Price became concerned over the direction that *Rockford* seemed to be taking early in the second season, particularly with respect to its approach to humor. A pattern seemed to be developing. Whereas in the first season, much of the humor of the series was derived from Rockford's character, in the early going of the second season, much of the humor came at Rockford's expense. Four of the first five shows produced that season ("Aaron Ironwood School of Success," "Great Blue Lake Land and Development Company," "Chicken Little is a Little Chicken," and "Pastoria Prime Pick") all revolved around the following theme: Rockford is either duped/swindled (in some cases, by his own friends) or otherwise thrust into a set of circumstances in which he is the last to know what's going on.

There is nothing wrong with taking the conventions of a genre and turning them inside out — after all, that's what Roy Huggins had done with *Maverick*. Unlike most TV heroes, Maverick didn't always come up on top, and by the end of any given episode, he was likely to find himself broke, or swindled, or even tied up in the middle of nowhere. And episodes like "Chicken Little is a Little Chicken" are admittedly fun to watch, because they usually provide Rockford with an opportunity to display some of his *Maverick* qualities (he'll hatch a scheme designed to cheat the cheater).

But Huggins also knew that the key to playing with conventions was to do so with restraint — the audience would grow tired of watching if Maverick ended up with egg on his face every week. That, ultimately, is why NBC and Universal were concerned that the broad approach to humor in the second season might ultimately hurt the appeal of *The Rockford Files*. After watching a few of these stories, the audience might wonder just how smart Rockford is if he continues to fall for such cons (particularly from his friends) time and again.

This was the exact problem NBC had encountered with *Nichols*. The ASI Program Test Report for that series indicated that the Nichols character "lacked a very important quality for the protagonist of a series—intelligence. [Nichols] did not project an impression of

Garner and Cannell.

intelligence to the viewers and came across as a well-liked but dumb hero." Calling to mind those findings, NBC's Program Research Division specifically recommended that "great care should be taken to highlight Rockford's cleverness and to insure that the character's casualness is never mistaken for lack of intelligence."

Word of the network and studio's concerns over the direction *Rockford* seemed to be taking in its approach to humor eventually made its way to James Garner. Apparently, however, either Garner misunderstood the problem, or someone had miscommunicated it to him, because Garner thought that NBC and Universal wanted *all* the humor taken out of the show. Garner requested a meeting with Price, which took place at the Riviera Country Club in West Los Angeles, where the series was on location filming the episode "Joey Blue Eyes."

"We had a meeting in Jim's motor home," Price said. "I told him that I thought that the shows were headed in the direction of broad farce, which is what I had seen on *Nichols* — and that I thought that was wrong for *Rockford Files*. You can't play Rockford for a chump every week — Rockford has got to be a sophisticated guy. He is *smarter* than everybody else, not dumber.

"Jim became very angry over the position I was taking — and he was particularly offended that I cited *Nichols* as an example of what I didn't want done, because he thought *Nichols* was the best thing he'd ever done. I said, 'Jim, I don't know what to say, because I saw *Nichols*, and I don't agree with you about that.' All I know is that last year, we did the kinds of shows we wanted to do on *Rockford*; now we're moving into silly stuff this year, and if we don't do anything about it, it will kill the series.'"

Although Garner works hard to maintain a laidback, easygoing personality, he does have a temper which (by his own admission) occasionally gets the best of him. When Price mentioned *Nichols*, Garner lost his temper. "I was sitting in the driver's seat of the motor home, and Jim was standing between me and the door," Price continued. "Once I brought up *Nichols*, he became angry, and he took the coffee table that was in the motor home and started smashing it against the rest of the furniture.... At that point, the argument had really ended, and so, I began to say things to Jim, to calm him down, and I eventually eased by him and made my way out the door."

To understand this incident requires examining it from both sides' point of view. One of the most respected men in the motion picture industry, Frank Price is a rarity — an executive who came from a creative (as opposed to a legal- or business-oriented) background. Price had spent many years as a writer-producer on such shows as *The Virginian*, *It Takes a Thief*, and *Ironside*, so that certainly qualified him as a good judge in the area of storytelling. It was Price's responsibility as head of television production at Universal to sell series and to keep them on the air as long as possible, so he was simply doing his job.

Nichols was still a sore spot with Garner, so the mere mention of the show was likely to set him off—and Garner did overreact in this instance. However, his outburst can be tempered in light of his numerous other exceptional instincts. As discussed earlier, Garner has absolute trust in the abilities of his writers; because he would never tell them how to do their jobs, he may have felt compelled to protect them from what he perceived to be outside interference. (Price and Garner have remained amicable in the years since the incident at the Riviera Country Club.)

Fortunately, as far as Price and the network were concerned, Garner was not the key decision-maker in the area of story and script—that was left in the hands of Stephen J. Cannell. "The key was talking to Steve," said Price. "From a creative standpoint, you had to get to Steve, to try to make sure he agreed with and understood what needed to be done."

What NBC wanted were more shows that reflected the sophisticated humor of the first season and less of the pattern they had seen in the early second-year episodes—to the extent that it was possible. (By the time the matter was addressed, not only were six episodes already filmed, but most of the scripts for the remaining 16 shows were drafted and being readied for production.) It would have been practically impossible (not to mention very expensive) to order new scripts. Cannell had to work with what he had — and to his credit, he corrected the problem. For the most part, the rest of the episodes produced in 1975-1976 were "on target," so far as the network was concerned—they portrayed Rockford more as a problem solver than as a patsy, and featured less evidence of the broad humor that the network and the studio found off-target.

NBC, which ultimately determined the broadcast schedule, decided to refrain from airing the problem shows until later in the year. That meant that many of the episodes that were produced later in the summer were often broadcast almost immediately upon completion. For instance, "The Farnsworth Stratagem" and the two-parter "Gearjammers," which were both filmed in August, each aired in September; while "A Bad Deal in the Valley," another early-made show in which Rockford is duped, was held back until the very last week of the season.

However, because the date of the first September broadcast was only a few weeks away by the time the network voiced its concerns over the direction of the second season, NBC also had little choice but to open the year with one of those first five episodes and hope that it wouldn't have an adverse effect on the show. (Ironically, the network selected an episode that epitomized the problem—"The Aaron Ironwood School of Success," in which Rockford is duped by his own foster brother. Of the five episodes from which it had to choose, NBC would have been better off had it gone with "The Italian Bird Fiasco," a far more clever caper; although Rockford is duped in this episode as well, he is taken in by a man whom we're clearly not supposed to like.)

At any rate, that set the stage for the much ballyhooed competition between *The Rockford Files* and *Hawaii Five-O*. The first round went to *Rockford*, with *Five-O* finishing a distant 3rd (behind *The ABC Friday Night Movie*). *Rockford* not only took the time slot that night with a 35 share and a 24.4 rating; it also ranked No. 5 among all shows telecast that week.

Again, *Rockford* had a huge advantage over *Five-O* heading into the season because it had been averaging a 40 share in its time period throughout its first year. However, while

Rockford continued to beat *Five-O* during the next five weeks, *Five-O* steadily began to close the gap. By the end of October, *Five-O*'s total audience had increased by 10% from the first week of the season—which meant that *Rockford* had lost 10% of its audience during the same period of time.

The numbers get worse. After two months, *Rockford* dropped from 12th to 23rd in the overall rankings, and its average rating for that time (19.7) was 16% lower than its overall average for the first season (23.8). In terms of total audience, that's a loss of approximately 11,392,000 television households from the previous year. Although *Rockford* did come out on top in its head-to-head battle with *Hawaii Five-O* (CBS moved the show to Thursday nights in November), it was a pyrrhic victory at best. *Rockford* never recovered the sizeable chunk of its total audience it had lost during the first seven weeks of the season—despite the fact that the overall ratings improved slightly (the series finished with a seasonal average of 19.9). By the end of the year, *Rockford* was finishing third in the time slot it had once owned. For the 1975-1976 season, the series finished in 32nd place (out of 65 shows).

Yet the news on the second year is not all bad. Cannell may have made some mistakes in the early going, but he also demonstrated much of the promise and ability that made him the most sought-after producer in television at the time—and which ultimately propelled him into becoming one of the greatest talents the industry has ever known. In the years since *The Rockford Files*, Cannell has created and/or produced such critical and commercial successes as *Baretta, City of Angels* (co-created with Roy Huggins), *Baa Baa Black Sheep, The Greatest American Hero, Tenspeed and Brownshoe, The A-Team, Hunter, Wiseguy,* and *21 Jump Street*. It was under Cannell's guidance that the show won the Emmy for Best Dramatic Series of 1977-1978; in addition, the producer has been honored by the Writers Guild of America, the Mystery Writers of America, the International Film and Television Association, and Media Access.

In many respects, Cannell put his stamp on *Rockford* by virtue of the many singular characterizations he created for the show. For example, early in the episode "Foul on the First Play" (which Cannell wrote), we are introduced to a gangster who happens to have asthma. Later in the story, Rockford finds himself in a car chase with this same gangster. The chase takes them into L.A.'s Griffith Park, where Rockford pulls up in front of a museum and gets out of his car—forcing the gangster to continue the chase on foot. The asthmatic, of course, doesn't get very far, because he has to stop and administer his medication. Thus, Rockford is able to escape. What seemed at first to be a gimmicky detail (the gangster with asthma) ultimately contributed something very special to the story. "Steve can't write a scene that doesn't have character in it," said Roy Huggins. "He will not write a scene that is meaningless or that has someone who is characterless. The characters in his stories all have some bent or quirk that makes them terribly interesting."

Cannell also carried over the attitudes of *Maverick* to a new generation of viewers. In "The Great Blue Lake Land and Development Company," Rockford stores $10,000 overnight in a safe in a small town, only to discover the next day that the money's gone. He soon discovers that a corrupt real estate company has been bilking senior citizens out of their life savings through a phony land development project. The premise of this episode is straight out of *Maverick* (it's a variation of the classic "Shady Deal at Sunny Acres"). So is Rockford's reluctance to become involved in the matter (much to his father's chagrin) once he manages to get his money back. Rockford may really want to help the victims of the fraud, but he also realizes there's only so much he can do by himself. He's not out to be a hero (although he is pressed into becoming one by the end of the story). That is the *Maverick* attitude—the reluctant hero—which Cannell understood almost as thoroughly as Roy Huggins himself.

Prominent guest stars this season include Louis Gossett Jr., Linda Evans, Stefanie Powers, Joan Van Ark, Joe E. Tata, Robert Hays, Michael Conrad, Sherry Jackson, Ray Danton, James Hampton, Mitchell Ryan, David Huddleston, Charles Siebert, Blair Brown, Rob Reiner, Dick Butkus, John Saxon, Michael Ansara, Joseph Campanella, Robert Mandan, Veronica Hamel, and Susan Strasberg.

23. THE AARON IRONWOOD SCHOOL OF SUCCESS

Production Number: 42607

Original Airdate: September 12, 1975

Written by: *Stephen J. Cannell*
Directed by: *Lou Antonio*

Guest Cast: James Hampton (Aaron Ironwood), Ken Swofford (Federal Agent Patrick), Jonathan Lippe (Nino), Jerome Guardino (Vito Ginoso), Robert Broyles (Hauss), John Petlock (Dave), Gammy Burdette (Cabbie), Don Furneaux (Russo)

Hi, Jim. We couldn't reach you, so we went ahead with the job, and I know you're really gonna dig it—but if you don't, I supposed we could always tear it out ...

Synopsis. *Aaron Ironwood, an orphan who once lived with the Rockfords for many years, is now a self-made multi-millionaire who travels around the country giving motivational seminars that promote "Dare to Win," a $5,000 program that purports to teach people the secrets of his success. But Aaron is also a fraud artist, and Jim becomes his latest victim. After agreeing to take over control of Aaron's company on a temporary basis, Rockford discovers that Ironwood is wanted by both federal agents and the mob.*

The second season gets off to a fast start right off the bat. Three hoods try to abduct Rockford, but the plan stalls, literally, because the engine of their limousine won't start (a problem that recurs throughout the episode). When an elderly couple volunteers to help with the car, Rockford takes advantage of the delay and makes his escape by commandeering a VW Bug, although he soon finds the limousine hot on his trail. Because the car Rockford "borrowed" has a giant pizza plastered on top (it's the delivery vehicle for Pizza Dan's Restaurant), the chase sequence has an added element of fun.

Luis Delgado, who appears as the limousine driver, did his own stunt driving for this and other episodes of *The Rockford Files*. Delgado learned from one of the best in the business—formula race car driver Bob Bonderant, who had tutored James Garner years before for the motion picture *Grand Prix*. "Roy Clark, our stunt coordinator, had also taken lessons from Bob," said Delgado. "I thought that I could make a few extra bucks by doing some driving on the show, so I called Bob, and I spent about a week-and-an-half at his driving school at Sears Point. Bob was an excellent teacher, and he showed me everything I wanted to learn — how to do a 90° slide, a 180° slide, a reverse 180°, and to do chases. He easily could have taught me more, but I wasn't interested in getting into it that deep. I didn't want to learn how to flip a car over, or how to jump a car from one spot to another—those things, I did not care to do at all."

Delgado handles a car very well—although it took a while before some of the stuntpeople were convinced by what he could do. "I remember one show where I had to perform the same stunt four times because no one could believe it was me driving," he said. "I was driving a police car with a passenger, and I had to cut across a park in order to prevent the heavies from going into the park. I had to do a 90° slide between a tree and a fence, which left me about a foot-and-a-half in the front and a foot-and-a-half in the back.

"The stuntpeople didn't think I could do it, because they had never seen me drive a car or anything else before. But I brought the car in and, boom, dropped it right where they wanted it. They were amazed—they thought it was a fluke—and so they said, 'Well, let's see you do it again.' And I did it again—boom, right in the same spot. They still couldn't believe it. They made me do that slide four times—and all four times, I put the car right in the same spot. So I guess that convinced them that I knew what I was doing."

Rockford Facts. According to this episode, Becker is fifth on the list for lieutenant ("If I do well, I can make lieutenant in two or three months"). Although it took him a little longer than anticipated, Becker finally earned his promotion in the fifth season episode "Kill the Messenger."

Joe Santos as Becker.

24. THE FARNSWORTH STRATAGEM

Production Number: 42616

Original Airdate: September 19, 1975

Written by: *Juanita Bartlett*
Directed by: *Lawrence Doheny*

Guest Cast: Linda Evans (Audrey Wyatt), H.M. Wynant (Danzil), Paul Jenkins (Simon Lloyd), Pat Finley (Peggy Becker), John Crawford (Christian), Eric Server (William MacKenzie), Gerald McRaney (Manager), Al Hansen (Gardell), Steven Parr (Stewart Zilliox)

Rockford, this is Tony. Now, your car's ready—I couldn't reach you, so I went ahead and put in the new pistons. The tab's $527.54—and this time, we're talking cash!

Synopsis. Dennis and Peggy Becker apparently purchase 2-1/2% ownership of a posh hotel resort in a deal brokered by Simon Lloyd, a flim-flam artist who doesn't tell them the "hotel" actually houses condominiums, all of which are fully owned. To their embarrassment, the Beckers discover that they not only spent $7,500 (on a lobby!!), but they're indentured into paying a $700,000 trust deed. Dennis hires Jim to win back their money. Drawing on his own vast grifting skills, Rockford concocts an elaborate scheme designed to beat Lloyd at his own game.

Although we've seen Rockford the grafter in operation before (as Becker reminds us in this episode, he pulled off a couple of masterful scams in "Counter Gambit"), as a rule, he won't resort to such tactics unless either he himself or one of his friends has been cheated. (This is another characteristic taken straight out of *Maverick*.) Not only does Rockford run a "big store" con game in "The Farnsworth Stratagem," he also lays out the entire process (including the lingo) for the benefit of the viewers:

"In a con, there's always more than one grifter involved. Simon Lloyd was the operator, but somebody put up the marks [found the victim], and somebody roped 'em. A roper steers the marks to the inside man. They tell him the tale, show him the game, take off the touch, and blow him off."

Rockford will hold other "seminars" in the art of grifting in the episodes "There's One in Every Port" and "Never Send a Boy King to Do a Man's Job."

Rockford Facts. In this episode, we learn that Becker's rank is Investigator, 2nd Grade. Over the course of the series, Becker will be promoted to Investigator, 3rd Level (in the third-year episode "Piece Work") and finally to Lieutenant (in the fifth season's "Kill the Messenger").

Rockford Funnies. The name of the hotel assistant manager is "Zilliox" [named after Robert Zilliox, the series' set decorator].

25./26. GEARJAMMERS
(Two-parter)

Production Numbers: 42626/42627

Original Airdates: September 26 and October 3, 1975

Teleplay by: *Don Carlos Dunaway*
Story by: *Stephen J. Cannell*
Directed by: *William Wiard*

Guest Cast: Ted Gehring (Johnny LoSalvo), Scott Brady (Hammel), Rosemary DeCamp (Mary Ramsey), Jack Kruschen (John Koenig), Bobby Hoy (Scheib), Al Stephenson (L.J.), Peter Brocco (Hodges), Charles Cooper (Jack), Robert Ray Sutton (Paco), Joe E. Tata (Willie Thompson), Bucklind Beery (Officer Mazursky), Terry Leonard (John Smith), Reb Brown (Lifeguard), John Doulaghan (Sergeant Sullivan)

Hey, Jimmy, it's Angel. Don't pay no attention to my other message. You're out of it. You're clean. No trouble at all. Just ignore the first message ...

Okay, pal, it's Harry. I just checked my car. You kept the battery charged, all right. You also put 3500 miles on it!

Synopsis. *Rocky's life becomes endangered after he inadvertently witnesses an illegal business transaction between his trucker friend Johnny LoSalvo and LoSalvo's ruthless boss Hammel, who has plotted to hijack six of his own trucks as part of a master plan to steal an incoming cargo of valuable sable furs. Although Rocky has absolutely no idea what's going on, Hammel wants the old man eliminated simply because Rocky can identify him. LoSalvo tries to save Rocky, but Hammel has him killed. Jim protects his father from danger — while Rocky helps his son solve the case.*

The second act of Part One ends with an extensive chase in which Rockford is tailed by two of Hammel's goons. After Rockford pulls into a garage, he whips out his gun (he came prepared for trouble) and gets the drop on them, then pays the two men a compliment. "It's sort of an honor to be tailed by two people who drive so well," he said.

Rockford ought to know good driving when he sees it — his alter ego was one of the best in the business. James Garner not only did his own stunt driving on *The Rockford Files* and in many other motion pictures (including *Grand Prix* and *The Getaway*), he raced professionally for a time during the late 1960s/early 1970s. "Jim handles a car very well," said Luis Delgado. "He handles a car better than 99% of the stunt drivers in the business."

Rockford Familiar Faces. Joe E. Tata plays Nat, the owner of the Peach Pit, on *Beverly Hills 90210*. Also featured: Bucklind Beery, the son of series star Noah Beery Jr.

27. THE DEEP BLUE SLEEP

Production Number: 42620

Original Airdate: October 10, 1975

Teleplay by: *Juanita Bartlett*
Story by: *Chas. Floyd Johnson*
Directed by: *William Wiard*

Guest Cast: Robert Webber (Bob Coleman), Michael Conrad (George Macklan), Janet MacLachlan (Adrienne Clarke), Ric Mancini (Ray Porter), Melendy Britt (Millie), Doria Cook (Margaux Adams), Robert B. Hays (Darren Weeks), John Furlong (Medical Examiner), Ed Crick (Gas Station Attendant)

Hi, Jim — thanks for the dinner invitation. I'd love to, but does it have to be the taco stand?

Synopsis. *When the body of premier fashion model Margaux Adams is found at the scene of an apparent car crash, the police classify her death as either accidental or suicidal. But Beth, who was one of Margaux's best friends, suspects foul play — particularly since she received a frantic phone call from Margaux shortly before she died. Although clearly an open case, Beth convinces Rockford to probe the matter (by promising free legal services if the police hassle him). Jim's investigation uncovers a romantic triangle between Margaux, fashion designer Adrienne Clarke, and accountant Bob Coleman — and the likelihood that Margaux was killed upon discovering Coleman's link to organized crime.*

Two-time Emmy nominee Diahann Carroll was the original choice to play the female lead in "The Deep Blue Sleep." "When I first wrote the story, I did have her in mind — and Diahann wanted to do the show, too," said Charles Floyd Johnson. "But her schedule didn't work out. We just couldn't work out the dates." The role of the fashion designer went to Janet MacLachlan, who was excellent.

28. THE GREAT BLUE LAKE LAND AND DEVELOPMENT COMPANY

Production Number: 42603

Original Airdate: October 17, 1975

Produced by: *Lane Slate*
Written by: *Juanita Bartlett*
Directed by: *Lawrence Doheny*

Guest Cast: Richard B. Shull ("Fast Harry" Danova), Dennis Patrick (Walter Hart), Dana Elcar (Sheriff Mitchell), Mary Ann Chinn (Billie Carlton), Bob Hastings (Paul Tanner), Noble Willingham (B.J.), Ray Girardin (Murray Johnson), Bartine Zane (Mildred Jensen)

☎   *[Caller speaks in a robotic tone:] Hello, Jim Rockford's machine. This is Larry Doheny's machine. Will you please have your master call my master at his convenience? Thank you. Thank you. Thank you ...*

Synopsis. *En route to Los Angeles to deliver a client's $10,000 bail money, Rockford becomes stranded in the small desert town of Great Blue Lake after his car breaks down. Needing a place to store the money overnight, he deposits the cash with Murray Johnson, a salesman at the Great Blue Lake Land and Development Company (the only building in town with a safe). But when Jim arrives to pick up the money in the morning, he finds that the money is gone — and that nobody named Johnson works for the company. A determined Rockford plots a sting* *(and recruits Rocky and con artist Harry Danova for key roles) in order to recover his money, but he drops his plans when company president Walter Hart suddenly returns the $10,000. However, when the phantom Murray Johnson is found murdered, Rockford becomes the prime suspect. Rockford believes that Hart murdered Johnson, but he has to break himself out of jail in order to prove it.*

Juanita Bartlett found the basis for this episode in a segment she'd once seen on *60 Minutes*. "They had done a show on land fraud," she said. "One of the things that really got to me about that show was seeing how these people were selling land out in the middle of nowhere in Arizona. And I mean *literally*—there was a ribbon of a road, and desert on either side of the road. And it wasn't a matter where the investors were being taken in through the mail—they would actually go out there and look at it and say, 'No, that's too close to the road, or that's too close to the country club. I want my house to be over there.' In addition, the report showed that most of the people who were bilked were retired—people who were living on a fixed income, and who therefore had the most to lose.

"I found it so appalling (and infuriating) to see that people could be gullible. So I did 'The Great Blue Lake,' which had to do with the land fraud scheme. And my thinking was, 'If I can bring what has been happening to the attention of some of these people, maybe they won't bite if something like that comes their way.'"

Rockford Familiar Faces. Dana Elcar's best-known TV role is as *MacGyver*'s boss (prior to that, he had co-starred in *Baretta* and *Baa Baa Black Sheep*). Noble Willingham co-starred with James Garner in 1993's *Fire in the Sky*. Bob Hastings is the voice of Commissioner Gordon on *Batman: The Animated Series* (long before that, he played Lt. Carpenter on *McHale's Navy*).

29. THE REAL EASY RED DOG

Production Number: 42628

Original Airdate: October 31, 1975

Written by: *Stephen J. Cannell*
Directed by: *Ivan Dixon*

Guest Cast: Stefanie Powers (Christina Dusseau), Bruce Kirby (Aaron Friedler), Sherry Jackson (Jennifer Sandstrom), Wayne Grace (Deek), Larry Cook (Dave), George Wyner (Tom Brice), Nick Ferris (Pete Finch), Connie Bryant Milton (Policewoman)

Jim, it's Shirley at the cleaners. You know that brown jacket — the one that looks so great on you — your favorite? We lost it.

Synopsis. *A woman who identifies herself as Jennifer Sandstrom hires Rockford to delve into the apparent suicide of her sister Alice. Jim doesn't realize that his client is a private investigator, Christina Dusseau, who actually has paid him to play decoy. (An insurance company hired Tina to deliver a ransom payment to thieves who had stolen a $3 million jewelry collection — and to keep the authorities out of the matter. When Tina found herself followed by two police officers, she needed to create a diversion to throw the cops off her trail.) But Tina's charade turns up an unexpected dividend — although Tina pulled the Sandstrom suicide from a newspaper article, Jim stumbles onto evidence suggesting that Alice really was murdered. When Rockford and Tina link Alice's death to a black market baby racket, their lives become endangered.*

For a short time during the 1974-1975 season, Tom Atkins had recurring roles on two different series—in addition to playing the snarling Lieutenant Diel on *The Rockford Files*, he also played the delightfully dimwitted Sergeant Frank Cole on *Harry O*.

Rockford Facts. Although Atkins' character was known as "Alex Diel" throughout the first season, the lieutenant apparently underwent a name change, because according to this episode (as well as a later show, "The Battle of Canoga Park"), Diel's first name is "Thomas."

30. RESURRECTION IN BLACK AND WHITE

Production Number: 42629

Original Airdate: November 7, 1975

Written by: *Juanita Bartlett and Stephen J. Cannell*
Directed by: *Russ Mayberry*

Guest Cast: Joan Van Ark (Susan Alexander), William Prince (Arnold Newcomb), Sandra Smith (Shirley Atwater), Milton Selzer (Patrick Elber), John Lawlor (Dave Krueger), John Danheim (Roy Pierce), Elvin Howard (Police Officer)

☎

Hey, Jimmy, it's Cousin Lou! Gonna be in town a coupla days. Know you won't mind puttin' us up. It's just me, and Aunt Cissy, and B.J., and the kids, and little Freddie, and ...

Synopsis. *Investigative reporter Susan Alexander believes that Dave Krueger was wrongfully convicted six years ago of the brutal murder of his girlfriend Cheryl Wilson, and she wants Rockford to help her prove him innocent. First, Jim is skeptical — he suspects Krueger of playing Susan for a sucker, then doubts he could proceed far in a case whose principals are either long dead or long retired. He's also reluctant to stay involved when he learns that someone has been trying to kill Susan (although she's not fazed — the death threats actually convince her she's on the right track). But Rockford ultimately becomes curious when the police later identify a murder victim as Cheryl Wilson — the woman whom Krueger allegedly killed!*

Resurrection in Black and White" features several of the most memorable lines of the entire series. When Rockford discovers that Susan was nearly killed while investigating the Krueger case, he immediately wants out ("Physical violence has a tendency to put some people off"). Although Susan thinks that Rockford will protect her, she doesn't realize that Jim doesn't like to carry a gun. "You're not armed!?" she says in amazement. "But you're a private investigator—why don't you carry a gun?" "Because I don't want to shoot anybody," Rockford replies.

However, later in the story, Jim decides to pack his gun before he and Susan head out to Elber's boat. "I thought you didn't like to shoot people," Susan reminds him. "I don't shoot it," clarifies Rockford. "I just point it."

"Resurrection in Black and White" incorporates several elements from the first season episode "Tall Woman in Red Wagon," including a further explanation of the portable printing press Rockford keeps in his car. Jim tells Susan that he received the machine from a former client, who had been a printer.

31. CHICKEN LITTLE IS A LITTLE CHICKEN

Production Number: 42602

Original Airdate: November 14, 1975

Written by: *Stephen J. Cannell*
Directed by: *Lawrence Doheny*

Guest Cast: Ray Danton (Chester Sierra), Frank Campanella (Marty Frishette), Angelo Gnazzo (John Little), Sandy Ward (The Sheriff), Nicholas Worth (Kessler), Dave Cass (Sid), Kenneth Strange (Don), Charlie Horvath (Jose), Tom Williams (Minister)

Jim, it's Beth — you have the vet's number, the flea collar, and extra litter. One thing I forgot: keep him away from other cats. He's not very discriminating.

Synopsis. Angel finds himself in trouble with both the police and two rival crime lords after he innocently agrees to launder money for a former cellmate named John Little. Angel doesn't realize that Little, a convicted forger, swindled $30,000 from the newspaper where Angel works, then framed Angel by planting the counterfeiting evidence inside Angel's desk. Meanwhile, Angel's association with Little runs him afoul of underworld kingpins Chester Sierra and Marty Frishette, whom Little both doublecrossed. Rockford becomes stuck in the middle when he learns that Angel hid the $30,000 inside his car. In order to bail themselves out of trouble, Rockford fakes Angel's death, then plans a variation of the "shell game" designed to play Sierra and Frishette against each other at the "funeral."

Rockford is perfectly willing to walk away and let Angel sink in his own mess. "You were meant for this frame," he tells him in this episode. "It was built for a dummy, and it looks good on you!" However, Jim feels compelled to help Angel because, like Maverick before him, he has a conscience — or, at the very least, an ethical code. Rockford can't walk away once Angel appeals to him on a basic level — the man, after all, is his friend.

"That relationship has always puzzled me," James Garner told CBS in 1994. "I've never understood why Rockford likes this guy so much, even though he's just rotten to the core. I guess there is something loveable about Angel. I just don't know what it is."

Rockford Facts. In this episode, we learn that Angel had been court-martialed for desertion under fire during the Korean War, and served time in San Quentin and at the federal penitentiary at Railworth. Angel also reminds us that he and Jim served time together at San Quentin. "I guess you could say we owned a piece of the rock," he cracks (a reference to the popular advertising jingle for Prudential Life Insurance, "Get a piece of the rock").

32. "2 INTO 5.56 WON'T GO"

Production Number: 42630

Original Airdate: November 21, 1975

Written by: *Stephen J. Cannell*
Directed by: *Jeannot Szwarc*

Guest Cast: Jesse Welles (Shana Bowie), Charles Napier (Billy Webster), Mitchell Ryan (Colonel Hopkins), Frank Maxwell (Colonel Daniel Hart Bowie), William Boyett (Sergeant Harvey Slate), Harvey Gold (Quentin Davis), Carol Vogel (Terri), John Carey (Lieutenant Doug Fenton), Kenneth Washington (Guard), Eddie Firestone (Dwight Davis)

Jim, it's Maria over at the laundromat. There's a yellow dress in with your things — is that a mistake, or a special handling, or what?

Synopsis. *Moments after leaving an urgent message on Rockford's phone machine, Colonel Daniel Bowie is abducted by his aide, Sergeant Harvey Slate, and a former soldier named Quentin Davis. Bowie is later found dead, the victim of an apparent car accident. When the military discover that Bowie had contacted Rockford prior to his death, they question Rockford (who had also served under Bowie during the Korean War) for possible involvement. Meanwhile, Bowie's daughter Shana, who believes her father was murdered, hires Jim to investigate. When Rockford determines that Davis, a mortician, has been teaming with Slate to steal military weapons (by smuggling them inside funeral caskets), he suspects that Bowie was killed after he stumbled onto the operation.*

Rockford apparently had a colorful career in the Army. According to his military file, after he was wounded in action (an injury also mentioned in the episode "The Hawaiian Headache"), he received a Silver Star and was promoted to sergeant; however, six months later, he was bumped down to PFC (private first class) after he was busted for trading 400 cases of sea rations for a North Korean tank. (What the file doesn't mention, though, is that Rockford was merely following orders. Colonel Bowie had told Rockford to commandeer a tank *fast* because the troop needed to blow their way out of a pocket — and he wasn't specific about whether it had to be a U.S. tank.) For his fast thinking, Rockford received a battle field promotion to sergeant, although he was demoted to private once again after he was caught setting up a string of pool halls in Puo Sang and stealing a major general's staff car right in front of the Seoul Korean Hilton.

In real life, James Garner was wounded on two occasions during the Korean War, and was awarded two Purple Hearts. He was also something of a "dog robber" (Army lingo for someone who operates just barely within the law); during an interview with *Playboy* in 1981, he recounted some of the exploits he pulled off while stationed at a base postal office in Japan. "Guys in the Army like their mail and they become very unhappy if they don't get it," he said. "I decided to spruce up our unit, and if they didn't give me what we needed, they didn't get their mail. The base post office was stationed in a bombed-out shoe factory, and I turned it into a showplace. In exchange for their mail, other units got us the materials to build a bar and then kept it stocked with whiskey. Nobody over there had ice except us, courtesy of the Graves Registration Unit. I built us a theater in the biggest room in the shoe factory, got a baseball diamond laid out, got us hot water and showers. My crowning achievement was a swimming pool.... The smallest room in the shoe factory was the basement. We cleansed it all out, whitewashed it, cemented the floor, put a ladder up the side and filled that sucker up with water."

Rockford Facts. Mitchell Ryan starred in *Chase*, a police drama that Stephen J. Cannell created for Jack Webb in 1973.

33. PASTORIA PRIME PICK

Production Number: 42609

Original Airdate: November 29, 1975

Written by: *Gordon Dawson*
Directed by: *Lawrence Doheny*

Guest Cast: Warren Kemmerling (Vern Soper), Richard Herd (Sheriff Gladish), William Lucking (Officer Pete Kolodny), Kathie Browne (Mayor Karen Sanders), Smith Evans (Rita Sanders), William Zuckert (Emmett Byrd), Don Billett (Gilbert Univaso), Bill Quinn (Judge Russell Cline), Robert Ward (Honcho), Bill Tuthill (First Hood), Barbara Collentine (Waitress)

Hey, Jimbo — Dennis. Really appreciate the help on the income tax. Do you want to help on the audit now?

Synopsis. *Rockford becomes the latest victim of an horrifying blackmail scheme orchestrated by the mayor and sheriff of a small community called New Pastoria. Lured into town to find a man who allegedly abandoned his family, Rockford finds himself stung by a hornet's nest of manufactured charges ranging from grand theft auto to possession of narcotics and statutory rape. The county prosecutor, who is also in on the scheme, then offers to drop the charges if Jim pays an outlandish fine of $15,000 — money which is intended to "build a better New Pastoria." Rockford, however, finds an ally in retired sheriff Emmett Byrd, who helps the P.I. uncover evidence that could bring down the operation.*

Early in this episode, Rockford calls himself collect in order to retrieve his messages. Although he asks the operator to dial 555-9000, according to the ad in the Yellow Pages (as well as the closeup of his phone that appears at the beginning of each episode), Rockford's phone number is 555-2368.

34. THE REINCARNATION OF ANGIE

Production Number: 42631

Original Airdate: December 5, 1975

Written by: *Stephen J. Cannell*
Directed by: *Jerry London*

Guest Cast: Elayne Heilveil (Angie Perris), Wayne Tippit (FBI Agent Dan Shore), David Huddleston (Sherm Whitlaw), Sharon Spelman (Susan), Eugene Peterson (Tom Perris), Charles Siebert (Bettingen), George Skaff (Bundy), Jenny O'Hara (Operator), Jeanne Bates (Lady in Bank), Louise Fitch (Maid)

Hi, Jim. It's Jamie at the Police Impound. They picked up your car again — lately, they've been driving it more than you have ...

Synopsis. *Angie Perris receives a late night phone call from her brother Tom, who asks her to remove an envelope from his safe, but Tom is abducted before he can give her the combination. Angie hires Rockford. After disarming both the man who had seized Tom, as well as another man who had been following Angie, Jim retrieves the envelope — which contains $500,000 in* *cash. Rockford later learns that Tom, a stockbroker, had been working with a federal agent named Bettingen to determine who had been selling forged stock certificates to Tom's firm. Bettingen provided Tom with $500,000 to make the purchases; when Bettingen is found dead, and both Tom and the money disappear shortly thereafter, the feds become suspicious. Meanwhile, the kidnapers notify Rockford that they'll release Tom in exchange for the money. Jim arrives at the appointed place, only to find himself set up — federal agents converge on the scene and discover Tom's dead body stuffed inside the trunk of Rockford's car.*

When Rockford meets Angie at a bar, he confronts the man who had been following her. The man claims to be a federal agent, but Rockford quickly determines that the man is lying after noticing that the picture on the man's I.D. card was taken against a blue field — as it would appear on a drivers' license. "Feds have their pictures taken against a yellow field," Rockford later explains to Angie. "What that guy did was cut his picture out of his drivers' license, paste it into a federal I.D. and encase it in plastic."

Angie is impressed. How did Rockford know about that trick? "I tried it once myself," he said.

35. THE GIRL IN THE BAY CITY BOYS CLUB

Production Number: 42632

Original Airdate: December 19, 1975

Written by: *Juanita Bartlett*
Directed by: *James Garner*

Guest Cast: Blair Brown (Kate Doyle), Joel Fabiani (Tompkins), Stewart Moss (Burton Kimball), Paul Stevens (George Welles), William Phipps (Sergeant), William Bryant (Paul Flanders), Sharon Ullrick (Clerk), Julio Medina (Gardener), Stacy Keach Sr. (Cy Mosher), Todd Hoffman (Young Man), Byron Morrow (Ted Thatcher), Norman Bartold (Thatcher)

Hi, Sonny. It's Rocky. I got the bill — I've been trying to figure out what everybody owes on L.J.'s birthday party. Tell me, did you have the Pink Lady?

Synopsis. A man named Phelps hires Rockford to determine if the weekly Thursday night poker game held at the Bay City Boys Club is fixed. Rockford doesn't realize that his client is really Burton Kimball, a prominent deputy district attorney heavily in debt to racketeer George Welles, who founded the club as a front to his operation. Kimball, who has been blackmailed by Welles into fixing cases, needs evidence against Welles in order to escape his grasp. When Kimball is later found dead, Jim deduces that the D.A. was close to obtaining the proof he needed. With the help of fellow investigator Kate Doyle, Rockford tries to put Welles and the Bay City Boys Club out of business by determining how the game was rigged.

Isaac Hayes and James Garner.

According to James Garner, the matter of his directorial debut on the series was little more than an accident. "We lost a director," he explained. "The person who was scheduled to direct that show, for some reason, couldn't do it, and had to pull out. It was a last-minute situation, so I went ahead and did it myself."

It is a challenging task for an actor to direct a film in which he or she is also appearing. That task becomes even more difficult when the actor/director has to appear in 90% of the scenes — which was the case with Garner and *The Rockford Files*. "That show asked a great deal of him," said Juanita Bartlett. "As the director, he had to get everything going in each scene; and then he'd have to pop into it and play Rockford, while still directing the other actors in the scene. It was an extremely hard thing for him to do, and he came through."

That he did. Garner kept the story moving at a brisk pace, and elicited a sparkling effort from Blair Brown (*The Days and Nights of Molly Dodd*, in one of her early roles). And while the added burden of directing can sometimes affect an actor's own performance, that wasn't the case with this episode — Garner as Rockford was definitely "on."

Although "The Girl in the Bay City Boys Club" was one of Garner's first "official" efforts behind the camera, he is often looked upon as a second director on the set. His input and suggestions, coming from over 40 years in the business, are welcomed. But Garner never imposes himself on the director. That's never been his style.

"I talk a lot with the directors, so I know what they're doing," he said. "Sometimes, I'd make suggestions. But I'd never, ever say, 'You've got to do it this way.' When I hire people, I let them do whatever they do, because I think you get better work that way."

Garner has proven that he can direct and star in the same picture. However, he also knows that doing so is an extra burden that he could do without. "After that show, Jim said, 'I am never going to do this [star and direct] again,'" said Bartlett. "However, he did say that he might direct again — so long as he wouldn't have to appear in the picture."

Garner and Brown would later co-star in the 1985 miniseries *Space*.

Rockford Facts. In this episode, we learn that Rockford always carries a lock-pick inside his billfold.

36. THE HAMMER OF C BLOCK

Production Number: 42622

Original Airdate: January 9, 1976

Written by: *Gordon Dawson*
Directed by: *Jerry London*

Song *"Gandy's Theme"*
Music and Lyrics by: *Isaac Hayes*
Sung by: *Isaac Hayes*

Guest Cast: Isaac Hayes (Gandolf Fitch), James A. Watson Jr. (Arthur Bingham), Annazette Chase (Debbie Bingham), Jack Somack (Oliver Prey), Lynn Hamilton (Eunice Charles Bingham), Allan Rich (Charles "Pebbles" Runkin), Bill Walker (Rosie), Sandy DeBruin (Receptionist), Hank Stohl (Wino), Helen Schustack (Betty)

It's Jack. The check is in the mail. Sorry it's two years late. Sorry I misfigured my checking account and I'm overdrawn. Sorry I stopped payment on it. So when it comes, tear it up. Sorry!

Synopsis. *Gandolf Fitch received the death penalty after he was convicted of the brutal murder of his girlfriend Lila McGee, but the sentence was lifted to life imprisonment after one year. Released after serving 20 years, Fitch calls on former prison mate Rockford to collect a five-year-old debt (Jim lost $1,500 in a crap game one night). But Gandy, who claims he was framed, makes Rockford a deal: he'll waive the debt if "Rockfish" (as he calls Jim) can help him find the real killer. Although their trail starts cold, Rockford and Gandy eventually locate a former prostitute named Eunice Charles who may have proof of Gandy's innocence. But Eunice also holds a secret that, if revealed, could absolutely devastate Gandy.*

Grammy and Academy Award-winning vocalist/composer Isaac Hayes had just started his acting career around the time "The Hammer of C Block" was being cast. "Isaac's agency contacted us, and they recommended that we let him read for the role of Gandy Fitch," said Charles Floyd Johnson. "He was in Memphis at the time, and he wanted to do it — his agent told us that he was going to fly himself in. So we said, 'Sure.' It was near the beginning of his acting career — in fact, I remember that I kept saying, 'Isaac Hayes, *the singer?*' But when we heard him read, we all knew he was perfect for the part. Isaac helped create a very, very interesting character, and we brought him back to do two more shows."

Hayes apparently composed the haunting "Gandy's Theme" exclusively for *The Rockford Files*. The song does not appear on any of the artist's charted albums (i.e, albums that made the official Billboard charts).

Rockford on the run in "No-Cut Contract."

37. THE NO-CUT CONTRACT

Production Number: 42615

Original Airdate: January 16, 1976

Written by: *Stephen J. Cannell*
Directed by: *Lou Antonio*

Guest Cast: Rob Reiner (Larry "King" Sturtevant), Dick Butkus (Himself), Wayne Tippit (Agent Dan Shore), Milt Kogan (Norman), Sharon Cintron (Sharon), Gene Tyburn (Bill), Barbara Flicker (TV Coordinator), J. Jay Saunders (Agent Prizer), Mary Angela (Lisa), Kathy Silva (Judy)

Horas fantasticos. La unique opportunidad en su vida la frescia rosaria llantas realiades. Call toll free — cinco-cinco-cinco, tres-uno-dos-uno.

Synopsis. *Larry "King" Sturtevant, starting quarterback for the Southern Illinois Warriors (a second-rate team in a third-rate pro football league), knows that team owner Dale Fontaine has ties with the Chicago underworld, so he had Fontaine's conference room bugged in order to gain leverage in case he ever needed any. Sturtevant recorded a conversation in which Fontaine sold mob information to federal agents; when he learns that Fontaine planned to replace him with another quarterback, Sturtevant threatens to turn over the tapes unless Fontaine cancelled the deal. However, when word of the tapes leaks out, Sturtevant finds himself on the run from both sides of the law. The weasely Sturtevant, who claims he'd stashed the tapes with a private detective, supplies the mob and the FBI with a name he'd randomly plucked from the Yellow Pages — Jim Rockford.*

The No-Cut Contract," featuring actor/director Rob Reiner (*All in the Family, This is Spinal Tap, Stand by Me, A Few Good Men*) is available through MCA/Universal Home Video as part of its *Rockford Files* collection.

38. A PORTRAIT OF ELIZABETH

Production Number: 42633

Original Airdate: January 23, 1976

Written by: *Stephen J. Cannell*
Directed by: *Meta Rosenberg*

Guest Cast: John Saxon (Dave Delaroux), Wayne Tippit (Agent Dan

Shore), Cynthia Sikes (Susan Valero), Kate Woodville (Karen Silver), Robert Riesel (Mickey Silver), Ned Wilson (Arnold Adams), Joe E. Tata (Solly Marshall), James Murtaugh (Tom Hanson), Angus Duncan (Morey Dayton), Michael Thoma (Maitre D'), Victor Izay (Garvey), Chuck Winters (Fred Marley), Peg Stewart (Maid)

Jim, it's Harry. We've been waiting on you two hours. The forks — where's the forks?!? Lasagna ain't no finger food.

Synopsis. *Beth's client (and new boyfriend) Dave Delaroux, the controller for the local branch of a national corporation, wants Rockford to determine whether someone in his office has been stealing cashier's checks. Although Rockford is suspicious (and a little jealous) of Dave, he agrees to look into the matter — and finds nothing amiss. Meanwhile, Dave, who along with two men swindled a San Diego bank out of $2 million (using cashier's checks from his company), not only frames Rockford for that crime, but uses Rockford's gun to kill his two partners. But the real kicker is that Rockford has an alibi he can't use — Beth, who cannot reveal anything that could incriminate Dave without violating attorney/client confidentiality.*

Gretchen Corbett comes from an extensive theater background. In the seven years prior to signing with Universal in 1974, she appeared in numerous stage productions (on and off-Broadway), including *Arms and the Man, After the Rain, Forty Carats, The Effects of Gamma Rays on Man-in-the-Moon Marigolds,* and *The Master Builder.* She has also performed in such classics as *Othello* (as Desdemona), *Romeo and Juliet* (as Juliet), and *Saint Joan* (as Joan of Arc).

Although Corbett had done some films and television shows prior to *The Rockford Files*, "I was still relatively new to the world of camera when I first started the series," she recalled. "There are a lot of technical things that you need to be aware of when you're being filmed, and having come from stage, I didn't know all the technical stuff. Jim Garner was particularly helpful to me in that regard — he was like a mentor. He taught me where shadows were, and when I was in a light or not in a light, and when I was being lit well or when I wasn't being lit well.

"And Jim also taught me how to walk and talk at the same time. That may sound funny, but it's hard to do at first, particularly when you've got 150 technicians walking with you as you're being filmed."

Corbett also recalls the atmosphere of family that emanated from Garner. "Jim is an angel," she said. "He's a really wonderful man. His crew loved him. Whenever you're working on a film set, or a television set, the feeling on that set always comes from the top. And the feeling on *Rockford* was one of family, of looking out for each other, of caring for each other in a personal way. And that all came from Jim."

Rockford Funnies. Watch closely and listen carefully during the scene in which Rockford visits the Biometrics office early in this episode, and you'll catch the names of several key behind-the-scenes people. As Rockford examines the ledger, we can see via an insert of Rockford comparing the check numbers in the ledger to his own list of allegedly missing checks—that some of the names in the ledger include "George Rohrs" (*Rockford*'s film editor) and "Charles F. Johnson" (the associate producer). Also, Rockford claims that he was sent by "Mr. Swerling of the Central Office," a reference to supervising producer Jo Swerling Jr.

39. JOEY BLUE EYES

Production Number: 42613

Original Airdate: January 30, 1976

Written by: *Walter Dallenbach*
Directed by: *Lawrence Doheny*

Guest Cast: Michael Ansara (Joseph DiMina), Suzanne Charny (Paulette DiMina), Robert Yuro (Gannon), James Luisi (Bert Striker), Eddie Fontaine (SweetTooth London), James Lydon (Barrow), Sandy Kenyon (Mitchell), Michael Lane (Fred), Norman Bartold (Evans), Ril Raden (Fulton)

☎

Sorry, Jim — this is for Rocky. Hey, Rock — Stan. I got that redhead and her sister. Ten-thirty, Stacy's Grill. [Chuckles.]

Synopsis. *Joseph "Joey Blue Eyes" DiMina, a reformed hood who has become a successful restaurateur, finds himself the victim of a conspiracy between his business partner Bert Striker and his attorney Larry Mitchell to force him out of his own business. To make matters worse: Joey borrowed money from loan shark Sweet Tooth London, who has Joey's daughter Paulette beaten up as a warning in case Joey fails to make payment. An enraged Joey assaults Sweet Tooth's thugs and ends up in jail. Although Rockford initially clashes with Joey, Beth (a friend of Paulette's) implores him to help. When Rockford learns that Striker also has financial problems, he sets up an elaborate con aimed at forcing Striker to pay Joey's loan with his own money.*

Guest stars in this episode include James Luisi, who would join the cast of *The Rockford Files* as Lieutenant Chapman starting in the third season.

Rockford Funnies. The following names are paged over the loudspeaker at the golf course: "Howard Berk" (who had written the episode "Counter Gambit") and "Walter Jenevein" (one of the sound effects editors on the show).

40. IN HAZARD

Production Number: 42634

Original Airdate: February 6, 1976

Written by: *Juanita Bartlett*
Directed by: *Jackie Cooper*

Guest Cast: Joseph Campanella (Arnold Bailey), Ben Frank (Howard Nystrom), Richard Venture (Fred Metcalf), Joe E. Tata (Solly Marshall), Frank Campanella (Marty Jordan), Melendy Britt (Connie), Skip Ward

(Walt Raynor), Anne Weldon (Police Matron), Linda Dano (Marie), Bruce Tuthill (Murray Gaines)

Mr. Rockford, Miss Miller of the Bartlett Book Club. "Great Detectives of America" is not in stock, so we sent you "Cooking Made Easy." Hope you enjoy it.

Synopsis. *Shortly after representing Arnold Bailey, a stockbroker accused of tax fraud, Beth is arrested on contempt-of-court charges. She learns that her office was burglarized, and then is nearly killed after drinking cyanide-laced coffee. Rockford finds that the attempt on Beth's life is tied to the partnership between Bailey and another of Beth's clients in a scheme to skim money from the pension fund of a textile workers' union controlled by syndicate leader Marty Jordan.*

"In Hazard" features another inside joke: in Act II, when Rockford bumps into Bailey at the hospital, you can hear a page for "Dr. Robert Crawley" over the loudspeaker. Robert Crawley was the art director on *The Rockford Files*.

Rockford Familiar Faces. Joseph Campanella, a mainstay in television (and a familiar voice in radio commercials) for over 40 years, starred as Mickey Ryder in "I Still Love L.A.," the first new *Rockford Files* movie that aired in November 1994.

41. THE ITALIAN BIRD FIASCO

Production Number: 42605

Original Airdate: February 13, 1976

Written by: *Edward J. Lakso*
Directed by: *Jackie Cooper*

Guest Cast: William Daniels (Thomas Caine), Camilla Sparv (Evelyn Stoneman), William Jordan (Jeffers), Peter Palmer (Stack), Ron Silver (Ted Haller), Ivon Barry (Cryder), Dean Santorro (Collins), Eric Server (Whitlock), Karl Lukas (Officer), Gerald S. Peters (Edward Barrows), Peter Ashton (Clerk), D'Mitch Davis (Guard)

Jim — Sally. Hey, I just found out you're an Aries. Listen, if you have Virgo rising, give me a call.

Synopsis. *Thomas Caine, a shady dealer in objects d'art, hires Rockford to purchase a sculpted cormorant that is reportedly one of three priceless originals by Italian sculptor Giacopo Lambrighni. Rockford doesn't realize that Caine's true interest lies in recovering a fortune in stolen jewelry that he had smuggled inside a series of imitation Lambrighni birds. Rockford makes the purchase, but the cormorant is destroyed after two men attack Jim outside the gallery. (Neither Caine nor Rockford realize that the cormorant was in fact a genuine Lambrighni.) A determined Caine blackmails Rockford into purchasing another allegedly original Lambrighni. Meanwhile, the woman who helped Caine plan the theft starts her own search for the phony Italian birds.*

Emmy and Tony Award-winning actor William Daniels (*1776*, *St. Elsewhere*, *Boy Meets World*) co-starred with James Garner in 1969's *Marlowe*, and also appeared in the third season's "So Help Me God." Ron Silver was nominated for an Academy Award for his brilliant portrayal of Harvard law professor Alan Dershowitz in 1990's *Reversal of Fortune*.

Rockford Facts. Like his alter ego, James Garner is also an Aries — his birthday is April 7. (Rockford's birthday, according to the episode "Beamer's Last Case," is April 14.)

42. WHERE'S HOUSTON?

Production Number: 42625

Original Airdate: February 20, 1976

Written by: *Don Carlos Dunaway*
Directed by: *Lawrence Doheny*

Guest Cast: Lane Bradbury (Houston Preli), Robert Mandan (Charles Blackhorn), Del Munroe (Charlie), Dabbs Greer (Peter Preli), Raymond O'Keefe (Hal), Murray MacLeod (Jerry Specht), Thomas Bellin (Clerk), Rodolfo Hoyos (Carlos Santoro)

Jim — Madame Arcana at the Zodiac Restaurant. You don't pay that dinner tab, we're gonna repo your birthday....

Synopsis. *Peter Preli, a longtime friend of Rocky's, hires Rockford after he believes his granddaughter Houston has been kidnapped. Early in his investigation, Rockford is beaten badly by three men who warn him to drop the case. When Jim reports back to Preli, he finds the old man dead, and the front door broken; however, when the police investigate the scene, they find no signs of forced entry, so they arrest Rockford for Preli's murder. Meanwhile, Houston returns unharmed — she'd been in Mexico on a geological expedition. Rockford soon realizes that the kidnapping hoax and Preli's murder are connected to a real estate conglomerate that plans to build a multi-milliondollar entertainment complex on the old man's property.*

W here's Houston?" contains more inside humor: among the tenants who live in the Sunset Marquis Hotel, which Rockford investigates in this episode, are "R. Zilliox" (named after set decorator Robert Zilliox) and "R. Crawley" (art director Robert Crawley).

43. FOUL ON THE FIRST PLAY

Production Number: 42635

Original Airdate: March 12, 1976

Teleplay by: *Stephen J. Cannell*
Story by: *Charles Floyd Johnson and Dorothy J. Bailey*
Directed by: *Lou Antonio*

Guest Cast: Louis Gossett Jr. (Marcus Hayes), Dick Davalos (Manny Stickells), David White (Martin Eastman), Pepper Martin (Greg Smith), James Ingersoll (Steve Sorenson), Al Ruscio (Tom Corell), John Mahon (Todd Morris), Chuck Bowman (Commissioner Bob Tremayne), Vincent Cobb (Ray Fairchild), Pamela Serpe (Receptionist), Ji-Tu Cumbaka (Sherm Addison), Al Checco (Leasing Agent), Janet Winter (Secretary), Jayne Kennedy (Janice)

Jim? It's Eddie. You were right about Sweet Talk in the 7th — he breezed in, paid $7,250. But I didn't get your bet down ...

Synopsis. *Rockford learns that his conniving parole officer Marcus Hayes has become a private investigator (after he was fired by the Parole Board). Marcus was hired by NBA Commissioner Bob Tremayne to find out which of the three prospective bidders for the Santa Monica expansion franchise has been using pressure tactics to influence the Commissioner's decision on who will get the new team. To get a lead on the case, Marcus tricks Rockford into acting as a decoy, but when Jim catches on, he forces Hayes to surrender half of his $10,000 fee. When Tremayne is found dead on the night before the announcement of the final decision — and one of the bidders implicates Marcus — Rockford must clear Hayes of the charges.*

T he cagey Marcus Hayes was tailored specifically for Emmy and Oscar winner Louis Gossett Jr. (*Roots, An Officer and a Gentleman*), who had previously co-starred with James Garner in the 1971 Western satire *Skin Game*. "I was looking for any excuse to get Lou and Jim together again, because they had played so well off each other in that picture," said Charles Floyd Johnson. "And I think that when Dorothy Bailey and I wrote that story together, we did have Lou in mind — we pretty much designed Marcus as a character who was very similar to what Lou had played in *Skin Game*. And, fortunately, Lou was available to play it."

Other familiar faces in this episode include David White (Larry Tate on *Bewitched*), Ji-Tu Cumbaka (Jason on *Room 222*) and model/actress Jayne Kennedy.

Rockford Facts. Dorothy Bailey, who co-wrote the story for "Foul on the First Play" with Charles Floyd Johnson, worked as an assistant to Roy Huggins for many years at Universal. Bailey occasionally wrote under the pseudonym "Chris Wesley."

Chuck Bowman, who plays NBA Commissioner Tremayne, has produced and directed many of Stephen J. Cannell's other series, including *Baa Baa Black Sheep, Tenspeed and Brownshoe,* and *The Greatest American Hero.* David Menteer (the name of the third—and unseen—bidder in this story) was one of *Rockford*'s assistant directors.

44. A BAD DEAL IN THE VALLEY

Production Number: 42618

Original Airdate: March 19, 1976

Written by: *Donald L. Gold and Lester William Berke*
Directed by: *Jerry London*

Guest Cast: Susan Strasberg (Karen Stiles), Jack Colvin (The Preacher), Veronica Hamel (Sandy Lederer), David Sabin (Murray Slauson), Rod Cameron (Jack Chilson), John Lupton (Tony Lederer), Gordon Jump (Appleby), Fritzi Burr (Maid), Russ McGinn (Fred Sutherland), Reg Parton (Jerry Sutherland), Dudley Knight (Agent), Laurence Haddon (Robert L. Braverman)

Uncle Jim? It's Ralph! I got your letter — but I moved out here anyway. I really want those detective lessons ...

Synopsis. *Rockford dates Karen Stiles, whose father Sam Stiles served time with him at San Quentin. Karen, a real estate agent, asks Rockford to deliver a suitcase containing escrow papers for a major property transaction (but doesn't tell him that the suitcase actually contains $100,000 in phony money). Later, after Rockford's release from jail, Karen is apparently abducted; but when Jim learns that Karen's father was a premier plate artist, he deduces that Karen staged her abduction so that the authorities would not suspect her of the counterfeit money fiasco. After linking Karen's real estate deal to a $500,000 jewel theft, Rockford tries to trip up Karen by recovering the jewels himself and collecting the finder's fee.*

Unit production manager Les Berke also teamed with Donald L. Gold to write the episodes "Feeding Frenzy" and "Deadlock in Parma." Berke, who also contributed several teleplays for *Quincy*, returned as the second assistant director for the new *Rockford* movies for CBS.

The production team. Clockwise: Charles Floyd Johnson, Stephen J. Cannell, Meta Rosenberg, David Chase, Juanita Bartlett and James Garner.

Third Season: 1976-1977

J ames Garner likes to joke that he never set out to become Number One in movies or on television, because "once you've reached the top, you have nowhere to go but down. I'd much rather settle in at around Number Seven or Eight, and just hang in there."

By the start of the 1976-1977 season, *The Rockford Files* had become a "middle-of-the-pack" show. Over the course of the next three years, the series would place somewhere between 40th and 50th [out of 100 shows] in the overall Nielsen series rankings. During that period of time, *Rockford* would average about an 18-19% weekly audience rating; translated into raw numbers, that means, despite sustaining a huge loss in audience during its second season, the series continued to draw approximately 13 million television households every week.

Granted, by television industry standards, those figures aren't spectacularly large — particularly when compared to the numbers *Rockford* pulled during the Spring of 1975, when the series was at the peak of its popularity. Yet, *Rockford*'s audience numbers during its third, fourth and fifth seasons remained remarkably steady, and that's what makes them intriguing. Although *Rockford* sustained a huge loss in audience (18%) over the course of the 1975-1976 season, the series would not suffer any other significant decreases in audience throughout the remainder of its network run. Put another way, while the show never regained the viewers it had lost, it held onto the viewers that it still had. In Garner's parlance, *The Rockford Files* "hung in there."

Those viewers who stayed with the show through the end did so to watch James Garner, who was ably supported by solid writing that remained tailored to his strengths. "Because television is such a character-driven medium, a lot of what you do with a character depends upon the actor you're working with," said Charles Floyd Johnson, who (along with newcomer David Chase) became co-producer of *Rockford* during the third season. "When you have an actor like James Garner, who has such a distinctive personality — which we've seen in *Maverick* and in the many other things that he's done — a lot of what you write is based on what you know he can bring or will bring to the material.

"In television, especially in developing episodic series, you draw on the character and the actor, in the sense that a lot of Jim Rockford may be a lot of Jim Garner. What happens, inevitably, in a series is that the actor and the writers expand upon each other — the writers see what the actor can do, and write that into the material; then the actor takes the material and brings it to a new level; and with each subsequent week, you try to continue to build from that level.

"I used to watch *All in the Family* all the time. A lot of what was Archie Bunker was really Carroll O'Connor; the writers would write Archie Bunker as Carroll O'Connor, and you could just see that character grow and develop each week. I think the same holds true for Angela Lansbury in *Murder, She Wrote*, and Peter Falk in *Columbo*. In series where you have major personalities that dominate the screen, you get a lot of 'building' onto the main actor with each week."

In the case of *The Rockford Files*, a kind of synergy developed between a performer with particular strengths (Garner's ability to deliver wry, character-driven humor) and writers (Huggins, Cannell, Bartlett and Chase) who knew how to bring out that strength. But, as Johnson points out, the "building" of actor traits onto the character did not stop with Garner and Rockford. "You try to 'build blocks' with your other actors and the characters they play," he continued. "For example, the relationship between Rockford and his dad was just gold to begin with [on paper]. But after watching Jim and Noah Beery play those roles, you see that they would each bring nuances to the characters, and you start thinking, 'Wouldn't it be great to do a scene where you'd have Jim and Rocky bickering, because Jim and Noah play off each other so well.'"

The sheer nature of episodic television is not only volume-driven (you have to produce 22 one-hour films a year), but also speed-oriented (you have only six days to make each film). It's an industry where you never seem to have enough time, but you can never use that as an excuse — you simply try to make the best shows possible within the parameters. Under these circumstances, the presence of a James Garner as your series lead is invaluable, both before the camera and behind the scenes. Garner's leadership on the set, as we have seen, inspires the members of his staff and crew to work hard because they know that he will support them. Similarly, Garner's uncanny knack for turning otherwise ordinary-sounding lines into "Christmas presents" provided the writers with an added incentive to deliver the best scripts possible. "When you have James Garner as your lead (or others who are as good as he is), you know that there'll always be something wonderful to watch — even if the episode or the writing isn't quite the way you want it — because Jim would make it work," added Johnson.

The Academy of Television Arts and Sciences recognized Garner's efforts by honoring him with the Emmy Award for Best Dramatic Actor of 1976-1977. Since that time, Garner has won several other major awards, including a People's Choice Award in 1979; a second Emmy in 1987; a Golden Globe in 1994; and induction in the Television Academy Hall of Fame in 1990. In addition, *TV Guide* named Garner television's All Time Best Dramatic Actor in 1993.

Truly, Garner has received the recognition he deserves for his enormous talent. "I think Jim feels that he's established in the business, and people today realize what he can do," added Luis Delgado. "Jim is an excellent actor. I would put him up against any actor or any actress in the business, and he would outshine them."

Juanita Bartlett echoed that sentiment. "I think that over the past few years, people have become more aware of how talented Jim really is," she said. "In the past ten years, he's done films like *Heartsounds*, where you can see his depth and appreciate some of the other things he can do."

Garner has modestly downplayed the importance of the individual awards. Although Garner realizes he is good at his craft, he never fails to remind himself of the important role his writers have played in his success. Johnson recalls discussing this very same matter with Garner during the planning stages of the 1994 *Rockford Files* episodes (of which Johnson and Garner are co-executive producers, along with Juanita Bartlett). "We were discussing how there are some actors who lose focus of what their jobs really are, so that they suddenly become very difficult to deal with," said Johnson. "Jim said to me, 'Well, it's a job you do. I don't write those words. I don't create that character — I embellish on it, and I know that the writers use a lot of me — but the words in the characters are from the writer. Without the writer, I don't have anything. So I never forget what the writers do — that they create Jim Rockford. Although I certainly have a big part in [the creation of Rockford's character], I don't let it become a focus of where I suddenly feel that I'm more important than the whole process.'"

Garner is one of the most esteemed performers in the business precisely because of this attitude. He recognizes and respects the contributions of his colleagues and workers, and that in turn brings him their respect. "I think that is what has kept Jim's feet on the ground over the years," Johnson continued. "He doesn't let himself get caught up in the hype — it's a job, and he enjoys it."

Noah Beery Jr. received an Emmy nomination for Best Supporting Actor in a Dramatic Series in the 1976-1977 season.

Familiar guest stars this season include William Daniels, Ned Beatty, Robert Walden, Burt Young, Kim Richards, Susan Howard, Robert Loggia, Vincent Baggetta, John Anderson, James Wainwright, Avery Schreiber, Michael Lerner, Howard Duff, Steve Landesberg, Jack Riley, John Dehner, Strother Martin, Alex Rocco, Jack Carter, Jon Cypher, Leslie Charleson, Kathleen Nolan, Conchata Farrell, Roger E. Mosley, Martin Kove, Simon Oakland, Cleavon Little, and Jack Kelly.

* * *

Prior to the 1976-1977 season, Garner amended his contract with Universal Studios. That in itself was not unusual; oftentimes, a lead actor in a successful series will use his clout as the star of the show in order to negotiate a substantial raise in salary and/or more creative control of the show. Peter Falk, for example, waged several such battles with Universal during the years he made *Columbo* (NBC, 1971-1978).

But Garner's case *was* unusual because he wasn't asking for more money — at least, more money up front. Under the terms of Garner's original contract with Universal Studios, Cherokee Productions was entitled to 37.5% of the net profits of *The Rockford Files*, while Garner received a base salary of $30,000 per episode (a figure that would increase by five percent in each subsequent season the series was in production). The contract also stipulated an arrangement made between Cherokee and an unnamed third party whereby 20% of Cherokee's percentage [or 7.5% of the total net profits] would be set aside for that third party — which meant, in essence, that Cherokee would actually only be receiving 30% of the total net profits of the series.

In February 1976, Garner renegotiated his contract — he reduced his salary in exchange for a percentage of Cherokee's actual percentage of the profits. Under the new agreement, Cherokee's 30% share of the series profits would be divided between Garner and the production company thusly:

"Such applicable percentage shall be divided between me and Cherokee in the same ratio as the number of photoplays produced hereunder bears to the number of Series photoplays produced prior to the term hereof and in which I appear (including the *Rockford Files* pilot). Thus, for example, if (i) the total applicable percentage of net profits otherwise payable to me and Cherokee hereunder is 30% of 100% after reduction by the aforementioned participations to third parties; (ii) 44 Series photoplays (including the pilot) have been produced prior to the term hereof; and (iii) 66 photoplays in which I appear are produced hereunder, then I shall be entitled to 60% of 30% of 100%, i.e., 18% of 100% of the applicable net profits, and Cherokee would be entitled to the 40% balance of 30% of 100%, i.e., 12% of 100% under your agreement with Cherokee."

Garner had apparently estimated that *Rockford* would run a total of five 22-episode seasons (which was the length of the contract between NBC and Universal with regard to the series).

Under the terms of the 1976 amendment, Garner's salary in 1976-1977 was $27,045 per episode — 18% lower than what Garner would have been entitled to that season under the terms of his original contract. (The new salary would be increased by 5% in each subsequent season the series was in production.) In essence, Garner took an 18% cut in salary in exchange for 18% of the total net profits from the series. In theory, he made a better deal for himself — although he was giving up about $1 million in salary over the final three years of the series (assuming that *Rockford* ran five seasons), he would more than make up that amount by receiving a personal share of the profits generated from the series once *Rockford* went into reruns.

The underlying assumption of this transaction, of course, was that *The Rockford Files* would indeed finish "in the black." This issue would come into play several years later, when the studio's claim that the series had lost over $9 million ultimately prompted Garner to take the matter to court.

45. THE FOURTH MAN

Production Number: 45004

Original Airdate: September 24, 1976

Written by: *Juanita Bartlett*
Directed by: *William Wiard*

Guest Cast: John McMartin (Timpson Farrell), Sharon Gless (Lori Jenevein), Michael Bell (Stegler), Dianne Harper (Susan), Candace Howerton (Airline Clerk), Barbara Collentine (Maid)

Hi. Just want to put your mind at rest — found your address book in the theater last week. It's in the mail. By the way, Carol's okay. But Linda ...?

Synopsis. *Rockford's neighbor Lori Jenevein, an airline reservations clerk, becomes the target of a hit man named Timpson Farrell whom she recognizes as a "regular" passenger on the commuter flight. Farrell fears that Lori will link him to the recent deaths of three witnesses who were scheduled to testify before a Senate committee on organized crime (murders which all took place within the past month in cities serviced by the commuter flight). Rockford is also threatened by Farrell, but he has no evidence linking Farrell to either the contract killings or the attempts on Lori's and his own life. Meanwhile, Farrell, who leads a double life as a respectable coin collector, sues Rockford for defamation of character.*

Early in this episode, Rockford temporarily rents a house (with Angel's help) as part of a plan to trap Timpson Farrell on trespassing charges. Rockford waits inside the house, hoping that Farrell will try to break inside — however, Angel upsets the operation (and nearly gets Rockford killed). This sequence sets up one of the most often-remembered lines of the entire series.

```
Rockford:      Angel? What are you doing here?

Angel:         You wouldn't shoot me for a lousy hundred
                 dollars, would you?

Rockford:      I ought to shoot you on general principles!
```

Rockford Facts. The character "Lori Jenevein" (played by Sharon Gless of *Cagney and Lacey*) is named after sound effects editor Walter Jenevein.

46. THE ORACLE WORE A CASHMERE SUIT

Production Number: 45006

Original Airdate: October 1, 1976

Written by: *David Chase*
Directed by: *Russ Mayberry*

Guest Cast: Robert Webber (Roman Clementi), Robert Walden (Barry Silverstein), Pepe Serna (Ray Ochoa), Terrence O'Connor (Eileen), Diane Sommerfield (Secretary), John Furlong (Detective Casselli), James Hong (Forensic Expert), Bonnie Bartlett (Casey Patterson)

Teddy's Treehouse — you've won our free landscaping services for one full year! We'll mow your lawn, top your trees, moat, seed, fertilize, and feed! Isn't that wonderful?

Synopsis. *Self-appointed "police psychic" Roman Clementi publicly accuses Rockford of withholding evidence that would link the investigator to the disappearance of a record company executive who, along with his girlfriend, vanished two days after Rockford was hired to surveil him. In fact, the grandstanding Clementi planted the rumor in order to make himself look good — and generate publicity for his upcoming book, Crime and the Third Eye. But the accusation causes Rockford no end of trouble. When he discovers that the record executive stashed away over $80,000 in cocaine, Rockford becomes the target of a drug-crazed drummer — and when the executive is found murdered, Rockford becomes the prime suspect.*

William Daniels was the original lead in "The Oracle Wore a Cashmere Suit," but he had to be replaced after he injured himself during the first day of filming. Filling in for Daniels was longtime TV villain Robert Webber, who narrowly avoids the dubious distinction of being the only guest star on *The Rockford Files* who is killed off in the third act in every episode he appeared in. (Midway through the story, Clementi takes what appears to be a fatal plunge down the hill; moments later, however, he emerges unscathed.)

William Daniels would return to *The Rockford Files* later this season — he played the ruthless federal prosecutor in "So Help Me God."

47. THE FAMILY HOUR

Production Number: 45002

Original Airdate: October 8, 1976

Written by: *Gordon Dawson*
Directed by: *William Wiard*

Guest Cast: Burt Young (Stu Gaily), Ken Swofford (Al Jollett), Kim Richards (Marin Rose Gaily), Paul Koslo (Pittson), Janice Carroll (Duty Clerk), Marge Wakely (Cecil Goss), Adrienne Ricard (Receptionist)

Hey, Jim, it's Frank. Me and Ellie's down here for our convention. Can't wait to see you. [Hiccups] We should be over at your place around 1:00 a.m. Bonzai, buddy!

Synopsis. *Jim and Rocky's fishing trip to Baja is interrupted when they discover nine-year-old Marin Rose Gaily sitting outside Jim's trailer. While Rocky takes care of Marin, Jim searches for her father Stu, a convicted drug smuggler on the run from Al Jollett, a crooked DEA agent. Although Jollett claims that Stu stole $100,000 in government front money, Rockford discovers Jollett had been using Stu and another convict named Marty Goss to plant evidence for a series of drug busts that Jollett had rigged in order to pad his arrest record. Goss tried to use a log he'd kept of Jollett's phony operations to negotiate a reduced prison sentence; instead, Jollett had him killed. Rockford must protect Stu, who has the book, from Jollett and his maniacal agents (one of whom wields a deadly electric cattle prod).*

Listen carefully to the game show and newscast that Marin Rose watches during the second act of this episode. The game show contestant ("Okay, Mrs. MaryAnn Rea of Sherman Oaks, let's see what you've won..."), game show host ("So until then, folks, Les Berke saying Good-bye and God Bless") and the newscaster ("Ladies and gentlemen, good morning, this is Robert Crawley with the morning news...") all are named after members of *Rockford Files* personnel. Rea is James Garner's personal assistant; Berke was the unit production manager on the series; and Crawley was the art director.

48. FEEDING FRENZY

Production Number: 45007

Original Airdate: October 15, 1976

Teleplay by: *Stephen J. Cannell*
Story by: *Lester William Berke and Donald Gold*
Directed by: *Russ Mayberry*

Guest Cast: Susan Howard (Sandy Blaylock), Eddie Firestone (Charlie Blaylock), Luke Askew (Al), Pepper Martin (Mickey Wanamaker), Richard Lepore (Lieutenant Dan Hall), Bill Phipps (Grady Northcourt), George Wyner (Max Steinberg), Roger Aaron Brown (Officer), Carmine Argenziano (Orin Wilson), Jon Seder (Agent Raval), Joseph Della Sorte (Lucy Carbone), John Dennis Johnston (Grady)

Hi, this is the Happy Pet Clinic. Your father gave us this number when he left town. The calico stray had six kittens. Please come get them — today?!?

Synopsis. *Charlie Blaylock, a former oil executive who now runs a bait stand on the pier, embezzled $500,000 from his company three years ago. Charlie has never spent the money, yet his conscience has gnawed at him ever since. Although the statute of limitations on the robbery is about to expire (which means that the police could not arrest him even if he confessed), Charlie hires Rockford to return the money to the company. But when mobsters kidnap Charlie's daughter Sandy, Rockford uses the money to pay the ransom. However, two factors complicate the matter further — first, Rockford is arrested after learning that the statute of limitations is still valid; and second, Sandy is kidnapped again, this time by the police lieutenant who worked with the insurance agent who originally investigated the heist.*

"Feeding Frenzy" features a clever twist at the end of the story. Although the statute of limitations on the robbery has passed, Charlie learns that he must pay as much as $250,000 in back income taxes for the three years in which the $500,000 was in his possession. The episode ends with slow motion footage of Charlie walking along the beach, as a cacophony of voices pounds inside his head. The final shot is a freeze frame of Charlie screaming in anguish — he realizes that by clearing his conscience, he has also ruined his life.

49. DROUGHT AT INDIANHEAD RIVER

Production Number: 45021

Original Airdate: November 5, 1976

Written by: *Stephen J. Cannell*
Directed by: *Lawrence Doheny*

Guest Cast: Robert Loggia (Dominic Marcon), Vincent Baggetta (David Marcon), Anthony Carbone (Brad Charlotte), Ronda Copeland (Delores), Nick Georgiad (Danny), Jerome Guardino (Carl Dorado), Laurence Haddon (Dr. Sager), Buddy Foster (Terry), Judith Searle (Norma), George Fisher (Lo-Ball Pete), Nick Dimitri (Sammy)

Jim, thanks for taking little Billy fishing. He had a great time. Turns out he wasn't even really seasick.... Have you ever had chicken pox?

Synopsis. *Angel suddenly becomes the major player in a multi-million dollar real estate deal that serves as the front for a major tax fraud scheme. Angel doesn't realize that his business partners, a trio of tax felons led by Dominic Marcon, plan to kill him, then use the money from the life insurance policy to pay the taxes on the property. Rockford learns about the plot against Angel from Marcon's nephew David — who then retracts what he said. When Rockford continues to investigate, Marcon implicates him in the murder of a prostitute. In order to negotiate a way out of trouble, Rockford and Beth freeze Angel's assets (by having him temporarily committed), so that Jim can make a deal with Marcon.*

Rockford demonstrates some of his golf prowess in this episode. In real life, Jim and Jack Garner are both avid golfers; in fact, Jack has been a senior member of the Professional Golfers Association for many years.

50. COULTER CITY WILDCAT

Production Number: 45009

Original Airdate: November 12, 1976

Written by: *Don Carlos Dunaway*
Directed by: *Russ Mayberry*

Guest Cast: John Anderson (Gerald O'Malley), Dennis Burkley (Howard), Patricia Stich (Phyllis), Noble Willingham (Claude Orzeck), Jerry Hardin (Walter Link), Sharon Compton (Beehive), Hal Bokar (Second Bidder), John Calvin (First Bidder), Gordon Hurst (Willie), Richard Kennedy (Third Bidder), Ed Deemer (Detective), Norman Blankenship (Russ), Terry Leonard (Driver), Don Nagel (Driver)

It's Shirley at the Plant and Pot. There's just no easy way to tell you this, Jim — we did everything we could. Your fern died.

Synopsis. *Rocky wins a parcel of land in Kern County in a public auction sponsored by the federal government. Two men pistol-whip Rocky into signing away all oil and mineral rights to the property, even though he'd apparently sold back the land for $2,000 two weeks before. A curious Rockford intervenes, and together with his father, he discovers that Rocky's parcel is worth a fortune in oil, and that the auction was part of a plan to cheat the government out of a valuable oil lease. Rockford determines that Claude Orzeck, who sold Rocky the parcel, organized* *the scam along with a silent partner. When Orzeck is murdered (presumably by his associate), and the Rockfords are held in suspicion, Jim auctions off Rocky's parcel in order to flush out the identity of the silent partner.*

Usually in series television, an episode begins by displaying the titles and credits for that particular show ("Guest Stars," "Written by," "Directed by," etc.). However, this isn't always the case with *The Rockford Files* — many episodes (such as "Coulter City Wildcat") cut right to the chase, immersing the viewer into the storyline for a good 5-7 minutes before eventually pausing to flash the opening credits. "The way the stories were written, there was often a lot of important exposition at the beginning of the show, and we felt that it might distract the audience if they had to contend with the credits flashing while there was important dialogue or action going on," explained producer Charles Floyd Johnson. "In those instances, we would wait until there was a break in the action, or some kind of transition sequence, where we could put in the credits without taking away from the story."

You can see the influence of a Roy Huggins in this approach. Huggins always advised his writers not to bother with writing "breaks" (i.e, "End of Act I," "End of Act II," etc.) into their teleplays because he believed that if the story was strong, it could be broken anywhere and still carry suspense. Similarly, it isn't necessarily important whether you show the opening credits at the top of the show or several minutes into it — what matters is that the story is good and that the picture works. If flashing the credits at the outset of the episode takes the audience away from the story, then wait until the first available opportunity.

The "delayed credits" became a signature element of *The Rockford Files*, particularly with regard to the episodes that aired after the first season. "It did become a kind of stylistic choice, because we did do that quite a few times, to the point where the audience noticed it," said Johnson. "But it was always our thinking, whenever we'd hold back the opening credits, that if we ran them earlier, we would be taking the audience away from exposition that we felt they didn't need to be distracted from. And I think that, once we'd done it a couple of times, we'd do the same in other shows whenever we felt it worked."

51. SO HELP ME GOD

Production Number: 45020

Original Airdate: November 19, 1976

Written by: *Juanita Bartlett*
Directed by: *Jeannot Szwarc*

Guest Cast: William Daniels (Gary Bevins), Sandy Ward (Henshaw), Ted Gehring (Warden Furtell), Jason Wingreen (Clarence Rohrs), Vernon Weddell (Mike Prescott), Robert Ray Sutton (Carl), John Lupton (Henry Franks), Lieux Dressler (Margaret Raucher), Cliff Carnell (Gordy), John B. Gowans (Doctor), Angelo Gnazzo (Pervis)

Dr. Soter's office. This is the third time you've cancelled. Now, you have to have that root canal — a sore foot has nothing to do with your mouth!

Synopsis. *Rockford sees the judicial system at its worst when he's subpoenaed to testify before a federal grand jury investigating the alleged kidnapping of union official Frank Sorvino. Although Rockford doesn't seem to know Sorvino, federal prosecutor Gary Bevins produces evidence of an apparent phone conversation between the two men that occurred on the day of the kidnapping. Rockford invokes the Fifth Amendment when Bevins brings up his prison record, but instead of protection, he finds himself victimized by an abuse of judicial power and ultimately jailed for civil contempt. Jim receives a temporary reprieve when Beth has him freed on a technicality (the subpoena was addressed incorrectly), but he could face continued harassment indefinitely unless he can refute Bevins' evidence. While awaiting a second summons, Rockford investigates the phantom phone call; later he deduces that Sorvino not only staged his own kidnapping, but actually hired Jim (while using an alias) to make sure that his accomplices had left town. Meanwhile, when he's called again to testify, Jim's caustic behavior lands him in the federal penitentiary — where Sorvino, whose embezzlement of union funds will become public if the phony kidnapping is exposed, arranges to have Rockford killed.*

Oftentimes there will be two or three stories going on over the course of a one-hour episode. The main story of the episode is known as the "A" story, while the subplot is called the "B" story. Juanita Bartlett had been looking for material around which she could build a "B" story for an episode she'd been developing when David Chase presented her with an item in the April 1976 issue of *The New Yorker* that pertained to the grand jury system. The article, "Annals of Law: Taking the Fifth," discussed a federal law passed under the Nixon Administration that provided for "use immunity," whereby persons who were compelled to testify before the grand jury could later be prosecuted themselves — provided that the government did not base its case on the persons' own testimony. Although the law was widely criticized by legal scholars who recognized its potential for abuse, it had not been repealed.

Although Chase suggested that the article might provide the basis for a possible "B" story, Bartlett thought, "This is more than just a possible subplot. This is a story on its own." After drafting "So Help Me God," she asked the local chapters of the American Civil Liberties Union and the American Bar Association to review the script for accuracy. Except for one change (Bartlett had overlooked one step of the procedure), both groups lauded the script. "So Help Me God" later received several commendations from other lawyers' groups.

Rockford Facts. The foreman Clarence Rohrs, who was named after film editor George Rohrs, was played by Jason Wingreen, who had appeared with James Garner in 1969's *Marlowe.*

52. RATTLERS' CLASS OF '63

Production Number: 45018

Original Airdate: November 26, 1976

Written by: *David Chase*
Directed by: *Meta Rosenberg*

Guest Cast: James Wainwright (Gene Chechik), Elayne Heilveil (Regine Boyajian), Avery Schreiber (Azie Boyajian), John Durren (Leo Kale), Rudy Ramos (Bobby Boyajian), Sandra Kerns (Robin Seidlitz), Stacy Keach Sr. (Reverend), Stanley Brock (Elliot Deutch), Ed Vasgersian (Hank Boyajian), Gerald Hackney (Jerryl)

Gene's 24-Hour Emergency Plumbing. Your water heater's blown? We'll have somebody out there Tuesday — Thursday at the latest.

Synopsis. *Angel marries his way into an Armenian family he had fleeced in a variation of the "red barn" con. Angel and another flim-flam artist pretended to purchase an old dumping grounds from the Boyajian brothers, pulled out of the sale, then conned the family into "bribing" them. The scam hits a snag when Angel learns his partner has been killed. Angel thinks the Boyajians are responsible, so he hastily pulls out of the marriage. Meanwhile, when Bobby Boyajian, who had disapproved of the marriage, also turns up dead, the family blames Angel (and, by association, Rockford, the best man at the wedding). In order to get out from under, Rockford must determine who killed Bobby Boyajian. He soon finds a connection between both murders and the bodies of two motorcycle gang members who were buried on the dumping grounds in 1963.*

Reportedly Stuart Margolin's favorite episode, "Rattlers' Class of '63" presents Angel in a rare light. For a brief moment at the end of the episode (when he admits to Regine that "he's always scared"), Angel reveals that there may actually a human being tucked inside his exasperating persona. "I like you," he tells Regine. "There's nothing phony there, you understand?"

53. RETURN TO THE THIRTY-EIGHTH PARALLEL

Production Number: 45003

Original Airdate: December 10, 1976

Written by: *Walter Dallenbach*
Directed by: *Bruce Kessler*

Guest Cast: Ned Beatty (Al Brennan), Veronica Hamel (Marcy Brownell), Paul Stevens (John Stabile), Normann Burton (Markel), Robert Karnes (Captain Hulette), James Congdon (Alvin Thomas), Jeff David (Funeral Director), Michael Ebert (Lee Nejman), John Mahon (Lieutenant Hayes), Bart Burns (Fire Department Chief), Chuck Winters (Kevin Lindsay), Tom Stewart (Aarons), Michael Alldridge (Cab Driver), Sam Vlahos (Deck Hand), Ted Noos (Agent)

Tompkins of Guaranty Insurance. About your burglary claim—major loss, all right. Funny—you remembered to file, but you didn't pay your premium...

Synopsis. *Rockford's former Army commander Al Brennan, whose work as an insurance investigator has run aground, wants to become Jim's partner. Meanwhile, a woman wants to hire Rockford to find her missing sister; before Rockford can decline, Brennan accepts the case. Jim soon discovers that his "client" actually works for Brennan, who wants Rockford to lead him to a $3 million Chiang Yin vase that was stolen from a New York museum two years ago. Rockford and Brennan compete with each other to recover the vase—and claim the 10% finder's fee.*

Apparently Rockford served under three commanding officers during the Korean War—Al Brennan (according to this episode), Daniel Hart Bowie ("2 into 5.56 Won't Go"), and "Howling Mad" Smith ("The Hawaiian Headache").

54. PIECE WORK

Production Number: 45022

Original Airdate: December 17, 1976

Written by: *Juanita Bartlett*
Directed by: *Lawrence Doheny*

Guest Cast: Michael Lerner (Murray Rosner), Ned Wilson (Robert Spiker),

Simon Scott (Gregory McGill), Ben Frank (Fred Molin), Frank Maxwell (Ciro Lucas), Jack Bannon (Herbert Deane), Michael Mancini (Angie Pictaggi), Deborah Landes (Lily Rosner), Harvey Vernon (Jerry Leedy), Ricky Powell (Junior Rosner)

It's Dr. Soter's office again, regarding that root canal? The doctor's in his office — waiting. He's beginning to dislike you ...

Synopsis. *Hired by an insurance company to investigate a suspicious accident at the Brent Air Health Club, Rockford stumbles onto a gun-running operation masterminded by club owner Ciro Lucas. Although arrested by federal agents (and, later, hassled by Lieutenant Chapman), Rockford finds his biggest threat in Murray Rosner, an incredibly paranoid informant who has been working with the FBI on the Lucas operation for over eight months. Rosner thinks Jim is an undercover agent whom the feds hired in order to circumvent paying Rosner for information. With a major gun shipment imminent (as well as a big score for himself), Rosner perceives Rockford as competition and decides to eliminate him permanently.*

According to this episode, the first name of Officer Billings (Luis Delgado's character) is Jack; however, in the fourth season's "Quickie Nirvana," Becker refers to Billings as "Officer Todd Billings."

Rockford Funnies. Over the hospital intercom, you can hear the page "Dr. Adler, Outside Call Please." This is a reference to Diane Adler, one of the film editors for *The Rockford Files*.

55. THE TROUBLE WITH WARREN

Production Number: 45008

Original Airdate: December 24, 1976

Written by: *Juanita Bartlett*
Directed by: *Christian I. Nyby II*

Guest Cast: Ron Rifkin (Warren Weeks), Paul Jenkins (Garrett Hudson), Joe Maross (Perry Lefcourt), John Dullaghan (Federal Agent Alpine), Tom Bower (Congressman), Ann Randall Stewart (Catherine Lefcourt), M.P. Murphy (Janitor), Jan Stratton (Hilda), Tom Williams (Wedding Guest), Ed Crick (Parking Attendant), Vince Howard (Kleinschmidt), Shirley Anthony (Secretary)

Jimmy, it's Phil in Puerto Rico. This is real important — [Inaudible due to poor phone connection.] He'll pay $20,000. Call me at — [Inaudible due to poor phone connection.]

Synopsis. *Beth implores Rockford to help her intellectually brilliant but socially inept cousin Warren, the prime suspect in the murder of his boss. The case lands Rockford in trouble with the police on a lengthy string of charges. Meanwhile, Jim's personal dislike for his client intensifies — first, he learns that Warren has been withholding information (he'd been fired from his job, plus he was fooling around with an executive's wife); then, when the executive is also found dead, Rockford finds himself accused of acting as an accessory to that murder. But Rockford sees a way out when he discovers a possible link between the two murders and a Senate committee investigating Warren's company regarding charges of corporate bribery.*

56. THERE'S ONE IN EVERY PORT

Production Number: 45026

Original Airdate: January 7, 1977

Written by: *Stephen J. Cannell*
Directed by: *Meta Rosenberg*

Guest Cast: Joan Van Ark (Christina Marks), Howard Duff (Eddie Marks), John Dehner (Judge Lyman), Steve Landesberg (Kenny Hollywood), John Mahon (Victor Sherman), Jack Riley (Adrian Lyman), George Memmoli (Blast Gillette), Michael Delano (Sharkey), Byron Morrow (Ray Fahasateur), Kenneth Tobey (Captain), Stanley Brock (Morris), Christopher Winfield (Waiter), David Pansaris (Ski Mask)

Bum - mer! I called up with some good vibes and some positive energies, and I talk to a robot? Forget you, man!

Synopsis. *Another con artist acquaintance plays Rockford for a chump. Jim learns that Eddie Marks could die of a kidney disorder unless he's treated with a $50,000 dialysis machine; but Eddie has only $10,000, and he doesn't qualify for welfare because of his prison record. Christina Marks begs Rockford to raise the money by playing in a highstakes poker game (using her father's money as a stake). Rockford gets into a game run by racketeer Blast Gillette. When three gunmen interrupt the game (and steal the $200,000 kitty), Blast suspects Rockford of orchestrating the robbery and threatens to kill him. When Jim realizes that Eddie and Christina set up the heist, he counters with an elaborate scheme designed to recover the money — and sting Eddie.*

Stephen J. Cannell often borrowed elements that he remembered from watching *Maverick* (his favorite TV show as a kid) and reworked them into his stories on *The Rockford Files*. As noted earlier, "The Great Blue Lake Land and Development Company" borrowed a plot device from the classic *Maverick* episode "Shady Deal at Sunny Acres," although the story for "Great Blue Lake" was completely different.

"There's One in Every Port," however, is a modern rendition of "Shady Deal," in that Rockford recruits several con artist acquaintances in order to engineer a sting aimed at the man who had cheated him (just as Maverick had done in the original story). In fact, the episode actually weds elements from two classic *Maverick*s. The setup of this episode calls to mind a *Maverick* story entitled "The Seventh Hand," in which Maverick is staked $10,000 to play poker, then becomes accused of staging a robbery that interrupts the game.

"There's One in Every Port" is a thoroughly entertaining hour featuring typically colorful Cannell characterizations, such as Kenny Hollywood (a con artist who is obsessed with washing his hands), and the Lyman brothers (who incessantly bicker with each other). There's also an inspired bit of casting: character actor John Dehner, who played Maverick's foil in "Shady Deal at Sunny Acres," appears as one of Rockford's cronies in this episode. Dehner also appeared with James Garner in the 1971 film *Support Your Local Gunfighter*.

Garner, Corbett and Beery.

57. STICKS AND STONES MAY BREAK YOUR BONES, BUT WATERBURY WILL BURY YOU

Production Number: 45025

Original Airdate: January 14, 1977

Written by: *David Chase*
Directed by: *Jerry London*

Guest Cast: Simon Oakland (Vern St. Cloud), Cleavon Little (Billy Merrihew), Val Bisoglio (Marv Potempkin), Anthony Costello (Ted Clair), Robert Riesel (Wass), James Karen (John LaPointe), Jim Storm (Officer), Katherine Charles (Susan Hanrahan), George Pentecost (Carl Colavito), Linda Dano (Gwen Molinaro), Fritzi Burr (Receptionist), Hal Stohl (Guard), Brian Levy (Garth McCreary), Henry Gayle Sanders (Hard Hat)

This is the Department of the Army. Our records show that you are the "Rockford, James" who failed to turn in his service automatic in May 1953. Contact us at once.

Synopsis. *Waterbury Security Systems, one of the largest detective agencies in the world, has been systematically disenfranchising independent P.I.s as part of its plan to reduce the small agencies' share of the market by 20 percent. Two victims, Billy Merrihew and Vern St. Cloud, hire Rockford to investigate the matter. (Jim would have been victimized himself had he not been away on vacation.) Rockford realizes that Waterbury means business when he discovers a third private investigator has been murdered.*

58./59. THE TREES, THE BEES AND T.T. FLOWERS

(Two-parter)

Production Numbers: 45012/45013

Original Airdates: January 21 and 28, 1977

Written by: *Gordon Dawson*
Directed by: *Jerry London*

Guest Cast: Strother Martin (Thomas Tyler "T.T." Flowers), Alex Rocco (Sherman Royle), Karen Machon (Cathy Royle), Scott Brady (Jack Meullard), Richard Venture (Dr. Ben Crist), Roy Jenson (Winchell), Paul Sylvan (Steve Fisher), Fred Stuthman (Homer Hobson), Jack Stauffer (Brubaker), Bob Hastings (Hank Gidley), Linda Ryan (Maid), Allen Williams (Dr. Norm Fellows), June Whitley Taylor (Nurse), Robert DoQui (SWAT Commander Willis), Tom Rosqui (Tom Brockmeyer), Dave Shelley (Division Commander), Ric Parrott (Attendant), Michael Lawrence (Newscaster), Fred Lerner (Lou), Dave Cass (Morris)

Jimmy, ol' buddy-buddy — it's Angel. You know how they allow you one phone call? Well, this is it.

Hello? He-hello? Hello ...? Hello?!?

Synopsis. *Rocky's friend T.T. Flowers, a slightly eccentric beekeeper, is spirited away to a convalescent hospital. Rockford intervenes and discovers a link between the abduction and Sherman Royle, T.T.'s son-in-law. Sherm borrowed heavily from several sources (including land developer Jack Meullard) to cover up a bungled investment scheme which he'd financed with embezzled funds. The ruthless Meullard, who has long coveted T.T.'s property (located next to an apartment complex Meullard owns), fronted Sherm $100,000 in exchange for the land. Sherm convinced his wife Cathy to have T.T. committed. But Cathy doesn't realize that her father is in the hands of diabolical physicians, bankrolled by Meullard, who are feeding T.T. hallucinatory drugs as part of Meullard's scheme to have T.T. declared legally incompetent. Jim breaks T.T. out of the hospital, then scores another victory when a judge strikes down the incompetency ruling. But Rockford knows that Meullard will stop at nothing — not even murder — to win T.T.'s property.*

A few years before *The Rockford Files*, Strother Martin had co-starred with James Garner in an episode of *Nichols* called "Zachariah," written by Juanita Bartlett. A mishap occurred during the filming of that show — Garner nearly had his foot broken—but you'd never know it from watching the episode. "That's because Jim is a consummate pro," said Bartlett. "There was a scene in which Jim and Strother are in a hotel room. Strother is supposed to come up to Jim and try to throttle him from behind, but instead Jim flips him over his head and onto the bed. Strother asked Jim, 'What can I do to help?' Jim said, 'Don't help. Let me do everything, and that way, nobody gets hurt. You just relax, and I will see that you go over my head and onto the bed.' Strother said, 'Fine.'

"The cameras started rolling, and the scene began. Jim reached back, grabbed Strother, bent over, flipped him over his head onto the bed—and the bed collapsed! Strother's weight had caused the frame of the bed to break—and it landed on Jim's foot. But you wouldn't have known it, because Jim continued to play out the scene as if nothing had happened. Finally, the director yelled 'Cut!' and Jim said, 'Will somebody get this damned bed off my foot?'

"The piece of the frame that fell on him was sharp. If Jim hadn't been wearing boots, he would be missing the front part of his foot—because there was this huge dent in the toe of his boot! And his foot hurt like hell."

Bartlett, who was on the set to watch the filming of that scene, couldn't believe Garner didn't say anything until after the scene had ended. "I went up to Jim," she continued, "and I said, 'My God, you didn't scream, you didn't tell the director to stop. Why didn't you tell him to stop?' And Jim said, 'Because I didn't want to have to do that scene again.'

"And I thought, 'My God, that is complete control.' They got it in the one take, and Jim went limping off."

Rockford Funnies. Early in Part One, Rockford cons his way into examining the admittance sheet at Horizons Crest residence so that he can find T.T.'s room. Among the names on the list is "William Fannon," which is also the name of the property master on *The Rockford Files*. Also, this episode mentions "Bartlett Oil" (named after Juanita Bartlett) and includes a reference to a patient named "Jackson" (as in Andrew Jackson, director of photography).

Rockford Facts. Joe Santos and Alex Rocco co-starred in the 1973 feature film *The Friends of Eddie Coyle*.

60. THE BECKER CONNECTION

Production Number: 45028

Original Airdate: February 11, 1977

Teleplay by: *Juanita Bartlett*
Story by: *Chas. Floyd Johnson and Ted Harris*
Directed by: *Reza S. Badiyi*

Guest Cast: Jack Kelly (Alex Kasajian), Jack Carter (Marty Golden), William Jordan (Officer Andy Dolan), Pat Finley (Peggy Becker), James B. Sikking (John Hickland), Lal Baum (Joey Holbrook), Rita George (Officer Hasty), Helen Schustak (Meter Maid), Warren Munson (Hotel Clerk), Bucklind Beery (Officer Al Mazurski)

Hi. I'm confused — is this Dial-a-Prayer? Well, should I come back when the Reverend's in the office, or what?

Synopsis. *Shortly after receiving a temporary transfer into the narcotics division, Becker finds himself suspended after someone stole heroin from the police property room and planted it in the spare tire of his car. A desperate Becker hires Rockford to find out who framed him. Rockford and Angel hit the streets and locate a dealer named Willie Hatton who may have information concerning "the Becker connection." But the matter becomes worse when Rockford finds Hatton dead and discovers evidence linking Becker to the murder.*

This is the first of two episodes featuring Jack Kelly, James Garner's co-star for three seasons on *Maverick*. In fact, Kelly "addresses" Garner in their only scene together — during Act IV, when Kasajian (Kelly's character) has Rockford cornered, Kasajian says to Rockford, "We're gonna put you on hold, Slick." For many years, "Slick" has been Garner's nickname. Jack Kelly also guest-starred in "Beamer's Last Case."

Rockford Facts. In order to stay active during his suspension, Becker takes a part-time job as a cab driver. In real life, Joe Santos drove a taxi for three years before he became an actor.

Jim Rockford, "The Taco King."

61. JUST ANOTHER POLISH WEDDING

Production Number: 45030

Original Airdate: February 18, 1977

Written by: *Stephen J. Cannell*
Directed by: *William Wiard*

Guest Cast: Louis Gossett Jr. (Marcus Hayes), Isaac Hayes (Gandolf Fitch), Pepper Martin (Mel), Walter Brooke (Germanian), Dennis Burkley (Bartender), Anthony Charnota (Dancer), Barney McFadden (Fred Koska), Jack Collins (Finn O'Herlihy), George Skaff (Maitre' D), Melendy Britt (Musicians Union Secretary), Sidney Clute (Funeral Administrator), Raymond Singer (Johnny Goodbye), Alfred Dennis (Mr. Koska), Boni Enton (Hildy Mitchell), Holly Irving (Mrs. Martin), Jeanne LeBouvier (Mrs. Mitchell), Bruce Tuthill (Yacht Club Attendant)

George DeBolt, Malibu Space Watch. Had three sightings last week. You see anything unusual? Your television reception interrupted? Call 555-1313.

Synopsis. *Gandolf Fitch finds that he needs a new line of work, so he decides to become a private investigator. Gandy offers his services to Rockford; although Jim declines, he proposes an alliance between Gandy and parole officer-turned-P.I. Marcus Hayes. While Marcus and Gandy work out the details of their unlikely partnership, Rockford travels to San Diego, where he tries to locate a missing heir on behalf of the Probate Department. When Gandy mentions the case to Marcus, the opportunistic Hayes also decides to find the heir — so he can ace Rockford out of the finder's fee.*

Normally, it took six working days to film a one-hour episode of *The Rockford Files*. But there were a few exceptions. In order to accommodate director William Wiard, "Just Another Polish Wedding" was filmed in less than five days. "Bill's daughter was going to be married about the time he was scheduled to direct this show," remembered Juanita Bartlett. "There was going to be a conflict, and so he went to Meta Rosenberg and asked her if she would release him from his commitment to do that show. Meta said, 'Well, we'll certainly look for another director, but it's going to be very difficult to find someone who's available to step in.' Which was true—because you always have to schedule your directors several weeks in advance of when you actually need them.

"Bill said, 'I'll tell you what. If you'll let me do the show in five days, then I can do it.' Meta asked, 'Can you do it in five days?' Bill said, 'Yes, I can.' And he did — he actually did that show in four-and-a-half days."

Considering the complex nature of "Just Another Polish Wedding," that was no mean feat. "That was a very complicated show, because it had so many different things happening," said Bartlett. "You had three stories going on—Rockford's search; Gandy and Marcus' partnership; and the wedding party. But Bill did a wonderful job on that show, because of the way he planned. He was very efficient, yet creative at the same time. He was just wonderful."

Wiard had already directed several episodes of *Rockford* up to that point, so he was very familiar with the exceptionally proficient crew at Cherokee Productions. In addition, Wiard had filmed one other episode ("Sleight of Hand") in five days, so there was a precedent. Still, the task at hand was not easy, but the crew came through.

"We were the fastest crew at Universal," said Luis Delgado. "We used to have the efficiency experts from the studio come down to our set and try to figure out what made us so efficient, why we did everything so fast, and got into less overtime, than any other show at Universal. And we did that show ['Just Another Polish Wedding'] in five days to show Universal how efficient we were and how fast we were—although we really had to crank that one out."

Needless to say, the studio was impressed by the crew's accomplishment on this episode—so much so, it apparently wanted to put the show on a permanent five-day shooting schedule. But James Garner wouldn't allow it. "Jim said, 'No way. We just did this to show you how efficient we are, and what can be done,'" Delgado continued. "We were all extremely tired after that show. And we stayed with our regular six-day schedule."

Rockford Facts. This episode served as the pilot for a possible spinoff series featuring Marcus Hayes (Louis Gossett Jr.) and Gandy Fitch (Isaac Hayes). Although the chemistry between Gossett and Hayes was promising, NBC did not express interest in any series. Hayes, however, returned to *The Rockford Files* for one more guest appearance in the fourth season ("Second Chance").

62. NEW LIFE, OLD DRAGONS

Original Airdate: February 25, 1977

Production Number: 45019

Teleplay by: *David C. Taylor*
Story by: *Bernard Rollins and Leroy Robinson*
Directed by: *Jeannot Szwarc*

Guest Cast: Kathleen Nolan (Cathy Hartman), Irene Yah-Ling Sun (Pham Vam Mai), Charles Napier (Mitch Donner), Charles Siebert (Gary Stillman), Luke Askew (Benson Kelly), James Callahan (Lew Hartman), Clyde Kusatsu (Nguyen), Al Stephenson (L.J.), Bruce Tuthill (Officer), Jim Ishida (Pham Vam Vinh), Herb Kayde (Guard), Jay Gerber (Deputy Chief), Robert Phalen (Will Dunning)

It's Pete. Hope you enjoyed using the cabin last week. Only next time, leave the trout in the refrigerator, huh? Not in the cupboard!

Synopsis. *Pham Vam Mai, a Vietnamese refugee, wants Rockford to find her brother Vinh, whom she believes was abducted by a trio of former American soldiers. Although Mai speaks*

English fluently, she addresses Rockford in pidginese because she doesn't want him to discover the real reason why she hired him — she has smuggled over $500,000 in American government payroll money that her brother and a Vietnamese colonel obtained through the black market during the Vietnam War. In addition to rescuing Vinh from the abductors, Rockford must protect his client from her American sponsor, a treacherous former Army CID agent who also has his sights on the money.

Rockford's ad in the Yellow Pages has changed since we first saw it in the pilot — the ad now features an actual photograph of Rockford (as opposed to the pen-and-ink drawing that appeared in the old version). Also according to the ad: Rockford's state investigator's license number is 9749; he speaks Spanish; and his phone number is 555-2867. (Previous episodes have listed 555-2368 and 555-9000 as his phone number.)

63./64. TO PROTECT AND SERVE
(Two-parter)

Production Number: 45027/45029

Original Airdates: March 11 and 18, 1977

Written by: *David Chase*
Directed by: *William Wiard*

Guest Cast: Joyce Van Patten (Lianne Sweeney), Leslie Charleson (Patsy Fossler), Jon Cypher (Michael Kelly), George Loros ("Anthony Boy" Gagglio), Pat Finley (Peggy Becker), Luke Andreas (Syl), James Coleman (Officer Haydu), Charles Parks (Officer Drumm), Jason Ledger (Sergeant Salcedo), Bob Peterson (Bartender), Lou Frizzell (Wes Wesley), Angus Duncan (John Fossler), Bucklind Beery (Officer Mazurski), Douglas Ryan (Deputy), Charles Bateman (First Detective), John Lucarelli (Bowling Alley Customer), Nick Dimitri (Dorsey).

This is Dusty, your father's friend. So you helped me move — that's it? You couldn't call, see if maybe I liked the new place? See if maybe there's some painting to be done?

This is incredible! Do you know last night I had one of my dreams? I dreamed that if I called you, you wouldn't be home — and you're not!

Synopsis. *New York attorney Michael Kelly hires Rockford to locate his fiancé Patsy Fossler, who apparently fled to Los Angeles after she abruptly cancelled their wedding a few days earlier. After two thugs from the East Coast who are also looking for Patsy break into Rockford's trailer and beat him up, Jim tries to quit the case, but Kelly won't let him — in fact, he threatens to kill Rockford if he can't find Patsy within 24 hours. The matter becomes clearer to Rockford once he tracks down Patsy: Kelly represents New York crime lord Joseph Manett, who was recently acquitted of jury tampering charges. Because Kelly told Patsy about many of the Manett family dealings, Manett wants her silenced for his own protection. Rockford must therefore protect Patsy from both his own client and Manett's goons. Complicating the situation: Lianne Sweeney, a meddlesome "police buff" whose efforts to assist the investigation nearly get Rockford and Patsy killed.*

J oyce Van Patten, who plays Lianne Sweeney (the police groupie who also runs a shoe concession stand in this episode), is the sister of Dick Van Patten (*Eight is Enough*); for a time in the late 1970s, she was married to Dennis Dugan (who later became *Richie Brockelman*).

65. CRACK BACK

Production Number: 45031

Original Airdate: March 25, 1977

Written by: *Juanita Bartlett*
Directed by: *Reza S. Badiyi*

Guest Cast: Joseph Mascolo (Gibby), Howard McGillin (Davey Woodhull), John Calvin (Coach Preston Garnett), Sondra Blake (Doreen Carpenter), Conchata Farrell (Ella Mae White), Nick Ferris (Cab Driver), Bo Kaprall (Willie Gunter), Robert Miller Driscoll (Defense Attorney Rosecrans), Norman Bartold (Judge Carroll), Glenn Robards (Doorman), Robert Ward (Reporter No. 1), Bill Woodard (Football Player), Gloria Dixon (Reporter No. 2), Bill Baldwin (Jury Foreman)

This is Dr. Soter. Now, my nurse tells me you've blown four root canal appointments. Well, you're finished in this office!

Synopsis. *Beth hires Jim to find a woman who allegedly could clear her client, pro football player Davey Woodhull, of first degree murder charges. Meanwhile, just as Woodhull's trial begins, Beth is harassed by crank phone calls, stalkings, and a series of sexually explicit gifts sent to her through the mail. When Woodhull's mystery woman is murdered shortly after Rockford locates her, Jim suspects Woodhull of masterminding an insidious scheme that would cover all bets in case he's convicted — by showing that Beth was distracted, Woodhull could appeal on the basis that she could not render an effective defense. Rockford then tries to prove that Woodhull orchestrated the harassment.*

Rockford frequently resorts to phony names and cheap disguises in order to wheedle information out of some of the people he investigates; he often uses the portable printing press in his car to print up business cards for his ruses. In this episode, we learn that Rockford will sometimes put his father's phone number on the business card he'll leave with his "mark." This makes perfect sense: he can't leave his own phone number, because if he's not at home, his cover would be blown as soon as his answering machine kicks in. (Rockford, of course, could solve that problem by changing his outgoing message every time he uses a phony name; however, as often as he goes through names, it wouldn't take long before he'd wear out the machine.)

66. DIRTY MONEY, BLACK LIGHT

Production Number: 45005

Original Airdate: April 1, 1977

Written by: *David C. Taylor*
Directed by: *Stuart Margolin*

Guest Cast: John P. Ryan (Dearborn), Wesley Addy (Agent Steiner), Roger E. Mosley (Electric Larry), Joshua Bryant (Agent Wolf), John Chappell (Blake), Martin Kove (Harry Smick), Victor Argo (Jud Brown), Michael Lane (Tony), Mary Carver (Receptionist), Dick McGarvin (Bank Teller), Craig Wasson (Steve), Edward Knight (Fed), Noami Grumett (Second Receptionist), Charles Hutchins (Trainer), Dani Heath (Switchboard Operator)

This is Tony. I forgot what I was calling for. Your recording is so boring. Spike it with some humor, some personality — something!

Synopsis. *Rocky wins an all-expenses-paid trip to Hawaii as part of a contest sponsored by a public relations company that serves as the front for an elaborate money racket. The company uses the addresses of the unsuspecting participants to funnel dirty money back and forth while the prize winners are out of town. Jim, who'd been collecting his father's mail while he was away, stumbles onto the scam when he opens four envelopes addressed to Rocky containing over $44,000 in stolen $100 bills. The complications increase when Angel steals two of the bills in order to repay a debt to loan shark Electric Larry — and promptly gets arrested once he tries to break them.*

The second of two episodes directed by Stuart Margolin, "Dirty Money, Black Light" features some very effective P.O.V. shots. For example, the sequence where Angel is being questioned by the two federal agents is filmed from Angel's point of view — the agents are filmed with the camera tilted slightly upward, as if the viewers are looking at them from where Angel is seated. Also, because Angel speaks quickly and acts very nervously throughout this scene, the camera frequently cuts back and forth from one agent to the other.

Rockford Facts. According to several television reference books, Angel resides at the Hotel Edison. However, the scene in this episode in which Jim and Beth visit Angel's apartment begins with an establishing shot of an apartment building; in the foreground, you can see a sign that reads "Hotel Madison."

Rockford owns an ultra-violet detecting mechanism that enables him to determine whether or not currency is marked.

Production meeting. Charles Floyd Johnson, Meta Rosenberg, David Chase and James Garner.

Fourth Season: 1977-1978

Judging from the numbers, *Rockford*'s fourth season would seem no different than its third. Although the series slipped five notches in the overall rankings (from 41st at the end of 1976-1977, to 46th at the end of 1977-1978), its overall average rating (18.3) was not appreciably different from its seasonal average of the third season (18.8). However, as we saw earlier (in the case of *Rockford*'s showdown with *Hawaii Five-O*), the raw numbers do not always reflect the entire story. In the case of the fourth season, *Rockford* started on par (averaging a 34 audience share and a 18.8 rating after three weeks), stumbled during the middle (sustaining a 10% loss in viewers from October through December), then finished strong (its audience numbers increased by 10% in the last two months of the season). *Rockford* also enjoyed its strongest season in three years with regard to the writing, which rivaled that of the outstanding first season in terms of overall quality. At the end of the season, the series reaped an Emmy Award—the Television Academy recognized *Rockford* as Best Dramatic Series of the year.

Still, it does seem ironic that *Rockford* should win the Emmy in a year when its overall ratings were low—particularly when you consider that in 1974-1975, when the show's popularity was at its peak, the series wasn't even nominated. In truth, many factors come into play when it comes to the Emmy Awards. Much depends on which shows are nominated; which particular episodes have been sent to the awards panel for consideration; and the makeup of the panel itself. There's also a great deal of lobbying that takes place in order to bring certain shows to the Academy's attention.

"I think it took a while for the Academy to recognize *Rockford* for what it was," said producer Charles Floyd Johnson. "By the time we were nominated, we'd been on four years, and the show had become a staple on Friday nights, and I think it was a matter of where people recognized how clever the show was. I think it kind of got to where [1977-1978] was its year."

Series co-creator Roy Huggins agrees that, while the quality of the fourth season definitely factored into the equation, the series was ultimately recognized for the characteristics it had developed over four years —including the many idiosyncratic characters that reflect the brilliant mind of Stephen J. Cannell. "It was more than just one year was better than the other," said Huggins. "It was a recollection of characters on the Academy's part, and not just the character of Rockford, but all the characters surrounding him—those that Steve created and those that Steve embellished. That's what kept the show going, and I think that's why it ultimately won the Emmy Award."

Another factor to consider was James Garner, who had won the Best Dramatic Actor Emmy for *The Rockford Files* for 1976-1977. While Garner's award in the previous season may not have had any actual bearing on the final selections for 1977-1978, it certainly couldn't have hurt *Rockford*'s chances. "Jim is one of a kind," said supervising producer Jo Swerling. "There's never been anybody like him, and there'll *never be* anybody like him, who has that unique personality that he has, and who has Jim's ability to read wry, ironic, humorous lines. He can do that like nobody else can. You can have another actor do the same role, and the same script, word for word, and it'll be the difference between it being ordinary, or being so good it sparkles."

The Emmy Awards program in 1978 does not list which episode of *The Rockford Files* was sent to the Blue Ribbon Panel for consideration. Although no one on the *Rockford* production staff can recall for certain which episode was submitted, the consensus is that it was one of two possibilities—"So Help Me God" and "Quickie Nirvana." In order to qualify for the Emmy, nominated programs must have been originally telecast during a specific period of time for the given season. In the case of the 1977-1978 awards, shows submitted for consideration had to have aired between March 14, 1977 and June 30, 1978. That would certainly favor "Quickie Nirvana," which first aired in November 1977 ("So Help Me God" was originally telecast in November 1976).

Either show is a worthy choice to represent the series. In "So Help Me God," Rockford is forced to do battle against the federal Grand Jury system. It's a marvelous showcase for Garner that demonstrates much of the appeal of the Rockford character. The other possibility, "Quickie Nirvana," is an excellent mixture of humor, drama and social commentary which pairs Rockford with an off-the-wall but not unrealistic character (Valerie Curtin as Sky Aquarian, a woman on a perpetual search for self-enlightenment). The humor comes out of Rockford's reactions to Sky's behavior, but never at Sky's expense. Yet the story ends on a somber note, because Sky is still very much a lost soul at the end of the episode.

Rockford's win was something of an upset — insiders had predicted that the Best Dramatic Series award would go to *Lou Grant*, the *Mary Tyler Moore Show* spinoff starring Edward Asner as the editor of a major Los Angeles newspaper. In fact, Charles Floyd Johnson recalls that he was as surprised as anyone that *Rockford* won. "Earlier that evening, we — Meta, David, Steve, Juanita and me — were all at Steve's house, getting ready for the awards ceremony," Johnson said. "Steve asked me, 'Do you think we'll win?' And I said, 'Give me a break! It's our fourth year on the air, we've never been nominated before — we're just lucky to be nominated!' And I really believed that. I didn't think at that stage of the game we'd get a win.

"We went to the auditorium that night. And I don't know whether it was a matter of wish fulfillment (in the sense that if I believed it wasn't going to happen, then it wouldn't happen), or that I just didn't want to be disappointed, but I honestly didn't believe we'd win. So.... when they opened the envelope later that night, and they announced '*The Rockford Files*,' I was the most nonplussed person in the world!"

Stephen J. Cannell, Meta Rosenberg, David Chase, and Charles Floyd Johnson all received Emmys on behalf of the show. Only Johnson nearly didn't made it to the podium — he was so dumbfounded by the announcement, he couldn't move from his seat. "Juanita sat next to me that night, and she started punching my arm: 'Charles! Charles, they said your name!'" he continued. "I looked up and I saw that David, Steve and Meta were all standing up on the stage — and I was still sitting in my chair! Juanita kept nudging me, and I finally got out of my chair. From that point on, I was sort of on automatic pilot, because I couldn't believe we had won. It was the strangest feeling — I remember, as I went down the aisle, that Lou Gossett reached out and grabbed my hand, and that I saw Rita Moreno, then Jim Garner. But it was as though I were in this dream. It was a wonderful feeling.

"And I remember that when I had the Emmy in my hand, I thought to myself, 'I know they want to take this back and have it engraved, but I'm never letting it go!'"

The fourth season is also marked by two cosmetic changes, and a subtle difference in the approach to Rockford's character. The opening credits sequence had been changed slightly. Inserted among the montage of Garner/Rockford in action are stills of Rockford interacting with Angel (Stuart Margolin), Beth (Gretchen Corbett) and Rocky (Noah Beery); then toward the end of the sequence, two stills of Rockford with Dennis Becker (Joe Santos) are also inserted. The closing credits sequence was also changed. During the first three years of the show, a head shot of Jim and Rocky was used as the background against which the closing credits were flashed. However, beginning with the fourth season, and continuing through the end of the series, the closing credits of each episode are flashed against still frames selected from that particular episode.

Also, whether by design or not, there's a subtle change in the perception of Rockford that is reflected in two nuances that appear in the fourth season episodes (and continue to recur throughout the remainder of the series). While Rockford always reminded his clients that he charged "$200 a day plus expenses," in truth he was more likely to be stiffed than be paid. However, that particular character facet changes somewhat beginning in the fourth season — Rockford not only gets paid more often than not, in one episode ("The Mayor's Committee from Deer Lick Falls") he even gets paid by a client who technically hadn't even hired him.

In addition, we learn in one episode ("The House on Willis Avenue") that Rockford has become a "living legend among the private eyes in the L.A. area," on the basis of front-page coverage in *The Los Angeles Times* of some of his cases. (Apparently, his reputation will soon spread — a character in the sixth-season episode "Lions, Tigers, Monkeys, and Dogs" refers to Jim as a "world famous private investigator.") And while the likes of Lieutenant Chapman may still sneer at the P.I., Rockford continues to merit the respect of his friends and peers, to the point where some people (like Richie Brockelman and Freddie Beamer) even want to emulate him.

These two nuances add to the appeal of Jim Rockford. "You're always looking for ways in which you can enhance your characters, and the series," added Charles Floyd Johnson.

Noteworthy guest stars in *Rockford*'s fourth season include Larry Hagman, Anthony Zerbe, Dionne Warwick, James Whitmore Jr., Gerald McRaney, Carlene Watkins, Ed Nelson, Malachi Throne, Ed Lauter, Gary Crosby, Chuck McCann, Jason Evers, Valerie Curtin, Barbara Babcock, Edward Binns, Charles Aidman, Richard Sanders, Priscilla Barnes, Jerry Hardin, Larry Linville, Arlene Golonka, Rick Springfield, Stephen Elliott, John Fiedler, Howard Hesseman, Pernell Roberts, and Rita Moreno.

67. BEAMER'S LAST CASE

Production Number: 47509

Original Airdate: September 16, 1977

Teleplay by: *Stephen J. Cannell*
Story by: *Booker Bradshaw and Calvin Kelly*
Produced and Directed by: *Stephen J. Cannell*

Guest Cast: James Whitmore Jr. (Freddie Beamer), Jack Kelly (Ralph Steel), Bibi Besch (Monica Steel), Robert Loggia (Manny Arturez), Cal Bellini (Pedro E. Ramirez), Howard George (Phil "Golf Bag" Moreno), Phil Hoover (Dallas Walker), John Davey (Delivery Man), Paula Victor (Receptionist), Arthur Eisner (Floyd Arturo), Raymond O'Keefe (Tony), Carlene Watkins (Girl on Bus)

Jimmy, this is Angel. Listen, I got this new pad, right over by the Hollywood Freeway, and some friends are coming. Can I borrow your record player?

Synopsis. *Rockford returns from an aborted fishing vacation in the Carribean to find that someone has wrecked his car, disturbed his home, used his credit card to purchase several expensive detection devices, and even impersonated him. The culprit: Freddie Beamer, a mechanic at Tony's Body Shop, but a private detective wannabe. Rockford not only has to clean up the mess Freddie made of his own life, he also has to save Beamer's neck after discovering that Beamer stumbled onto a taxicab company owner's plot to sabotage his own business.*

In this episode, writer/director Stephen J. Cannell borrows a concept from the classic *Maverick* episode "The Saga of Waco Williams" by pairing Rockford with a character with a penchant for landing in the middle of situations that Rockford would normally avoid. For example, when the rambunctious Beamer tries to take on the tempestuous Ralph Steel (*Maverick* star Jack Kelly), Rockford acts quickly to break up the fight.

```
Beamer:       I had the situation totally under control.
              I don't know what you pulled that guy off
              me for! I could've handled the guy.

Rockford:     Freddie, let me tell you something. A guy
                like that can go get a gun and shoot you,
                me, or both of us!

Beamer:       Well, sometimes a private detective's gotta
                take risks!

Rockford:     Well, not me! I make a habit of avoiding
                risks—that's why I've still got a full
                set of teeth.
```

When Beamer insists that he's "not the kind of guy you blow away with a threat," Rockford simply replies, "Well, I am."

Cannell would return to "Waco Williams" in the fifth season and carry it one step further by updating the entire episode (in the form of "White on White and Nearly Perfect").

Rockford Felines. Rockford "sort of" has a cat—Valentino, a stray who wanders in and out of the homes of the trailer park.

68. TROUBLE IN CHAPTER 17

Production Number: 47508

Original Airdate: September 23, 1977

Written by: *Juanita Bartlett*
Directed by: *William Wiard*

Guest Cast: Claudette Nevins (Ann Louise Clement), Ed Nelson (Edgar R. "Bud" Clement), Arthur Roberts (Jack Avery), Donna Bacalla (Jan Avery), Tasha Martell (Marty Bach), Al Checco (Sam), Michael Laurence

(Second Reporter), Bob Novarro (Third Reporter), Toni Berrell (Woman), Candace Howerton (Gloria), Mario Machado (First Reporter), Scott Ellsworth (Zinberg), Michael M. Steele (Lyle Van Houghton), Molly Dodd (Daisy)

[NOTE: The caller is calling from a pet center. You can hear dogs barking in the background.]

Jim, this is Donna. Boy, we've really been swamped today — No, sit! — We should be closing in about — Sit! — I'll meet you at — oh, get down!

Synopsis. *Author Ann Louise Clement, whose bestseller Forever Feminine advocates that "total happiness" for women lies in traditional feminine values, hires Rockford to investigate a series of threats that she believes have been carried out by militant women's liberation groups who resent the widespread acceptance of her book. Rockford soon realizes that he's been sucked into a publicity campaign (Ann Louise and her agent Marty Bach staged the "attacks" in order to generate publicity for the book); he also suspects the author of using him to help her win back her husband Bud, who has been fooling around with his secretary Jan Avery. But the matter turns into a real-life murder mystery when Marty is shot to death in Ann Louise's study.*

The Ann Louise Clement character was based on Marabel Morgan, a Miami housewife and author who attracted a tremendous amount of attention in the mid-1970s by exhorting women to behave in a manner that was decidedly against the feminist movement. Morgan's two books (*Total Woman* and *Total Joy*) suggested that housewives could only find happiness through total submission to their husbands; among other things, she thought women should try to "put sizzle back into their marriages" by wearing erotic costumes when they welcomed their husbands home from work. (Although Morgan herself thought that "a frilly new nightie and heels will probably do the trick," some readers followed her recommendations to the extreme — one woman greeted her husband wearing nothing but Saran Wrap and red ribbon.) Although both books were bestsellers, Morgan was soundly panned by critics who found her methods demeaning to women, because they ultimately suggested that happiness for women could only be found through deception and manipulation. Others found Morgan's ideology naïve and ridiculous on its face.

Juanita Bartlett chose to address the issue constructively by patterning a character after Morgan and placing her in a situation with the always discriminating Rockford. "Rockford was, and is, a no BS guy," explained Bartlett. "So if you put him with someone who is all BS, you're going to have fun. Something will happen (they may connect, or they may clash) that will be interesting and fun to watch. So I wrote 'Trouble in Chapter 17,' because I knew that Rockford would find a character like Marabel Morgan absolutely repulsive — he'd hate everything she stood for, because it was so manipulative. There's no honesty in that kind of a relationship. So, given that backdrop, that episode was particularly fun for me to write."

69. THE BATTLE OF CANOGA PARK

Production Number: 47505

Original Airdate: September 30, 1977

Written by: *Juanita Bartlett*
Directed by: *Ivan Dixon*

Guest Cast: Nora Marlowe (Viola Wenke), Adrienne Marden (Lee Ronstadt), John Dennis Johnston (Hank Schlaeger), Elliott Street (Leonard Wenke), Ted Gehring (Walter Chalco), John Perak (Pete Semple), Brion James (Clamshell), Charles Hallahan (Brian), James Parkes (Records Clerk), Art Koustik (Second Officer), Bruce Tuthill (Bomb Squad Officer)

It's Betty from up the street. I'm phoning all the neighbors because Spotty is loose. If you see him, call me. Oh, don't wear Musk cologne — leopards have a thing about that ...

Synopsis. *Jim's gun is stolen and used to murder Robert Reidy, a gas station owner and a member of a local paramilitary group. Without an alibi, nor any explanation for what happened to his gun, Rockford becomes the primary suspect in the killing. Although he and Reidy served in the same Korean War outfit, Jim never knew the man, and knows of nothing else that could link him to the murder victim. In fact, there is no link — the gun was stolen by Hank Schlaeger, another member of the paramilitary group, who had no idea that the weapon belonged to Rockford. When Lee Ronstadt, the group's leader, discovers Schlaeger's mistake, she orders the P.I. killed before he uncovers the connection between Reidy and the organization's radical activities.*

According to this episode, Rockford belonged to the 5th Regimental Combat Team, 24th Division of the U.S. Army — the same unit to which James Garner was assigned during the Korean War.

70. SECOND CHANCE

Production Number: 47503

Original Airdate: October 14, 1977

Written by: *Gordon Dawson*
Directed by: *Reza S. Badiyi*

Guest Cast: Isaac Hayes (Gandolf Fitch), Dionne Warwick (Theda Best), Malachi Throne (Shapiro), Tony Burton (Joe Moran), Sean Garrison (Lanark), Frank Christi (Brill), Richard Seff (Arnold Rose), Vivi Janiss (Pawn Shop Proprietor), Milton Oberman (Farnum), Janet Day (Secretary), Rudy Diaz (Raoul), Michael Jay London (Grizelli)

This is Globe Publications. Our records show you did not return your free volume of "The Encyclopedia of Weather," so we'll be sending you the remaining 29 volumes. You'll be billed accordingly.

Synopsis. *Gandolf Fitch now works as a bouncer at a dive in San Pedro — and he's in love with Theda Best, a onetime singer in Las Vegas who's now on the verge of getting another recording contract. Gandy and Theda's happiness is threatened when she is kidnapped by her ex-husband (and former singing partner) Joe Moran, who was convicted of murder five years earlier. Moran, who also was once involved in a counterfeit poker chip operation, received his parole through "Second Chance," a rehabilitation program that serves as a front for one of its sponsors, a shady industrialist named Shapiro, who arranges for the release of convicts so that he can use them to carry out his criminal operation. Shapiro has Moran kidnap Theda because she knows the whereabouts of the stereo system where Moran has hidden the counterfeiting equipment. Gandy and Rockford try to rescue Theda.*

Rockford wants to back out of the case once he and Gandy locate where Shapiro has hidden Theda — he's perfectly willing to let the police handle the matter from there. But Gandy begs Rockford to see it through to the end, and even offers Rockford 25% of the percentage he stands to make from Theda's contract with Pacific Records. Although Jim still wants out ("It's too dangerous"), he changes his mind once Gandy addresses him by his real name ("I really need your help, Rockford"). This is the only time in the series that Gandy calls Rockford by his given name.

Rockford Facts. "Second Chance" features Grammy Award-winning vocalist Dionne Warwick in a rare acting appearance. Warwick's hit singles include "Walk on By," "I'll Say a Little Prayer," "Do You Know the Way to San Jose?," "I'll Never Love This Way Again," and "That's What Friends are For."

71. THE DOG AND PONY SHOW

Production Number: 47502

Original Airdate: October 21, 1977

Written by: *David Chase*
Directed by: *Reza S. Badiyi*

Guest Cast: Joanne Nail (Mary Jo Flynn), Ed Lauter (Joseph Bloomberg), Walter Brooke (NIA Agent Simonds), George Loros (Tommy Lorentz), Michael Bell (NIA Agent Krasny), Gary Crosby (Beau), Al Ruscio (Vic Cassell), Howard Honig (Dr. Alan J. Adler), Bill Quinn (Judge Raymond Ordonez), Robert Lussier (Leo), Louisa Moritz (Helen), Dan Barton (Hal), Ken Sidwell (Attendant), Harriet Matthey (Girl)

Jimmy — Lou. You owe me five bucks. Matarozo's average in the '68 Series was .310, not .315. Oh, and — uh, Fran and I are getting divorced.

Synopsis. *Rockford meets his latest client in a group therapy session after a judge convicts him of petty theft and sentences him to undergo psychiatric counseling. (It was all Angel's fault — he stole $200 worth of silverware, then tried to haul the stash away in Jim's car.) While she was recently institutionalized for paranoid schizophrenia, Mary Jo Flynn met another patient named Joseph Bloomberg, who claimed to be an intelligence agent victimized by the U.S. government. But "Joey B" is really a renowned mob informer who was committed by his own family in order to prevent rival crime factions from killing him. Rockford must protect Mary Jo from Bloomberg's family, who perceive her as a threat because she could leak Joey's location.*

The premise of this episode is that Rockford is hired by a paranoid schizophrenic woman who believes someone is trying to kill her. Ironically, the woman turns out to be the sanest person Rockford meets over the course of the story. Rockford soon finds that both the NIA agents and the mobsters (particularly, the hit man Tommy Lorentz) all display more signs of paranoid schizophrenia than his client does.

72. REQUIEM FOR A FUNNY BOX

Production Number: 47511

Original Airdate: November 4, 1977

Teleplay by: *James S. Crocker*
Story by: *Burt Prelutsky*
Directed by: *William Wiard*

Guest Cast: Chuck McCann (Kenny Bell), Robert Quarry (Lee Russo), Jason Evers (Paul Sylvan), Judian Rousseau (Maxine), Meredith McRae (Lori Thompson), Gilbert Green (August Sylvan), Thomas A. Geas (Waiter), Del Hinkley (Poco), Hank Stohl (Officer), Joel Lawrence (Newscaster)

Mr. Rockford? Sue Ellen. Our class is having that great scavenger hunt I told you about — if you're wondering what happened to your trailer door, it's gonna win me first prize!

Synopsis. *Moments before comedian Lee Russo is about to deliver a brand new monologue on national television, his former partner Kenny Bell scoops him by performing the routine first (and taking all the credit). Kenny placed a bugging device in Lee's home in order steal material for his own "funny box" (a catalog of jokes and funny material). But Kenny also stumbled onto a well-kept secret — Lee is a homosexual who has been involved with his personal manager Paul Sylvan, whose father is a major crime lord. Later, Kenny's funny box in stolen in exchange for $10,000. Kenny suspects that Russo and Sylvan were behind the theft, so he hires Rockford to make the drop. After discovering Russo dead at the place of exchange, Jim finds himself arrested on suspicion of murder. Rockford explains that he was hired to retrieve Kenny's funny box, but when the police question Kenny, the comedian denies the entire story.*

At the beginning of the episode, Rocky is extremely excited to be part of the audience at a live television show. In real life, Noah Beery Jr. was quite at home in front of a camera. He came from a family of actors; in fact, many of his early roles were in action serials that were filmed at Universal Studios, where *The Rockford Files* was produced. Beery once said, "I feel as though I'd been born [at Universal]."

73. QUICKIE NIRVANA

Production Number: 47513

Original Airdate: November 11, 1977

Written by: *David Chase*
Directed by: *Meta Rosenberg*

Guest Cast: Valerie Curtin (Sky Aquarian), Kenneth Gilman (Alan Bayliss), Quinn Redecker (Gordon Borchers), Dick Anthony Williams (Maceo Prentiss), Larry Cook (Dijon), Patricia Pearce (Girl at Ashram), Carl Crudup (Eddie McBrare), Elta Lake (Ann), Aesop Aquarian (Cook), Michael Grandcolas (Panhandler), Dan Magiera (Conga Drummer)

Hey, I saw your ad in the classified — three African goats for sale. I keep calling. All I get is a machine. Is that a typo in the paper, or what?

Synopsis. *Rockford becomes embroiled in the perils and anxieties of Sky Aquarian (a.k.a. Jane Patton, a 40-year-old waif on a perpetual search for personal fulfillment). Sky's failure to deliver an envelope for her boss, attorney Alan Bayliss, may prove fatal. The envelope contained $30,000 in hush money intended for a witness who can link Bayliss' client, recording star Maceo Prentiss, to the murder of musician Joe Vivyan. Rockford returns the envelope to Bayliss — without realizing that someone had stolen the money. When he learns that Sky had told her "consciousness guru" Gordon Borchers about the $30,000, Jim suspects that Borchers took the money and ran. Meanwhile, an impulsive Maceo decides that, without the money, his only option is killing the witness — as well as Rockford and Sky.*

Part of the fun of "Quickie Nirvana" lies in watching Rockford's (and James Garner's) reactions whenever Sky begins to speak in tongues (i.e., sing the praises of whatever new age ideology she's into). "I'm not into structured living or accumulated things," she tells Rockford. "I'm into my consciousness." "Consciousness!?" retorts Rockford. "You're practically unconscious 24 hours a day."

Rockford Facts. Becker's police handle is "1Y9."

James Garner and Tom Selleck at a private eye awards banquet.

74. IRVING THE EXPLAINER

Production Number: 47507

Original Airdate: November 18, 1977

Written by: *David Chase*
Directed by: *James Coburn*

Guest Cast: Barbara Babcock (Katarina Korper), Paul Stewart (Buddy Richards), Maurice Marsac (Chief Inspector Jeneau), Irene Tsu (Daphne Ishawahara), Robert Etienne (Inspector Mage), Peter Von Zernick (Ruprecht), Byron Morrow (Irving), Lester Fletcher (Gertler), Brooke Palance (Gilda), Alex Rodin (Willie Schindler), Shep Sanders (Desk Clerk)

So you put your machine on at night, huh? Just because I call you at 3:00 a.m.? You know how bad my insomnia is! Thanks a lot, Jim.

Synopsis. *A woman who is apparently writing a biography of controversial film director Alvah Korper hires Rockford to help her research the book. Rockford doesn't realize that his client is really Korper's daughter Katarina, who hopes that the private investigator will lead her to a priceless painting by 17th-century artist Antoine Watteau that Alvah Korper allegedly purchased and hid during the 1940s. Rockford soon finds himself thrust into a convoluted mess involving French police officers and German spies (both of whom also want to find the painting) and the long unsolved murder of Korper's wife, which may hold the key to the entire puzzle.*

I rving the Explainer" was directed by James Coburn, who co-starred with James Garner in *The Great Escape*, *The Americanization of Emily*, and the motion picture version of *Maverick*. The episode also features future *Hill Street Blues* star Barbara Babcock.

75. THE MAYOR'S COMMITTEE FROM DEER LICK FALLS

Production Number: 47506

Original Airdate: November 25, 1977

Written by: *William R. Stratton*
Directed by: *Ivan Dixon*

Guest Cast: Edward Binns (Everett Benson), Richard O'Brien (Art Kelso), Charles Aidman (Noah Deitweiler), Priscilla Barnes (Lauren Ingeborg), Jerry Hardin (Knute Jacobs), Clark Howat (Mr. Rankin), Richard Sanders (Samuel Rooney), Fritzi Burr (Miss Hornick), Ian Sander (Christian), David Rupprecht (David)

Jim, this is Manny down at Ralph's Bar. Some guy named Angel Martin just ran up a 50-buck bar tab, then he wants to charge it to you. You gonna pay it?

Synopsis. *Four eccentric businessmen from Michigan hire Rockford to help them purchase a used fire engine on behalf of their town's mayor. Rockford soon discovers his clients have a much more horrifying proposal in mind: they offer him $20,000 to arrange for the murder of actress Lauren Ingeborg (the niece of one of the men), who has threatened to report them to the Michigan IRS after she uncovered their scheme to pocket over $750,000 in falsified tax deductions. The businessmen retaliate viciously after Rockford reports them to the police — they not only deny the charges, but arrange to have Rockford's P.I. license suspended. In order to clear himself, Rockford must find Lauren and get her in touch with the local IRS before the mayor's committee has her killed.*

76. HOTEL OF FEAR

Production Number: 47514

Original Airdate: December 2, 1977

Written by: *Juanita Bartlett*
Directed by: *Russ Mayberry*

Guest Cast: Gerald McRaney (D.A. John Pleasance), Frank DiKova (Nova), Vincent Baggetta (Murray Riddle), Madison Arnold (Del Kane), Eugene I. Peterson (Louie Gaedel), Barry Atwater (Roach), Barbra Rae (Teddy), Fred Carney (Howe), Stephen Coit (Thompson Welles), James Whitworth (Krauss), Rene Djon (Waiter), Peter Forster (Judge Bertram Hovis), Sal Acquisto (Bailiff)

Hey, am I too late for those African goats? Haven't got the whole $300 in cash, but, like, I got a lot of homemade cheese. Maybe we can work something out ...

Synopsis. *Del Kane, a syndicate hit man from New Jersey, was hired to a kill a bookie named Gaedel, but the contract was cancelled at the last minute. However, Kane, a decidedly loose cannon, decided he had to kill someone in order to save face, so he shot a prostitute named Muriel Nafac. Angel witnessed the murder, and later agrees to testify against Kane at a preliminary hearing (in exchange for nonstop police protection). But after the D.A. fails to present a prima facie case against Kane, the killer is set free — and sets after Angel.*

According to this episode, Angel's address is 21150 Sierra Bonita, Apartment 202, in Los Angeles. Also according to this episode, fear makes Angel hungry, which explains why he's constantly eating in this story.

77. FORCED RETIREMENT

Production Number: 47512

Original Airdate: December 9, 1977

Written by: *William R. Stratton*
Directed by: *Alexander Singer*

Guest Cast: Larry Hagman (Richard Lessing), Margaret Impert (Susan Kenniston), Denny Miller (Chris Jenks), Ron Masak (Virgil Cheski), William Joyce (Harcourt), Conrad Bachmann (Rundstedt), Derek Murcott (Maitre' D), John Davey (Sergeant Jacobson), Doug Hale (Restaurant Manager), Bill Hart (Benish)

Hi, there. If you're interested in selling your product via computerized telephone sales, stay on the line, and one of our representatives will speak with you.

Synopsis. *Beth asks Jim to investigate the Minerva project, a highly speculative offshore drilling venture whose investors include Beth's boss. Beth's concerns stem from her relationship with the project's engineer (longtime college rival Susan Kenniston), but they intensify considerably, first after her apartment is broken into, then after an attempt is made on her life. Meanwhile, Rockford becomes curious after discovering that Richard Lessing, the primary investor, has a shaky credit history — and a string of businesses that all folded after the CEO died under accidental circumstances. After Chris Jenks, the president of Minerva, dies in a plane crash, Jim deduces that Lessing manufactured the accident in order to collect the insurance money. When Rockford learns that Lessing also took out a life insurance policy on Susan, he tries to prevent another fatal accident from happening.*

Forced Retirement" marks the first appearance of Jimmy Joe Meeker, the Oklahoma oilman who's "smoother than oil on a blister." Rockford adopts this alter-ego on several occasions over the course of the remainder of the series. In many ways, "Jimmy Joe" resembles the Maverick character — not only does Rockford as Meeker dress in Western duds and wear a ten-gallon pushed back (very much like the way in which Maverick wore his hat), he also speaks in folksy aphorisms, such as "When you're looking at a man right in the eye, it's hard to get your hand in his wallet."

As a running gag in this episode, Richard Lessing (Larry Hagman, in one of his many post-*I Dream of Jeannie*/pre-*Dallas* roles) derisively refers to Rockford/Meeker as "Joe Jimmy." Rockford, in turn, counters by sardonically addressing Lessing as "Dick."

Rockford Facts. In this episode, Beth decides to quit her job at Harcourt & Lowe and begin her own law practice. Because she can't raid the client list at her old law firm, Beth is concerned whether she can develop enough of a client base to survive as a sole practitioner. "Well, you've always got me as a client," reminds Jim. "Thanks, Jim," replies Beth, "but I mean paying clients."

78. THE QUEEN OF PERU

Production Number: 47519

Original Airdate: December 16, 1977

Written by: *David Chase*
Directed by: *Meta Rosenberg*

Guest Cast: George Wyner (Stephen Kalifer), Ken Swofford (Karl Wronko), Christopher Cary (Ginger Townsend), Joe E. Tata (Mike Trevino), Luke Andreas (Lou Trevino), Hunter Von Leer (Skip), Jennifer Markes (Shareen Wronko), Michael Morgan (Sean Wronko), Susan Davis (Dot Wronko), Paul Cavonia (Donnie B. Waugh), Tara Buckman (Girl)

Jim, it's Grace at the bank. I checked your Christmas Club Account. You don't have $500. You have $50. Sorry — computer foulup.

Synopsis. *An insurance company hires Rockford to assist in the recovery of a stolen diamond worth over $1 million. Rockford and insurance agent Stephen Kalifer deliver the ransom money to Donnie Waugh and Mike Trevino (two of the thieves), but learn that Waugh hid the diamond inside the ashes of Rockford's barbecue grill. Jim returns home, only there's no grill — it was inadvertently stolen by the Wronkos, a family from Indiana who had spent the night on the beach near his trailer. When Waugh clubs Kalifer and runs off with the money, Rockford must recover both the diamond and the ransom. Complicating the matter: Ginger Townsend, the mastermind of the theft, who wants the diamond back (he was doublecrossed by Waugh and Trevino); and the Wronkos themselves, who kept the grill, but lost the diamond (without realizing it) after they emptied the ashes at a roadside dumping grounds.*

Christopher Cary, who later appeared in "The Hawaiian Headache" (also featuring Ken Swofford), previously co-starred with James Garner in *Marlowe* (1969). Also featured in this episode: George Wyner, who co-starred with Garner in the *Man of the People* series.

79. A DEADLY MAZE

Production Number: 47521

Original Airdate: December 23, 1977

Written by: *Juanita Bartlett*
Directed by: *William Wiard*

Guest Cast: Larry Linville (Dr. Eric Von Albach), Corinne Michaels (Tracy Marquette), J. Pat O'Malley (Billy Baines), Lance LeGault (Phil D'Agosto), Johnny Seven (George), Cliff Carnell (Max Savatgy), Jack Collins (Victor Kreski), John McKinney (Nick Commandini), Ken Anderson (Tom Posner), Gail Landry (Student Receptionist)

Hey, Jimmy, I tried to catch you before you left. Hey, buddy, I was wrong—you know that rally in Mexico? That was yesterday.

Synopsis. *Facing a serious cash flow stoppage, Rockford agrees to find a man's missing wife — a case he'd decline under normal circumstances. Rockford doesn't realize that his client, Eric Von Albach, is a behavioral scientist who is using him as a guinea pig in a government-funded study to determine how monetary reinforcement influences certain people's ability to complete their work under stress. The "missing wife" case was part of the charade Von Albach concocted in order to measure Rockford's reactions. The experiment hits a snag, however, when the woman Von Albach hired to play his wife is later found murdered.*

Larry Linville was an inspired choice to play the cold, calculating, eccentric and ever scientific Professor Von Albach. At the time of this episode, Linville had just completed his five-year stint as Major Frank Burns on *M*A*S*H*.

80. THE ATTRACTIVE NUISANCE

Production Number: 47520

Original Airdate: January 6, 1977

Written by: *Stephen J. Cannell*
Directed by: *Dana Elcar*

Guest Cast: Victor Jory (Eddie LaSalle), Ken Lynch (Vince Whitehead), Dick Balduzzi (Don Silver), Hunter Von Leer (Skip Speece), Rudy Bond (Bennie), John Morgan Evans (Vinnie), Jess Nadelman (Bruce Weinstock), Jeanne Fitzsimmons (Joy Silver), Joey Tornatore (Sid), Paul Sorenson (Inspector Claybourn), Jerome Guardino (Hank), Joseph Della Sorte (Dave Young), Will Gill Jr. (FBI Agent), Anne Gee Byrd (Woman on the Beach), Richard Doyle (Paramedic)

Jimmy Scott? This is Aunt Bea from Tulsa. Cousin Randy just gradu-ated high school and wants to be a movie producer. Now, you live out in Hollywood — you just do something!

Synopsis. *Rocky opens a truckstop diner with a man named Vince Whitehead. Neither Jim nor Rocky realize that Whitehead, a onetime major mob figure, is using the garage located behind the restaurant to market stolen auto parts. Jim soon discovers that he and Rocky have been under the surveillance of Eddie LaSalle, a retired FBI agent who has long been obsessed with apprehending Whitehead — the man who murdered his partner over 40 years ago. Meanwhile, Rockford finds himself sued by a man whom LaSalle hired to bug his home (the man fell off the roof of Jim's trailer after planting an electronic bugging device).*

According to this episode, Rockford's middle name is Scott, which means that the character's full name (James Scott Rockford) is similar to the given name of his alter ego (James Scott Bumgarner).

81. THE GANG AT DON'S DRIVE-IN

Production Number: 47516

Original Airdate: January 13, 1978

Written by: *James S. Crocker*
Directed by: *Harry Falk*

Guest Cast: Anthony Zerbe (Jackson Skowron), Arlene Golonka (Jeanne Rosenthal), Lawrence Casey (Bob Atcheson), Mills Watson (Stan Collier), Dick Bakalyn (Porter), Elaine Princi (JoAnn), Connie Sawyer (Mrs. For-nechefski), Jordan Rhodes (Dr. Kozoll), Paul Pepper (Don Brakeman Jr.), Al Rossi (Fred Stassi), Fredd Wayne (Curtis Meyer), Chuck Hicks (Walton Hettie), Lynn Hurst (Reporter)

Jim, I have finally finished 12 long years of psychotherapy and I am now able to tell you just what I think of you — would you please call me?

Synopsis. *Author Jackson Skowron, whose career has run aground in the 20 years since his only success (the bestselling novel Free Fall to Ecstasy), hires his old friend Rockford to help him research his new book on the John C. Fremont High School graduating class of 1962. Rockford doesn't realize that Jack has discovered that onetime classmate Bob Atcheson — whose powerful family owns the Los Angeles Tribune newspaper — accidentally killed young Nancy Fornechefski, then covered up the homicide with the help of two other classmates. If Jack can prove that Fornechefski was murdered, he'll have the makings of a guaranteed best seller. But Jack may never live to write that book, because Atcheson will resort to anything, including murder, to protect his secret.*

The running gag of this episode: while everyone has heard of *Free Fall to Ecstacy* — a 1,040-page stream-of-consciousness narrative whose protagonist jumps off a roof in the first chapter (while the rest of the novel depicts the character's random thoughts as he continues his descent) — nobody's ever managed to finish it. Although many readers apparently gave up after approximately four chapters, Rockford himself only finished 15 pages (he tells Jack that someone stole his copy). Jack Skowron is played by Emmy winner Anthony Zerbe (*Harry O*, *The Young Riders*), who had played the man who killed James Garner's character in the final episode of *Nichols*.

Rockford Facts. According to this episode, Skowron and Rockford once worked together as carpet layers for two years. In real life, James Garner had once worked with his father (a carpet layer) prior to becoming an actor.

82. THE PAPER PALACE

Production Number: 47522

Original Airdate: January 20, 1978

Written by: *Juanita Bartlett*
Directed by: *Richard Crenna*

Guest Cast: Rita Moreno (Rita Capkovic), Bruce Kirby (Sid Loft), Pat Finley (Peggy Becker), David Lewis (Burton Woodrup), Trish Donahue (Eleanor Loft), Rena Assa (Jeannot Turner), Shirley O'Hara (Maggie Gilson), James Jeter (Officer McRainey), Norwood Smith (Henry Helpern), Gene Scherer (Rudy Ganse)

This is Mrs. Owens with the Association for a Better Malibu. Thanks for your contributions. We've made great strides, but it would help, dear, if you could move your trailer!

Synopsis. *Rita Capkovic is a career prostitute who aches for genuine friendship—she's so lonely that she often wheels an empty cart around a supermarket just to socialize with other people. After meeting Rockford at a disastrous dinner party with Dennis and Peggy Becker, Rita finds herself needing his help after two French-speaking men nearly kill her inside her own apartment. Rita then stays at the home of her friend Maggie Gilson—who is murdered the following night by the same two men. Rita assists Rockford as he tries to find a connection between the two attacks.*

There's a built-in advantage in writing for a television series, regardless of whether the writer is a freelancer or a member of the show's staff: you know who the regular characters are and the actors who play them, and that often proves helpful in writing the story. However, the freelancer and the staff writer both face the same obstacle when it comes to writing "guest" characters. "You usually don't know who your guest stars are going to be when you're writing your story—those decisions aren't made until long after the script is finished," said Juanita Bartlett. "You have to write the character that you feel is correct for the story, and then you cast it. That's the way you always do it."

Sometimes, though, it's helpful to have a particular actor in mind as you create a character. "When I wrote the Rita Capkovic character, I did have Rita Moreno in mind—but that didn't mean we were going to get Rita Moreno," said Bartlett. "In that case, as it turned out, we did. But for the most part, you write the character, and then after that character is fully realized, you start saying, 'Who could play this? Well, so-and-so would be excellent, or do you think we could get this person, or that person?' So, usually, it's a matter of writing the character out of your head, and casting it."

Rita Moreno won an Emmy for her performance in this episode.

83. DWARF IN A HELIUM HAT

Production Number: 47524

Original Airdate: January 27, 1978

Written by: *Stephen J. Cannell and David Chase*
Directed by: *Reza S. Badiyi*

Guest Cast: John Pleshette (Jay Rockfelt), Rebecca Balding (Carol Lansing), Gianni Russo (Gianni Tedesco), Milton Selzer (Irving Rockfelt), Rick Springfield (Keith Stuart), Ted Markland (Mel), Scott Ellsworth

(Norman Appet), Robina Suwol (Amy Rockfelt), Bea Silvern (Edith Rockfelt), Mary Nancy Burnett (Susan), Marie Reynolds (Janaique), Robert Mayo (Santo)

Here's the tally, Jimbo. You had Atlanta on even money —tough break— and you got bombed on the new Wake Forest fiasco, and you split the Cornell at Hollypark, so you're in the book $4.50. Any time before Friday, huh, buddy?

Synopsis. *After receiving a strange phone call from a man who tells him "your dog is dead" and that "you and that Lansing girl are next," Rockford determines that the message was meant for Jay Rockfelt, whose name appears directly above Jim's in the phone book. After rescuing Rockfelt's dog (Romanoff) and girlfriend (Carol Lansing), Jim learns that the problem stems from a lavish birthday bash Rockfelt threw for Gianni Tedesco, an aspiring actor who also has connections with the mob. Gianni suffered the embarrassment of having to pay the $30,000 tab for his own party — an incident which has made him a laughingstock in Hollywood. Gianni blames Rockfelt, who left the party early to fly to Puerta Vallarta; the irresponsible Jay, however, blames his parents, who have refused him to loan him any money after cutting off his inheritance. Although Rockford doesn't like Jay, he feels compelled to help him after learning that Gianni has kidnapped Rockfelt's sister.*

"Rockford's attitudes toward the police, the FBI, the CIA, the Mafia, or any other American authority figures present a consistently anti-authoritarian viewpoint," observed Tom Stempel in *Storytellers to the Nation* (Continuum, 1992). "This was usually present in traditional private eye shows, but *Rockford* takes it a step further. It also goes further than Roy Huggins did in *Maverick*. In the Western, the authority figures were those of the past, while on *Rockford* they are contemporary. In other series, representatives of the Federal Government and the Mafia are both treated seriously. In *Rockford*, they are not."

Rockford certainly knows his way around the legal system, so he doesn't easily succumb to whatever pressure tactics that some police officers or FBI agents may try to exert. In one particular instance ("The Girl in the Bay City Boys Club") when a cocky deputy district attorney who had hired him threatens to have his P.I. license suspended, Rockford not only didn't flinch, but dared the D.A. to make the call: "Go ahead and do it — I'll appeal, of course, and there'll be a hearing, and our relationship will have to come out in the open. Unless you're completely clean, everything you've got at stake will have to come out, too."

Rockford's writers may have thumbed their noses at the system from time to time, but they never completely ridiculed it. "We always tried to give Rockford worthy opponents, because his triumph wouldn't mean much if it wasn't against a formidable foe," said Juanita Bartlett. "There's no triumph in outwitting a stupid person."

The one exception would appear to be Lieutenant Chapman (James Luisi), who was much more thickheaded than Rockford's previous police foil, Lieutenant Diel (Tom Atkins). Chapman has a penchant for either sticking his foot in his mouth, or simply setting himself up for some of Rockford's ridicule, as is the case in this episode ("Come on, Chapman, does this keep coming, or are you really just a giant bag of gas in a three-piece suit?").

But Bartlett says that's not the case. "Chapman isn't a stupid character," she explained. "He didn't like Rockford, but a lot of police don't particularly like private investigators.

Chapman wanted to run things his own way, because he was on his own turf. He also knows that whenever Rockford's on a case, he's making one hell of a lot more money than he is, and he's putting in less hours, and he can quit whenever he wants to, and he doesn't have any of the restrictions that a cop has. Rockford doesn't have to go by the book — he just has to stay out of trouble. But Chapman wasn't stupid, by any means. Of course, he could be impossible to deal with...."

84. SOUTH BY SOUTHEAST

Production Number: 47523

Original Airdate: February 3, 1978

Written by: *Juanita Bartlett*
Directed by: *William Wiard*

Guest Cast: Dorrie Kavanaugh (Christine Van Deerlin), Don Chastain (John Van Deerlin), Carlos Romero (Agent Sam Goroll), Don Diamond (Coelho), Jim B. Smith (Agent Whitaker), Isaac Ruiz Jr. (Jorge), Bert Rosario (Second), Mark Roberts (Agent Kleinhoff), George Clifton (Agent Mallardi), Jim Scott (Agent Ben Bast), Eric Mason (Emilio Rivera), Don Dubbins (Agent Frazee), David Panceri (Bodyguard), Robert Clockworthy (Tommy), Yolanda Marquez (Hotel Operator), Gloria Dixon (Party Guest)

Bill Skelly with ICO. I'd like to interest you in some new private detection, including the 440A Telephonic Bug. We'll demonstrate it in a friend's home for one full week, at no charge.

Synopsis. *Government agents who have mistaken Rockford for an operative named Terence Halsey fly the P.I. to Mexico to prevent heiress Christine Van Deerlin from selling 50,000 shares of her father's aircraft company to Arab countries—a move which could adversely impact both the economic structure and strategic defense of the United States. Without any choice, Rockford meets Christine and discovers that she's being blackmailed by her fortune-hunting husband John, who threatens to expose the unsavory truth behind her father's "legend" unless she carries out the sale. Although Rockford has a chance to walk away once the matter of his identity is straightened out, he decides to stay—even at the risk of his own life—when he learns that Christine's safety is endangered.*

South by Southeast" is ostensibly an espionage story, but it's also a very poignant love story that brings out the rarely-seen tender side of Rockford. Although Rockford has shown that he's capable of falling in love without losing sight of how to make a profit, in this episode, he is willing to risk his life for someone he cares about—without any consideration of his own personal gain.

85. THE COMPETITIVE EDGE

Production Number: 47504

Original Airdate: February 10, 1978

Written by: *Gordon Dawson*
Directed by: *Harry Falk*

Guest Cast: Stephen Elliott (Dr. Herb Brinkman), Jim McMullan (Perry Brauder), Robert Hogan (Lester Shaw), John Fiedler (James Bond), Neile McQueen (Joyce Brauder), George Murdock (Doc Holliday), Pepper Martin (Gustav), Logan Ramsey (Dr. Carl Brinkman), John Lupton (Marty Sloan), Harold Sakata (John Doe), Anthony Charnota (Robert W. Zachary), Dennis Fimple (Phino), William Boyett (Morris), Charles Howerton (Councilman Moore), Dick Gjonola (Security Guard), Barbara Leigh (Sylvia), Sandie Newton (Gail)

Okay, Jimbo — Dennis. I know you're in there. And I know you know it's ticket season again — Policeman's Ball, and all that. So come to the door when I knock this time — I know you're in there!

Synopsis. *Joyce Brauder hires Jim to find her husband Perry, an accused embezzler who has jumped bail. After infiltrating an affluent men's health club directed by Dr. Herb Brinkman, Rockford discovers that Brinkman has been running a drug-and-extortion racket — he laces his clients' "vitamin treatments" with amphetamines financed by exorbitant monthly membership fees. When Rockford suspects that Perry's disappearance may be linked to his membership in the health club, Brinkman intervenes by drugging the P.I. and imprisoning him in a mental institution run by Brinkman's equally heinous brother.*

While he is incarcerated in the insane asylum, Rockford encounters a Stetson-wearing inmate who thinks he's Doc Holliday (and that Rockford is Wyatt Earp). James Garner actually played Wyatt Earp in two films — *Hour of the Gun* (1967) and *Sunset* (1988).

Rockford Familiar Faces. This episode features John Fiedler (Mr. Peterson on *The Bob Newhart Show*); and Neile McQueen, former wife of Steve McQueen (Garner's co-star in *The Great Escape*).

86. THE PRISONER OF ROSEMONT HALL

Production Number: 47510

Original Airdate: February 17, 1978

Teleplay by: *Stephen J. Cannell and David Chase*
Story by: *Chas. Floyd Johnson and MaryAnn Rea*
Directed by: *Ivan Dixon*

Guest Cast: Frances Lee McCain (Leslie Callahan), Kenneth Tobey (Max Kilmore), Joyce Easton (Valerie Douglas), Danny Ades (Machmoud), Maurice Sherbanee (Kadahfi), Barney McFadden (Bert Hannon), Bill Thornberry (Paul Lowe Douglas), Paul Coufos (Thomas Tate), Ric Carrott (Pledge Miller Claussen), Buck Young (Jake Sand), Michael Swan (Cal Morris), Kathy Richards (Judy), Julia Ann Benjamin (Melinda), Douglas Ryan (Herb)

That No. 4 you just picked up from Angelo's Pizza? Some scouring powder fell in there—don't eat it! Hey, I hope you try your phone machine before dinner ...

Synopsis. *Rockford's friend Paul Lowe Douglas, a promising journalism student at Rosemont University, is abducted outside of Jim's trailer by members of a popular college fraternity. With the help of Leslie Callahan (Paul's teacher—and lover), Rockford discovers that Paul had gathered evidence of a plot to kidnap student Mustahfa Ben Ali, the son of a prominent Arab ruler. Max Kilmore, the head of campus security, had hoped to exhort $2 million from the boy's father, but the plan backfired when Ali died of a heart attack. While the paranoid Kilmore tries to fend off the Arab agents who are investigating the matter, he also tries to eliminate Rockford and Leslie.*

In the "B" story of this episode, Rocky asks Jim to help him prepare his income taxes. Rockford, however, reminds his father that he'll only "help" him by allowing him to use his adding machine. Perhaps it wasn't a pleasant experience for Jim when he last helped his father with his taxes (in the episode "Claire").

Rockford Facts. MaryAnn Rea, who collaborated with series producer Charles Floyd Johnson to write the story on which this episode was based, has been James Garner's personal assistant for many years.

87. THE HOUSE ON WILLIS AVENUE
(Two-hour episode)

Production Numbers: 47597/47598

Original Airdate: February 24, 1978

Written by: *Stephen J. Cannell*
Directed by: *Hy Averback*

Guest Cast: Dennis Dugan (Richie Brockelman), Jackie Cooper (Garth McGregor), Simon Oakland (Vern St. Cloud), Howard Hesseman (Albert Steever), Philip Sterling (Supervisor Thomas Nardoni), Pernell Roberts (B.J. Anderson), Paul Fix (Joe Tooley), Irene Tedrow (Mrs. Tooley), Lou Krugman (Sam Detonis), Brett Hadley (Computer Operator), Vince Howard (Billy Mayhew), Vince Milana (Tim), Brian Culhane (Second Deputy), Jay Fenichel (Mourge Attendant), Nancy Conrad (Receptionist), John Van Dreelan (Hans Gunderson), Robert Hogan (Sergeant Ted Coopersmith), Russell Thorson (Arthur Kenner), Hank Brandt (Mr. Davis), Ben Wright (Derek Halsted), Tom Stovall (Baker), Larry McCormick (Newscaster)

Good morning. This is the telephone company. Due to repairs, we're giving you advance notice that your service will be cut off indefinitely at 10 o'clock — that's two minutes from now.

Sonny, this is Dad. Never mind giving that talk about your occupation to the Gray Power Club. Hap Dudley's son is a doctor, and everybody sort of—would rather hear from him. But, thanks ...

Synopsis. *Rockford and greenhorn investigator Richie Brockelman probe the suspicious circumstances surrounding the accidental death of their mentor, veteran P.I. Joe Tooley, who died in the middle of a case involving a series of properties housing an extensive computer system. After questioning Tooley's last client, political activist Albert Steever, Rockford and Richie determine that Tooley had run afoul of Garth McGregor, an electronics expert who plans to install a national computer network capable of providing access to personal information on over 250 million Americans—for his own means. Rockford and Richie try to pull the plug on McGregor's operation.*

Richie Brockelman is amazed to see how much information Rockford can elicit from people through sheer blarney. But Richie himself has a little bit of "Rockford" in him, insofar as he's capable of changing his opinion in a second if need be:

Richie: This guy actually lives in a trailer.

Rockford: What does that mean?

Richie: Oh, I don't know — it just seems to me like
               living in a trailer is kind of the bottom.

Rockford: I live in a trailer.

Richie: Well, no, not exactly the bottom—more
               like the middle, and, of course, depending
               on the trailer, it could be more like the
               upper middle.

Although Richie clearly looks up to Rockford, it's also apparent as the story unfolds that Jim respects Richie on his own terms. This is particularly important to Richie, who is extremely aware of the fact that, because of his age (he's 23) and his appearance (he looks like he belongs in high school), he isn't always taken seriously as a private eye. In fact, Richie is a little too sensitive about the impression people have of him—at one point, he jumps all over Rockford for saying "Good boy, Richie" (when Jim was actually *complimenting* him on a particularly brilliant piece of deductive reasoning). However, Richie also admits that he uses that perception as an advantage ("I count on people underestimating me," he tells Rockford).

This episode was the second pilot for the *Richie Brockelman, Private Eye* series, which ran in *Rockford*'s time period for five weeks during the Spring of 1978. (Stephen J. Cannell had first introduced Richie in the 1976 TV-movie *The Missing 24 Hours*, starring Dennis Dugan and Suzanne Pleshette.)

Rockford Facts. Rockford's trailer is 50 feet long, and can be transported by a rig. Richie drives a red Ford Mustang.

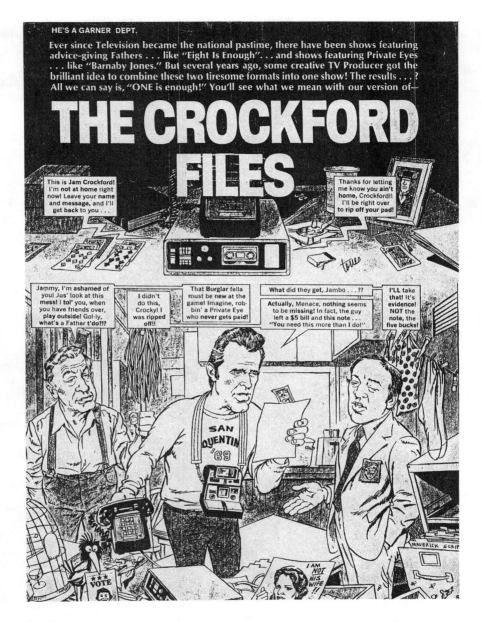

In 1979, *Mad Magazine* published "The Crockford Files," a parody of *The Rockford Files* written by Lou Silverstone and illustrated by Angelo Torres. Notice the photo of Bret Maverick on Rockford's desk top, and the open filing cabinet drawer filled with "*Maverick* scripts." (The parody also includes a panel in which Rockford is laid up in a hospital; among the items on his night stand is a Get Well Soon card signed "Brother Bart.") Also: the camera around Rockford's neck, as well as the caricature of Gretchen Corbett and its accompanying caption ("I am not his wife!"), allude to the enormously popular commercials for Polaroid cameras featuring James Garner and Mariette Hartley in the late 1970s. The lighthearted banter between the two actors in those TV spots was so believable, many viewers were convinced that Garner and Hartley were actually married — which prompted Hartley to print a special T-shirt with the disclaimer "I am *not* Mrs. James Garner." (A character resembling Hartley also appears in the parody.)

Fifth Season: 1978-1979

Beginning in September 1978, reruns of the first four seasons of *The Rockford Files* aired Monday nights as part of *The CBS Late Movie*. In addition to generating more revenue for the studio, the late night reruns broadened the demographics by introducing the Emmy Award-winning show to a new audience. Throughout its first four years, *Rockford*'s primary audience consisted of older viewers. However, by the end of the 1978-1979 season, a survey conducted by the Nielsen Television Index indicated that the series was becoming increasingly popular among young adults as well—a development that did not surprise Roy Huggins. "*Rockford* gradually became strong with young adults because of its attitude," he said. "It had the *Maverick* attitude—which Steve understood beautifully—and I'm sure that Steve tried to keep that alive throughout the show."

Cannell did just that, not only by incorporating elements of classic *Maverick* episodes into *Rockford* stories, but by continuing to bring out facets of the Maverick character (such as the reluctant hero and Maverick's basic concern with his own self-interest). With an Emmy Award under his belt, Cannell believed he could now take risks and experiment—just as his mentor Huggins had done, years before, during the peak of *Maverick*'s success. So it's fitting that the fifth season of *The Rockford Files* introduces one of the series' most memorable characters, Lance White—whom Cannell patterned after a character from one of the most famous *Maverick* episodes of all, "The Saga of Waco Williams."

"The Saga of Waco Williams" paired Maverick with gunslinger Waco Williams, an honorable, brave soul with a knack for landing in the middle of situations that the pragmatic Maverick would normally avoid at all costs. For instance, if Waco picked a fight, Maverick would tell him, "Waco, don't do that—they could *kill* you." Waco would say, "Well, what would you expect me to do? Run away?" And Maverick would say, "By all means, yes", because, like Rockford, Maverick's philosophy is that "being brave doesn't get you anywhere but dead real fast."

However, by the end of the show, everything manages to work out for Waco—he becomes engaged to the daughter of a big rancher, and becomes such a hero in the eyes of the townspeople that they consider electing him sheriff. Even Maverick, who had been steadfastly warning Waco not to live so recklessly, can't help scratching his head. In fact, the episode ends with a dumbfounded Maverick looking straight into the camera and asking the audience, "Could I be wrong?"

Similarly, "White on White and Nearly Perfect" pairs Rockford with fearless Lance White (Tom Selleck), "a guy who was sickeningly heroic—which was exactly what Waco Williams was," said Cannell. "The story for that show was different, but the concept of that character was absolutely out of 'Waco Williams.' I thought that was one of the funniest *Maverick*s of all. And it was also something that you couldn't do early in the show. It was definitely a Year Four or Five kind of show, where you've fed the audience fastball after fastball—in terms of, you've done *Rockford* and done *Rockford*, and the audience knows what the platform is. Then you can throw this changeup pitch."

Although Cannell didn't actually screen "The Saga of Waco Williams" prior to writing "White on White," he knew the concept of the character so well that he didn't really need to. Lance White behaves as if he's a character in a spy novel or an action movie. Just like those characters, Lance operates in a world of incredible coincidences, where you can go back to your office and find a clue just at the time when you need it most. Understanding Lance's world requires a willful suspension of disbelief. Rockford, on the other hand, operates in perpetual disbelief; not surprisingly, he spends most of the episode telling Lance that everything he's doing is "wrong" (just as Maverick had done with Waco Williams).

In "White on White," Rockford and Lance investigate the disappearance of the daughter of a wealthy industrialist named Teasdale. The trail runs aground midway through the story—until a voluptuous beauty named Belle Labelle suddenly shows up with an apparently vital clue! Because Lance (like Waco Williams) goes about his business oblivious to the possibility that he could get himself killed, he's ready to pounce on the lead. However, the discriminating Rockford (who is always more concerned with staying alive than acting heroic) advises Lance not to move so fast:

```
Rockford:    It hasn't occurred to you that this is a trap?

Lance:       A trap? Come on, Jim, I doubt that.

Rockford:    You know, I can't explain why you're still
                walking around! It's not going to last long.
             You're näive, Lance—you really are. You
             have to be cynical. You have to question
             things. You can't trust someone named
             "Belle Labelle" on face value. What's
             her angle, huh?  Whose payroll is she on?
             You find out the answers to those things,
             and you start moving fast and crooked.
             You go through doorways sideways, and low,
             at all angles. You look for the big lie.
             You question everything.
```

Although Rockford is right—as a matter of self-preservation, you have to be a little cynical and skeptical—he is ultimately proven "wrong," just as Maverick was proven "wrong" in "The Saga of Waco Williams."

Although it is Rockford who risks his life to rescue Teasdale's daughter, it's Lance who reaps the reward—at the end of the story, he gets the girl (along with complete control of Teasdale's company), simply because Teasdale believes that Lance is more capable than Rockford of providing for his daughter in the way to which she was accustomed. Teasdale even admits the unfairness of it all to Rockford, and offers Jim some kind of compensation (in addition to his hourly fee). Rockford politely declines, knowing that (under normal circumstances) Teasdale would probably insist on giving him the bonus. However, this is the world of Lance White, where normal circumstances do not occur; thus, Rockford is proven "wrong" once again when Teasdale promptly withdraws the gesture ("I just thought I'd offer"). This is one time where Jim would have been better off accepting Teasdale's offer at face value.

One of the real treats of "White on White" is watching James Garner's reactions to Lance's straight-out-of-a-spy-movie behavior. "Jim kept coming up to me and saying, 'You know, I just feel as if all I'm doing is mugging,'" said Cannell, who also directed the episode. "I kept telling him, 'Jim, you're doing great.' Because that was the point of the whole show—all the jokes were geared to Jim's reactions. And Jim was terrific."

Selleck would return to play Lance White once again in the sixth season. Other familiar guest stars in 1978-1979 included Hector Elizondo, Mary Frann, Abe Vigoda, Ed Harris, Janis

Paige, James B. Sikking, Nicholas Coster, John Pleshette, Allan Arbus, Denny Miller, Kenneth McMillan, Rene Auberjonois, Erin Gray, Glenn Corbett, Marge Redmond, Patricia Crowley, Ted Shackelford, Mills Watson, Harold Gould, John Considine, Reni Santoni, Leo Gordon, Lane Smith, and Kim Hunter.

Meanwhile, as production began on the fifth season of *The Rockford Files*, Universal's hardball stance with regard to Gretchen Corbett resulted in the loss of one of the series' most popular characters.

Corbett was the only cast member of the series who was under contract to Universal Studios. As such, that meant that her salary was paid by the studio—in order to have her on *The Rockford Files*, Cherokee Productions had to pay Universal whatever fee the studio charged for use of her services. (The studio would then pay Corbett her salary out of that fee.) Corbett contributed a great deal to the success of *The Rockford Files*—her character "Beth Davenport" was among the most popular of the entire series—and as a result, the studio raised its fee on Corbett after each of the show's first three seasons.

"What happened with Gretchen was that Universal wanted more money from us in order to continue using her on the show," said James Garner. "But at the same time, they wanted us to cut the budget by reducing the sets and the like, yet they still jacked up the price on her. I forget how much it was, but it was outrageously high. We couldn't afford it, and so, unfortunately, we had to eliminate her character.

"It was a difficult decision to make, because Gretchen was one of the family. But we couldn't afford to pay what the studio wanted."

Corbett was not aware of the negotiations between Garner and Universal regarding the use of her services; however, she does recall experiencing her own frustrations with the studio. "By that time, I was going crazy being under contract," she said. "I felt that I was not a 'typical contract player,' in that I had a lot of stage background, particularly on the New York stage, and it was therefore hard for me being lumped in with all the other 'kids under contract.' And so, I had asked out of my contract."

Although Universal had initially refused to accommodate Corbett, the studio changed its mind—on one condition. "In order to get out of my contract, I had to agree not to do *Rockford*," she said. "I don't really know what went down between Jim and the studio. But, as far as I know, that's why I did not return to the show after the fourth year."

Fans of Beth Davenport can take comfort in this: it essentially took two characters to replace her. Bo Hopkins (*Walking Tall*) appeared in three episodes as disbarred attorney John Cooper, Rockford's new legal counsel, while Kathryn Harrold (*MacGruder and Loud*, *The Larry Sanders Show*) starred as Rockford's new love interest, blind psychologist Megan Dougherty.

The departure of Corbett was also reflected in a cosmetic change in the opening sequence of the fifth season episodes. The still of Garner and Corbett—which had been added only one year before—was eliminated. A solo still of Garner smiling and laughing (from the episode "A Good Clean Bust with Sequel Rights") was inserted in its place.

Stuart Margolin won an Emmy for Best Supporting Actor—the first of two successive seasons in which he would be so honored. Joe Santos and Noah Beery Jr. also received nominations for Supporting Actor; James Garner was nominated for Best Actor, and the series was nominated once again for Best Dramatic Series.

After maintaining steady audience figures during its third and fourth seasons, *The Rockford Files* suffered a overall decrease in audience of nearly 10% in its fifth year, and dropped 13 notches in the overall Nielsen ratings. However, the decrease is attributable to the show's temporary move to Saturday nights in February 1979. Prior to the move, *Rockford* had been averaging a 17.5 rating and a 29.2 audience share in its regular Friday 9:00 p.m.

time slot—slightly lower figures from what the show had averaged the year before, but still respectable. But when the series was moved to Saturdays at 10:00 p.m. (where it competed against ABC's top-rated *Fantasy Island* for seven weeks), the audience figures dropped dramatically Rockford averaged a 26.7 share (8% lower than its Friday night figures) and a 14.8 rating (15% lower) during that period of time. (Interestingly enough, when *Rockford* was returned to its customary Friday night time slot in April, the show's audience figures increased by 10%.)

In Fall 1979, MCA/Universal distributed the first 107 episodes of *The Rockford Files* to independent television stations across the country. During *Rockford*'s first year in syndication, the reruns aired under the title *Jim Rockford, Private Investigator* because the series was still producing new episodes for NBC. However, in Fall 1980, after the series had ended its network run, MCA added the sixth-season episodes to the package, and the reruns reverted to their original *Rockford Files* title. As noted earlier, the 90-minute pilot film was re-edited and included in the rerun package as a two-part episode entitled "Backlash of the Hunter."

Mariette Hartley and James Garner.

88. HEARTACHES OF A FOOL

Production Number: 51106

Original Airdate: September 22, 1978

Written by: *Stephen J. Cannell*
Directed by: *William Wiard*

"Good Hearted Woman"
Music and Lyrics by Waylon Jennings and Willie Nelson
"Heartaches of a Fool"
Music and Lyrics by Willie Nelson
Both Songs Performed by Willie Nelson

Guest Cast: Taylor Lacher (Charlie Strayhorn), Lynne Marta (Carrie Strayhorn), James Shigeta (Clement Chen), Norman Alden (Roland Eddy), Joe E. Tata (Norman Abbott Kline), Leo Gordon (Clark), Mark Roberts (Hillman Stewart), Robert Phillips (Mike Thomas), Donald "Red" Barry (Shorty McCall), Herb Armstrong (Union Official), James Jeter (Mel), John Davey (Deputy Farnsworth), Raymond O'Keefe (Jake Sand), George Kee Cheung (Harry Lee), Byron Chung (David), Ben Jeffrey (Deputy Patino), Jayson Caine (Howard Freeman), Fred J. Gordon (Mel Willis)

Say, I'm the one who hit your car at Ford City. I've got no insurance — I'm broke. But I really wanted you to know how sorry I am. If it makes you feel any better, I hurt my arm....

Synopsis. *Country-western recording star Charlie Strayhorn is beset with financial and personal problems: production on his new album has been delayed; he has tax troubles; and his marriage is ending. Apparently, the only thing Charlie has going for him is the popular brand of smoked sausages that bears his name — but that's also a fraud. Charlie doesn't realize that his unscrupulous business partner, Clement Chen, has been circumventing the FDA and the Teamsters by producing the sausages in Mexico and arranging for non-union transportation of the product into the United States. Rocky becomes victimized by Chen's operation after he innocently agrees to pick up a load of the sausages in San Diego — he not only has his truck overturned and destroyed by two men, but loses his drivers license and has his union pension and medical benefits suspended. After Jim confronts him with the truth about his sausage company, Charlie helps Rockford investigate the matter.*

The fifth-season opener features two numbers performed by Grammy Award-winner Willie Nelson, whose title track is used in a particularly effective manner. The somber lyrics of "Heartaches of a Fool" provide a poignant backdrop to the breathtaking aerial footage of the San Fernando Valley that closes the episode.

Rockford Facts. "Heartaches of a Fool" appears on *Willie Nelson's Greatest Hits [and Some That Will Be]*, a Top 30 album first released by Columbia Records in Fall 1981.

89. ROSENDAHL AND GILDA STERN ARE DEAD

Production Number: 51103
Original Airdàte: September 29, 1978

Written by: *Juanita Bartlett*
Directed by: *William Wiard*

Guest Cast: Rita Moreno (Rita Capkovic), Abe Vigoda (Phil Gabriel), Robert Loggia (Dr. Russell Nevitt), Sharon Acker (Edie Nevitt), Robin Gammell (Donald Pilmer), John Karlen (Leo), Ron Gilbert (Freddie), Joanne Meredith (Ceil), William Joyce (Dr. Neil Rosendahl), Jason Wingreen (Earl Stagen), George Planko (Sergeant Curcio), Rick Goldman (Attorney), Clint Young (Harry the Doorman), Rod Masterson (Oscar Weinberg)

Hello? Are you the guy who lost his wallet in the Park Theater? Well, I'm kind of, like, into leather, so I'll be returning the money — but I'm gonna keep the wallet.

Synopsis. *Rockford once again comes to the aid of Rita Capkovic, the prostitute he befriended in "The Paper Palace." Although Rita witnessed the murder of arthroscopic surgeon Neil Rosendahl, the police arrest her on circumstantial evidence (she escorted the doctor at a medical convention dinner). In fact, Rosendahl was killed by noted crime king Phil Gabriel, who became permanently disabled after an unsuccessful hip replacement operation which Dr. Rosendahl performed. Rockford tries to gather evidence that will link Gabriel and clear Rita.*

This is the first of two sequels to "The Paper Palace," the Emmy Award-winning episode that introduced Rita Capkovic (Rita Moreno). Since we last saw her, Rita has managed to spend nearly all of the $300,000 she inherited from her neighbor. Rita tells Rockford that most of the money went for new clothes, a new apartment, a microwave oven, capped teeth for her friend Ceil, and hospital expenses for Ceil's mother. "But you could have paid for all that on the interest of $300,000," Rockford points out. "What happened to the principal?" Finally, Rita explains that she spent the rest of her money on "this guy." Rockford is about to admonish her. "But, Jim," she explains, "I had such a good time spending it..."

90. THE JERSEY BOUNCE

Production Number: 51109

Original Airdate: October 6, 1978

Teleplay by: *David Chase*
Story by: *Stephen J. Cannell & David Chase & Juanita Bartlett*
Directed by: *William Wiard*

Guest Cast: Bo Hopkins (John Cooper), Sorrell Booke (Wade Ward), Greg Antonacci (Eugene Conigliaro), Eugene Davis (Mickey Long), Luke Andreas (Artie Nodzak), Elta Blake (Celeste), Jim Scott (D.A. Cowan), Doney Oatman (Dawn Nodzak), George Planko (Cop), Tony Brand (Judge Carmine Rossi), Walter Olkewicz (Mac Amodeus), Paul Teschke (Carl Gibbons)

Jimmy—Angel. Here's the tip, but his handwriting's bad: Third Son in the fifth race at Bell Meadows. Wait a minute—could be Fifth Son in the third. Wait —his might be next week's race...

Synopsis. *Rocky and his neighbors have been harassed by Eugene Conigliaro and Mickey Long, a pair of lowbrow hustlers who are anxious to ingratiate themselves with mob boss Artie Nodzak. Conigliaro and Long intimidate the community with their wild parties, loud music and overt drug dealings. Jim intercedes on behalf of his father and nearly gets in a fight with Conigliaro. Later, Rockford unwittingly becomes an integral part of Conigliaro and Long's plans to coax their way into the mob. When they discover that Nodzak's sister dates a man who beats her, Conigliaro and Long kill the boyfriend—and pin the murder on Rockford.*

91. WHITE ON WHITE AND NEARLY PERFECT

Production Number: 51105

Original Airdate: October 20, 1978

Produced, Written and Directed by: *Stephen J. Cannell*

Guest Cast: Tom Selleck (Lance White), Jason Evers (Brad Davies), Frank R. Christy (Vincent), Peter Brecco (Meyer Ziegler), Bill Quinn (Armand Teasdale), Eddie Fontaine (Augusto DePalma), Raynold Gideon (Tuner Watson), Jay Rasumny (Manolo), Karen Austin (Veronica Teasdale), Carolyn Calcote (Angela), Julienne Welles (Belle Labelle), Freddye Chapman (Maggie)

*Pacific View Lots — Perpetual care by people who care." At an unbeliev-
ably low price. Call Monteith & Snell, the Full Service Mortuary — "We won't
rest easy until you do."*

Synopsis. *Millionaire industrialist Armand Teasdale hires Rockford to locate his daughter
Veronica, who has apparently eloped with her boyfriend Joey Blackwood, a seedy nightclub owner.
Veronica's disappearance soon becomes linked with the plight of Meyer Ziegler, a notorious
criminal who has been exiled from Israel. Ziegler kidnaps Veronica and threatens to kill her
unless Teasdale, an arms manufacturer on the verge of selling 25 defense missiles to the Israeli
government, can arrange for Ziegler's naturalization and acceptance into his homeland. When
neither the U.S. nor Israeli governments will interfere in the matter, Rockford becomes Teasdale's
only hope of seeing Veronica alive. Meanwhile, Rockford must also contend with Lance White, a
rival P.I. whose intrepid yet oblivious approach to their profession nearly gets them both killed.*

While Lance White clearly has his origins in Waco Williams, he also has characteristics that are similar to those of a character from another classic *Maverick*
episode—Jack Vandergelt, the character played by Roger Moore in "The Rivals."
Like Lance, Jack is totally oblivious to reality—he acts as if he's a character in a
romance comedy, someone who is in love with the idea of committing suicide in
order to win the heart of the woman he loves. Similarly, Lance White loves the idea
that he's a private investigator in the middle of a caper, and has no concept of the
fact that his impulsive reactions could very well get himself (and Rockford) killed.
Lance's credo is "Things have a way of working out—they always do."

In both instances (as Bret Maverick in "The Rivals," and as Jim Rockford in "White on
White"), James Garner's role is the same—the voice of reason, a reactor who steps back
from the action and asks himself, "Am I really in the same room with this person?" In both
instances, Garner plays this part superbly.

Coincidentally, Tom Selleck (a few years away from *Magnum, P.I.*) bears a striking
resemblance to Wayde Preston, the actor who played Waco Williams on *Maverick*. "I think
that, when they were casting Waco Williams, they were looking for an actor who looked like
James Arness on *Gunsmoke*," said Stephen J. Cannell, who also directed this episode. "I didn't
have a James Arness in mind. I just wanted someone who 'looked heroic.' We found Tom
Selleck, who was the perfect guy for the part. He was terrific."

92. KILL THE MESSENGER

Production Number: 51110

Original Airdate: October 27, 1978

Written by: *Juanita Bartlett*
Directed by: *Ivan Dixon*

Guest Cast: W.K. Stratton (Lieutenant Frank Dusenberg), Byron Morrow (Chief Everett Towne), Pat Finley (Peggy Becker), Alex Colon ("Captain Crunch"), Ed Harris (Officer Rudy Kempner), Tony Crupi (Bandit), Don Diamond (Lieutenant Alverez), Lee Farr (Booking Suspect), Robert Cleaves (Leo Benbrook), Nancy Parsons (Miss Buettner), Frank McRae (Junior), Michael LaGuardia (Officer Shumway), Sterling Swanson (Store Manager), Bucklind Beery (Officer Mazursky), Tiger Williams (Little Den), Joey Miller (Scotty), Doris Donaldson (Maude), John Wheeler (Cliff), Edward Dogans (Guard)

Jim — Chet, returning your call. Sorry I missed you, but I appreciate your calling back. Now, if you call again and I'm not in, just leave me a message, and I'll get back to you.

Synopsis. *As a nervous Becker prepares to take the examination for lieutenant, he's assigned a departmental hot potato — the homicide of parole officer Eileen Towne, wife of Deputy Chief of Police Eugene Towne. When Jim decides to help Dennis by conducting a preliminary investigation, he inadvertently jeopardizes their friendship and nearly sabotages Becker's chances for promotion. Rockford's disclosure that Eileen Towne frequently cheated on her husband (she fooled around with both parolees and young police officers) provides Deputy Chief Towne with a motive for killing her — but it also puts Becker in the awkward position of interrogating the very same man who presides over the examination proceedings.*

Dennis Becker (Joe Santos) has always been one of *Rockford*'s most appealing characters. Although he usually maintains a laidback, calm disposition, Becker is not immune to stress; as we have seen in the past ("The Becker Connection"), as well as in this episode, he will occasionally lose his temper. Becker certainly had to go through the wringer (not to mention three years of waiting) before making lieutenant, but he finally earned that promotion in this episode. Nice guys don't always finish last.

Rockford Funnies. Becker apparently has a friend at Universal Studios, because Peggy asked if Dennis could arrange a special tour of the studio for Bud and his son Den.

93. THE EMPTY FRAME

Production Number: 51114
Original Airdate: November 3, 1978

Written by: *Stephen J. Cannell*
Directed by: *Corey Allen*

Guest Cast: Richard Seff (John St. Clair), Paul Carr (Jeffrey Levane), Jonathan Goldsmith (Yossi Hindel), Dale Robinette (David Jones), Milt Kogan (Aaron Kiel), Troas Hayes (Carolyn Corkhill), Marianne Bunch (Cynthia Daskin), Dennis Robertson (John Jefferies), Eddie Ryder (Cateye Wilson), Lee Delano (Captain Salducci), Michael J. London (Norman Deekus), Sonny Kline (Pritzer), Douglas Ryan (Finta)

Jim, directions to the party: Left on Saugersfield, see a rock; left, left again, right, another left—there's kind of a hill. Keep going —y ou'll probably see a bunch of cars...

Synopsis. *Rockford's among the guests at a high-profile soiree honoring the appointment of Aaron Kiel (Angel's brother-in-law) to the Los Angeles Police Commission. Despite a security force led by Lieutenant Chapman, political activists crash the party and steal a set of paintings worth $2 million. John St. Clair and Jeff Levane, the hosts of the party, hire Rockford to recover the paintings. Meanwhile, Chapman's inept handling of the embarrassing incident lands him in the doghouse with the chief of police. The lieutenant is so desperate to save face that he swallows his pride and asks Rockford for help.*

This is the first episode in which we see Aaron Kiel, Angel Martin's often-mentioned but heretofore unseen brother-in-law, who publishes *The Los Angeles Tribune.*

94. A THREE-DAY AFFAIR WITH A THIRTY-DAY ESCROW

Production Number: 51101

Original Airdate: November 10, 1978

Written by: *David Chase*
Directed by: *Ivan Dixon*

Guest Cast: Janis Paige (Miriam), Richard Romanus (Sean Innes), Robert Alda (Cy Marguilles), Maria Grimm (Khedra Aziz), Gilbert Green (Talib), Joshua Bryant (Deputy Chief Gorman), Andrew Massett (Ahmad Ibshid), Maurice Sherbanee (Ishaak), Socorro Swan (Concepcion), Richard Moll (Ludes), James Gavin (Pilot)

Rockford? Alice, Phil's Plumbing. We're still jammed up on a job, so we won't be able to make your place. Use the bathroom at the restaurant one more night...

Synopsis. *A sheikh named Talib kidnaps Rockford and demands to know the whereabouts of his daughter, Khedra Aziz—a woman whom a gigolo named Sean Innes hired Rockford to find. After he manages to escape Talib's family, Jim locates Innes, and discovers a bizarre scheme designed by unscrupulous real estate broker Cy Marguilles to break up Khedra's marriage so that he could sell her home. Marguilles engaged women to seduce Khedra's husband Muhammed, but when he found that Khedra, a traditional Moslem woman, would never divorce Muhammed despite his infidelity, he contracted Innes to bed her. Later, Rockford discovers that Khedra's family intends to kill her because she cheated on her husband—an offense punishable by death under Moslem law. The complications increase when Rockford and Innes find Muhammed dead.*

95. A GOOD CLEAN BUST WITH SEQUEL RIGHTS

Production Number: 51102

Original Airdate: November 17, 1978

Written by: *Rudolph Borchert*
Directed by: *William Wiard*

Guest Cast: Hector Elizondo (Frank Falcone), James B. Sikking (Jeff Seals), Nicholas Coster (Augie Augustine), James Murtaugh (Bob Parsons), Jerry Douglas (Walt Wexler), Louisa Moritz (Debbie), Patricia Donahue (Board President), Hank Brandt (Captain Gene Lindner), Joanna Lipari (Mrs. Stern), Jenny Sherman (Linda), Derek Murcott (Manny Ables), Marland Proctor (Clerk), Loni Ackerman (Brochure Girl)

Jim, I have to thank you for talking over my problems with me last Tuesday night. I love you for it, but can you have lunch tomorrow and talk about the divorce? I'm real bummed out.

Synopsis. *Jim becomes a temporary "babysitter" for Frank Falcone, a superstar cop from Chicago whose legendary exploits have spawned a best seller, a major motion picture, and a popular network TV series. Jeff Seals, the image-conscious PR man for a toy company planning to launch a line of Falcone-related merchandise at a sales convention, hires Rockford to keep tabs on his rambunctious client. Seals is concerned that Falcone, who became irate when his former police partner Walt Wexler wrote a book that criticized the Falcone legend, might go after Wexler — and generate the kind of publicity that could kill the toy campaign. Although Rockford blows the account when he allows Falcone to slip away, he still finds himself in a position to protect the celebrity when he learns that Falcone may be the target of a contract killer.*

The character Frank Falcone was loosely patterned after David Toma, the New Jersey undercover detective whose exploits provided the basis for both the *Toma* and *Baretta* series. Falcone is played by Hector Elizondo (*Chicago Hope*), who had previously guest starred in "Say Goodbye to Jennifer."

96. BLACK MIRROR
(Two-hour episode)

Production Number: 51191/91192
Original Airdate: November 24, 1978

Written by: *David Chase*
Directed by: *Arnold Laven*

Guest Cast: Kathryn Harrold (Dr. Megan Dougherty), John Pleshette (Jackie Tetuska), Carl Franklin (Roger Orloff), Allan Arbus (Myron Katzen), Denny Miller (Norman), Alan Manson (Dr. Carl Rainer), Leo Gordon (Charles Martell), John Howard (Mort), Peter Tomarken (Commercial Director), Thomas Ageas (Maitre D'), Julia Ann Benjamin (Bonnie), Wallace Earl (Myra), Melvin F. Allen (Mr. Engle)

Jim, I leave London four o'clock, arrive L.A. nine — I guess that's London time. Yeah, four to nine is five, minus twelve hours flying — no, plus twelve hours — ah, but then there's a time change...

Rockford? Jake at the Sand Pebble. Sorry, old buddy, but there have been gun shots around your place once too often. The Neighborhood Association wants to have a talk with you.

Synopsis. *Megan Dougherty, a clinical psychologist who became permanently blinded in an accident ten years earlier, hires Rockford after she is menaced by a man in an elevator outside her office. Rockford suspects that one of Megan's clients is involved, but she won't compromise her professional ethics by allowing him to review their records. Megan does provide Jim with a writing sample of each client (in the form of cancelled checks), which Jim is able to present to handwriting expert Myron Katzen, a former cellmate of Rockford's who has now gone straight. To Megan's absolute disbelief, Myron finds the potential for violent behavior in an apparently docile client she knows as "Danny Green." But Rockford later determines that "Green" is really professional killer Jackie Tetuska, who created the mild-mannered personality as part of an elaborate insurance policy in the event he is ever arrested (he could always plead insanity, and call on Megan as a witness to testify on his behalf). When Tetuska realizes that Rockford's onto his scheme, he tries to eliminate Jim and Megan.*

Although Rockford can certainly handle himself in a fistfight, he doesn't have fists of granite—he gets hurt (sometimes very badly so) about as often as he inflicts pain. "I would get beaten up at least twice per show [on *Rockford*]," James Garner told Bob Costas in 1991. "I don't know what it is about people, but they like to see me get whipped—and I don't understand that. I guess it's because they know I'm gonna come back later and get my licks in."

Later, when Costas asked if Garner had ever been actually hit by another actor during the filming of a fistfight, Garner told this anecdote involving Leo Gordon, his co-star on *Maverick* (and who plays Charles Martell in "Black Mirror"). "Leo is a big, burly guy," Garner said, "and we had this a fight [scene early in the *Maverick* pilot], and he punched me in the gut. And I mean, he really nailed me. And I looked at him like, 'Whoa! What was that?' And I said, 'Okay.' But then the fight turns around, and I got to beat on him a little bit. And I buried my fist right up to his spine, and Leo looked at me and he kept trying to grin.... We got along well after that. We understood each other. If you can give it, you gotta take it."

97. A FAST COUNT

Production Number: 51108

Original Airdate: December 1, 1978

Written by: *Gordon Dawson*
Directed by: *Reza S. Badiyi*

Guest Cast: Kenneth McMillan (Morrie Hawthorne), Mary Frann (Ruth Beetson-White), Rocky Echevarria (Jesus Hernandez), Lawrence Casey (Don White), Bert Kramer (Skip LaForce), Carl Anderson (Tony Malavida), Woody Eney (F.I. Blassette), Don Starr (Bernard Kaplan), John Kerry (Dixon), Frederic Franklyn (Priest), John Yates (Second F.B.I. Agent), Tamara Eliot (Secretary), Lisa Marie Effler (Lucy), Rosa Turich (Mama Aguilar)

Jim, you give Peg the $200 for the painting. She owes me $70, and I owe you the $46 for the Christmas trees. Harry's still out $60 for the dinner, but at least it'll void that check.

Synopsis. *Rockford has a five-percent investment in promising light-heavyweight boxer Jesus Hernandez, whose road to the title has hit a major stumbling block. Manager Morrie Hawthorne can't get Jesus a match on the popular Tuesday Night Fights TV program, unless he sells car dealer "Right On" Ruth Beetson-White half-ownership of Jesus's contract in the event Jesus wins. (Ruth not only manages the leading contender, she's also the primary sponsor of the show.) When Morrie is suddenly besieged with problems — first, he's accused of bribing an immigration official; then, the Boxing Commission suspends his license; finally, he's accused of murder — Rockford suspects Ruth of putting the squeeze on Morrie in order to get him to sell.*

When he wasn't needed on the set, James Garner would relax in his motor home by playing backgammon, often with Luis Delgado. "When backgammon was the thing to do, we used to play it all the time," said Delgado. "When Jim wasn't working in a scene or something, we'd be playing backgammon. When he wasn't working during the summer hiatus, sometimes we'd pack some sandwiches and take a ride to the beach, park the car near some tables, and play backgammon all day."

Garner and Delgado first learned the game from actress Melina Mercouri (Garner's co-star in *A Man Could Get Killed*) and her husband, director Jules Dassin.

98. LOCAL MAN EATEN BY NEWSPAPER

Production Number: 51113

Original Airdate: December 8, 1978

Written by: *Juanita Bartlett*
Directed by: *Meta Rosenberg*

Guest Cast: Bo Hopkins (John Cooper), Scott Brady (Harold Witbeck), Kenneth Tigar (Jerry Simpson), Scott Marlowe (Augie Arnow), Rose Gregorrio (Natalie Arnow), Joseph Hindy (Leo Cotton), Gianni Russo (Johnny Bongard), Joe E. Tata (Sal), Pat Renella (Vincent), Harley McBride (Monica), Dallas Mitchell (Dr. Richard Hagans), Ed Crick (McNaughton), Bill Cross (Security Guard), Marland Proctor (Policeman)

Sonny, this message ain't for you — it's for me [Rocky]. I just want to remind myself to pick up the big ladder at the Paint Mart.

Synopsis. *Richard Hagans, the prominent Beverly Hills physician known as "the Doctor to the Stars," hires Rockford to infiltrate the tabloid newspaper The National Investigator after he suspects that someone at the paper broke into his office and raided his medical records. The Investigator recently reported that actor Johnny Bongard, one of Hagans' patients, was dying of cancer. Although Bongard is completely healthy (except for a minor case of skin cancer), the tabloid item could cause him irreparable damage—Bongard is also a prominent figure in the L.A. underworld, and he could lose control of his operation if his competitors perceive him as "weak." Bongard dispatches two men to check out Hagans' records; when Rockford and Hagans catch the goons breaking into the doctor's office, Hagans is shot. Complicating the matter further: when Harold Witbeck, the editor of the tabloid, discovers that Rockford was spying on the paper, he retaliates by running a libelous story in the Investigator. When Bongard reads the article, he suspects Rockford of leaking the cancer story—and puts out a contract on the detective.*

The Rockford Files was one of the first television series to feature characters that reflected some of the more colorful elements of the Southern California lifestyle—without resorting to stereotypes. "We tried to show that there's a lot more to Los Angeles than sun worshippers and movie stars and the like," said Juanita Bartlett. "They're certainly a part of the makeup of L.A., but there's also a richness to the populace that goes beyond that. There is a variety. We tried not to stereotype anyone because you have to look at your characters as human beings."

Rockford certainly met his share of off-the-wall people, but they were still believable—that is, the characters always behaved in a way that the viewers could identify with. For example, the heavies in each episode have to be threatening, but at the same time "you have to remember that they don't think they're doing anything wrong," explained Bartlett. "They're protecting their territory, and they feel justified."

For example, a mobster in one episode ("Chicken Little is a Little Chicken") describes himself in detail as "an urban horticulturalist," and by the time he's finished his speech, you can understand exactly what he meant by that. Or, in this episode, the ultra-Catholic Natalie Arnow lights votive candles and prays to St. Christopher for guidance in everything (even matters of murder). While the villains may commit acts that are vile and repulsive, their behavior is often quirky enough to make them interesting to watch. "None of the heavies walk around thinking, 'Gee, I wish I didn't have this black hat on,'" added Bartlett. "We tried to give them characteristics that made them real."

99. WITH THE FRENCH HEEL BACK, CAN THE NEHRU JACKET BE FAR BEHIND?

Production Number: 51115

Original Airdate: January 5, 1979

Written by: *Rudolph Borchert*
Directed by: *Ivan Dixon*

Guest Cast: Rene Auberjonois (Masters), Erin Gray (Alta Hatch), W.K. Stratton (Lieutenant Dusenberg), Marisa Pavon (Sophia), Howard Witt (Bancroft), Christoper DeRose (Luigi), Chris Palmer (Carrols), Jim B. Smith (Officer Kline), John Zenda (Security Chief), Albert Carrier (Monty Barucci), Margarite Rae (Margo), Michael Des Barres (Keith), Frederick Castellano (Pietro), Sandy DeBruin (Nurse), Suzanne Copeland (Girl), Paula Victor (First Buyer), Dolores Quinton (Second Buyer), John Furlong (Dr. Bosca)

Jim, it's Coop. I'm at the address you wrote down for the poker game tonight. This is a gas station, it's closed, there's no one around, and now my car is stalled. Now you gotta call me at 466-3— [phone clicks].

Synopsis. *Rockford probes the apparent suicide of his friend Carol Calcote, a high-fashion supermodel who was found dead on the same night an international jetsetter named Consuela Hooper was murdered. With the help of former model Alta Hatch, Rockford discovers a link between both deaths and internationally renowned couturier Masters, whose designs are the cutting edge of the fashion industry, but whose financial troubles are so severe, he must borrow money from loan sharks to stay afloat—and even resort to murder to protect his reputation.*

It can be difficult sometimes to come up with 20 or 24 different stories a year, particularly after you've been on the air for several years [as *Rockford* had been, at this point]," said producer Charles Floyd Johnson. "Once in a while, you might receive a script (or an idea for a story) from an outside writer [i.e., a writer who was not a regular member of the staff] that's similar to one you had done on an earlier show. If the writer puts a different spin on the 'old' idea, and you like the script, you might decide to do it."

That's the case with "With the French Heel Back, Can the Nehru Jacket Be Far Behind?," which (like "The Deep Blue Sleep" before it) takes place in the world of *haute couture*. Although both episodes are centered around Rockford's investigation of the death of a top-flight model, the stories themselves are completely different.

100. THE BATTLE-AX AND THE EXPLODING CIGAR

Production Number: 51104

Original Airdate: January 12, 1979

Teleplay by: *Rogers Turrentine*
Story by: *Mann Rubin and Michael Wagner*
Directed by: *Ivan Dixon*

Guest Cast: Marge Redmond (Eleanor Bateman), Sully Boyar (Bernie Petrankus), Lane Smith (NIA Agent Donnegan), Charles Weldon (NIA Agent Watkins), Lawrence Casey (Echo Two), Glenn Corbett (FBI Agent Spelling), Mitzi Hoag (Margaret), Dawson Mays (Treasury Agent Musia), Mary-Nancy Burnett (Jill), Lindsay V. Jones (Susan), Antonie Becker (Stacy Hutchins), Roscoe Borne (Talliafero), James McAlpine (First Policeman), Dennis Holahan (Agent Kaiser), Joe Bratcher (Second Policeman), Bob O'Connell (Colonel Huxley), Kirk Mee (Agent Pearce), John Trujillo (Deputy)

Miss Hallroy, City Federal. Your lost check still hasn't arrived. It's impossible for us to lose checks, so unless we receive full payment by noon today, we'll foreclose.

Synopsis. *Down and out after a brutal gambling trip to Las Vegas, Rockford bums a ride back to L.A. from a man named Petrankus in exchange for doing most of the driving. But Jim's troubles only multiply: the Vegas police arrest Rockford and Petrankus on auto theft charges, then search the car and discover a horde of stolen weapons inside the trunk. The matter worsens in Los Angeles when Rockford discovers that not only has the FBI released Petrankus, but apparently no record of Petrankus' arrest even exists. After he manages to post bail, Rockford sets out to clear himself — and eventually stumbles onto a bizarre government conspiracy to sell defective weapons to third world nations.*

Here's a peculiar string of coincidences. This episode features Marge Redmond, who had co-starred with James Garner several years earlier in the final episode of *Nichols*, which was written by Juanita Bartlett (and, in fact, Redmond played a character named "Juanita"). Redmond's best-known TV role was Sister Jacqueline on the 1960s sitcom *The Flying Nun*, which starred Sally Field—who would co-star with Garner many years later in the motion picture *Murphy's Romance*.

Admittedly, none of these facts have anything to do with each other, but it is interesting how they all link together.

101. GUILT

Production Number: 51117

Original Airdate: January 19, 1979

Written by: *Juanita Bartlett*
Directed by: *William Wiard*

Guest Cast: Patricia Crowley (Valerie Pointer), Ted Shackelford (Eric Genther), Rita Gam (Cynthia Germaine), Robert Quarry (Joe Zakarian), Elisabeth Brookes (Jean Ludwig), Eldon Quick (Norman Singleton), Timothy Wayne (Allen Huff), James Lough (Brian Tage), Al Stephenson (L.J.), Ben Young (Mr. Goldstone)

Jimmy—Angel. Listen, Eddie Talliafero just gave me a hot tip on a class filly in the eighth down at Hollypark. Only trouble is, I need twenty ...

Synopsis. *Bittersweet memories of a failed love affair and unresolved feelings of guilt come to the surface when Rockford receives a cry for help from Valerie Pointer, the woman he nearly married 20 years ago. Valerie attempted suicide after Rockford broke off their engagement — an incident for which Rockford has never ceased blaming himself. In truth, though, Valerie is a master manipulator with an uncanny knack for pushing people's buttons. Despite the enormous emotional baggage brought forth by helping Valerie, Jim feels compelled to help when he learns that someone is trying to kill her.*

The highlight of this episode is the excitingly-filmed action sequence in which Rockford and Eric Genther (Ted Shackelford of *Knots Landing*) are chased by a hit man flying a helicopter. The scene intercuts footage filmed from inside the cockpit of the chopper, which provides the viewer with some very effective P.O.V. shots.

"Guilt" also features Patricia Crowley, who had also played opposite James Garner in "The Rivals," another classic episode of *Maverick*.

102. THE DEUCE

Production Number: 51118

Original Airdate: January 26, 1979

Written by: *Gordon Dawson*
Directed by: *Bernard McEveety*

Guest Cast: Mills Watson (George Bassett), Margaret Blye (Bonnie), Sharon Spelman (Karen Hathaway), Richard Kelton (Norman Wheeler), Patricia Hindy (Fran Bassett), Robert Sampson (Arthur Horvath), Edward Walsh (Van Sickle), Joe Maross (Al Corbett), James Karen (Martin Horvath), Michael O'Dwyer (Pete Johnson), Ed McCrady (Pete), Nancy Bond (Juror), Frank Downing (Jury Foreman)

Mr. Rockford? Arthur's Hi-Fi. Your stereo's ready, but since your warranty expired in the two months it was in our shop, you'll have to pay the $60 on the repair.

Synopsis. *Rockford is the lone juror who doesn't believe that George Bassett, a chronic drinker accused of vehicular manslaughter, was responsible for the victim's death, despite overwhelming circumstantial evidence to the contrary. After receiving a temporary reprieve (the judge ordered a new trial as the result of a hung jury), Bassett hires Rockford to clear him of the murder charges. After demonstrating that the accident could have been rigged, Rockford tries to determine who framed Bassett and why.*

Rockford admits that he took on Bassett's case primarily because he needed the money. He had to pull out of a case because of jury duty; by the time the trial ended, his client had already hired another investigator. However, his interest in the matter grows, particularly after he examines the accident victim's car at the police impound and finds evidence indicating that the accident could have been manufactured. He then provides a detailed description of how the accident was rigged, and you can see the excitement on his own face as he takes us through every step of the operation. "Usually detective work is not anywhere near this exciting," he said. "It's usually just sitting outside of somebody's house. But every once in a while you get one of these physical layout things. That kind of recharges your battery."

Rockford Facts. Rockford takes his civic duty seriously—he just doesn't like doing it, and would rather avoid it altogether (two reactions that most viewers can identify with). He even tried to get his doctor to write a letter recommending that he be excused from jury duty because it would have been bad for his back (which Rockford injured during the Korean War).

Also, the names of the baseball players mentioned at the beginning of this episode (Cecil "Rabbit" Garriott, Wayne "Twig" Terwilliger, Dom DeLaSandro, Bill Schuster) all played for the Los Angeles Angels minor league baseball team in the late 1940s. Jack Garner also played pro baseball—he was a pitcher for many years in the Pittsburgh Pirates organization.

103. THE MAN WHO SAW THE ALLIGATORS
(90-minute episode)

Production Number: 51197

Original Airdate: February 10, 1979

Written by: *David Chase*
Directed by: *Corey Allen*

Guest Cast: George Loros ("Anthony Boy" Gagglio), Luke Andreas (Syl), Sharon Acker (Adriana Danielli), Joey Aresco (Richie Gagglio), Joseph Sirola (Joseph Manett), William Bronder (Buster Hutchins), Diehl Burtee (Eddie Whitefeather), Penny Santon (Mrs. Gagglio), Joseph Perry (Murf Guellow), Howard Honig (I.R.S. Auditor Serra), Noel Conlon (Congressman Hartschorn), Julie Parrish (Jeanie), Michael J. London (Chin Jake), Lavina Dawson (Conchetta), Marc Bentley (Ethan), Raymond O'Keefe (Jake Sand)

Mr. Rockford, do you know what to do if you are attacked and killed? Ask for Albert Kim See, and Grand Opening of Happy Dawn School of Secret Arts. Win free lessons!

Synopsis. *Rockford must contend with three kinds of trouble. First, he's just had his wisdom teeth pulled; then, he faces an audit from the IRS; finally, he learns that "Anthony Boy" Gagglio (a contract killer whom he'd last encountered in the episode "To Protect and Serve") has just been paroled from San Quentin. Gagglio wants revenge against Rockford, whom he blames not only for his arrest, but also the chronic liver problem that resulted from a bullet wound he* *sustained in a shootout with Rockford. In the meantime, Joseph Manett, the New York kingpin who first hired Gagglio, wants him to come back to work; when Gagglio refuses, Manett dispatches two men to kill Gagglio — and Rockford. After barely evading Manett's goons, Jim flees to Lake Arrowhead, where he seeks refuge at a cabin owned by his accountant. Meanwhile, after Angel crashes Rockford's trailer, Gagglio arrives and forces Angel to reveal Rockford's hideout.*

Because Rockford frequently resorts to phony names and occupations in order to coax information out of people over the course of his investigation, the writers of the show needed a steady arsenal of names from which they could draw over the course of writing any given episode. Oftentimes, these names are borrowed from either actual street names in Los Angeles (as in "Jim Slauson"), or from members of the *Rockford Files* staff and crew (such as "This is Mr. Bartlett, from Chase Food Services").

With that in mind, you may have noticed that the name "Manett" was frequently used in a similar manner over the course of the show (often, as in this episode, as the name of a prominent mob figure). In fact, the name "Manett" was used in the same capacity in "I Still Love L.A.," the first of the CBS *Rockford Files* movies. "Steve, Juanita and David really liked the sound of that name, so they often threw it in whenever they needed a name," said producer Charles Floyd Johnson. "And, because Rockford was always dealing with gangsters and two-bit mob people, 'Manett' sort of became this mythical criminal figure — which was the case with the two-hour show we did in 1994 [where the character was mentioned, but not actually seen]. 'Manett' was a name that they liked to use, but I don't believe it was named after anyone in particular."

There was nobody named "Manett" on the staff or crew; however, the name "Manett" may have been derived from an actual person. "It probably stemmed from actor Larry Manetti, who's a friend of ours," said Juanita Bartlett. "We often looked for names unlike Smith, or Jones, or Thompson—something that sounded unusual. But we couldn't use 'Manetti,' because it sounds obviously Italian, so we got rid of the 'i' and made it 'Manett.' But 'Manett' doesn't refer to anybody in particular on the show—it just became a name that was convenient to use."

Rockford Facts. Although originally broadcast on NBC as a 90-minute segment, "The Man Who Saw the Alligators" was later edited into a one-hour show, which is how this episode appears in syndication.

104. THE RETURN OF THE BLACK SHADOW

Production Number: 51119

Original Airdate: February 17, 1979

Written by: *Stephen J. Cannell*
Directed by: *William Wiard*

Guest Cast: Bo Hopkins (John Cooper), Paul Koslo (Whispering Willie Green), Dennis Burkley (Animal), Laurie Jefferson (Gail Cooper), Andy Jarrel (Phil Dankus), Jerry Ayres (Robert Gries), Ken A. Anderson (Harry), Noah Keen (Dr. Greenberg), Paul Mays (Festus), Sandra DeBruin (Nurse), Scott Walker (Hilliard)

Jim, this is Florence Boyle. You worked for my husband last month in Glendale. You were so helpful then, and — well, I have a problem of my own I'd like to discuss. Confidentially, of course.

Synopsis. *Rockford's excursion with Gail Cooper (John Cooper's sister) turns ugly when they find themselves harassed by a sadistic gang of bikers known as the Rattlers. While the rest of the Rattlers converge on Rockford, ringleader Whispering Willie abducts Gail, steals Rockford's car, drives her to a secluded area, and rapes her. With both Gail and Rockford hospitalized as a result of the ordeal, Coop undertakes the investigation himself. Drawing on his experience as a member of the old Black Shadow motorcycle gang, Coop infiltrates the Rattlers in order to bring down their operation—and avenge the brutal assault on his sister.*

William Wiard (pronounced "wired") was as close to being a regular director as *The Rockford Files* had—he helmed 26 of the series' 118 episodes, including this one. "Bill Wiard had been a film editor before he became a director, and that was reflected in his approach to directing," said Jack Garner. "When he was directing, he was always 'cutting' the film in his own mind—he always seemed to know exactly the shot he wanted when he filmed it, and because of that, he never needed to shoot a lot of unnecessary film. He was really efficient, and extremely effective as a director, and he was just marvelous to work for."

105. A MATERIAL DIFFERENCE

Production Number: 51116

Original Airdate: February 24, 1979

Written by: *Rogers Turrentine*
Directed by: *William Wiard*

Guest Cast: Michael McGuire (Robert Bernard), Joshua Bryant (Holt), David Tress (Brother Bert), Rod Browning (Brother Leonard), Michael Alldridge (Dobson), John Davey (Cramer), Donald Bishop (Brother Randolph), Paul Chambers (Old Man), Alex Rodan (First Man), Ari Barakar (Second Man), Ron McCabe (Patrolman), Vance Davis (Cop), Lydia Kristen (Woman), Cynthia Nye (Receptionist)

Jim — Joel Meyers of Crowell, Fitch & Merriweather. We're going to court tomorrow on that Penrose fraud case, but the steno misplaced your 200-page deposition. Could you come down tonight and give it again?

Synopsis. *Rockford becomes embroiled in Angel's latest, most bizarre get-rich-quick scheme. Advertising himself as a hit man named Jones, Angel figures he can make a fortune without ever killing anybody — simply by collecting the front money. Angel thinks the plan is foolproof (his "clients" can't send the police after him without incriminating themselves), but the operation hits a snag with the very first client — a Russian undercover agent who wants "Mr. Jones" to assassinate a Soviet defector believed to have a secret formula for denim. Rockford and Angel soon find themselves on the run from Russian agents (who want Angel for not killing the defector) and U.S. Naval Intelligence officials (who want the formula for use in making Navy dungarees). The matter becomes further convoluted when the man Angel was supposed to have killed turns up dead.*

Occasionally (as in this episode), Dennis Becker is put in a position where his personal friendship with Rockford becomes secondary to his duties as a police officer. Rockford telephones Becker for information—just as Chapman discovers that Rockford is wanted in connection with the shooting of Cramer. Chapman instructs Becker to stay on the line with Rockford long enough to have the call traced. However, Rockford senses what's going on, and he cuts the conversation short. Becker, a little defensively, tells Chapman he did the best he could—and we can see that he did. Becker was, once again, in a no-win situation.

"We felt it would be realistic if we sometimes put Becker in those kinds of situations," said Juanita Bartlett. "He was Jim's friend, but he was also a police officer, and there were rules he had to follow. But you could understand why Becker did what he had to do in those circumstances, without losing respect for him."

106. NEVER SEND A BOY KING TO DO A MAN'S JOB

(a.k.a. "The Return of Richie Brockelman")

(Two-hour episode)

Production Number: 51198/51199

Original Airdate: March 3, 1979

Written by: *Juanita Bartlett*
Directed by: *William Wiard*

Guest Cast: Dennis Dugan (Richie Brockelman), Harold Gould (Mr. Brockelman), Kim Hunter (Mrs. Brockelman), Robert Webber (Harold "Jack" Coombs), Trisha Noble (Odette Lependeaux), Pepper Martin (Harry Stone), Gary Crosby (Larry Litrell), David Hooks (Frederick Doyle), Salt Walther (Drew), Stanley Brock (Cowboy Mickey), Jack Collins (Dr. Wetherford), Todd Martin (Robert Wendkos), Stephanie Hankinson (Toulie), Bob Basso (Auctioneer), Danny Ades (Egyptian Consul), Michele Hart (Maggie), Jennifer Holmes (Amy), John Wyche (Museum Guard), Robert Ward (Second Workman), Shirley Anthony (Receptionist)

Mr. Rockford? Miss Collins from the Bureau of Licenses. We got your renewal before the extended deadline, but not your check. I'm sorry, but at midnight you're no longer licensed as an investigator.

Jim — Denny, from Denny's Pest Blasters. I've a great deal for you. We'll rub out your rodents at a tremendously low cost, so call us. We're in the Yellow Pages, and we mean business.

Synopsis. *Ruthless sports promoter Harold "Jack" Coombs strongarms Richie Brockelman's father into selling the family printing plant, which he plans to turn into a race track. Coombs not only bought the family business for a fraction of its worth, but he soundly humiliated the elder Brockelman in the process—first by buying off the City Council and City Zoning Commission, then by bribing Brockelman's lawyer, and finally by having the old man brutally beaten. An angry Richie implores Rockford to intercede. Although initially reluctant to take on the powerful Coombs, Rockford decides to help the Brockelmans get their money back. With the help of Richie, Angel, and a cast of grade-A grafters, Rockford tries to ensnare Coombs with a "big store" con designed around a bogus agreement with the Egyptian government and the Cairo Museum to arrange a second exhibit of the treasures of Tutankhamen.*

Never Send a Boy King to Do a Man's Job" is also very similar to the classic *Maverick* episode "Shady Deal at Sunny Acres," in that Rockford employs several expert grafters as part of an elaborate sting operation designed to upend an unscrupulous opponent. The expanded two-hour length enables the episode to provide the viewer with a look at some of the preparation that goes into running a con game (including a sequence in which Rockford holds a "casting call" for some of the grafters), and adds a sense of realism to the proceedings.

Rockford Facts. "Never Send a Boy King" marks the third appearance of Rockford's Oklahoma oilman alter ego, Jimmy Joe Meeker.

107. A DIFFERENT DRUMMER

Production Number: 51120

Original Airdate: April 13, 1979

Written by: *Rudolph Borchert*
Directed by: *Reza S. Badiyi*

Guest Cast: John Considine (Dr. Lee Yost), Jesse Welles (Sorel Hender-son), Carmen Arganziano (Dumas), Walter Brooke (Dr. Bosca), Dave Cass (Casey), Reni Santoni (Perry), Harland Warde (Evan Grange), Fritzi Burr (Tax Assistant), Patrick Culletin (Patrolman), Sandy Freeman (Dr. Ad-dison), Anne Bellamy (Nurse), Ray Stricklyn (Dr. Stark), Lesley Woods (Lucy Grange), Will Gill Jr. (Orderly), Glenn Robards (Father), Don Furneaux (Janitor)

☎

Jim, this is Andrea, Todd's Food Mart. Listen, there's a guy down here by the name of Angel Martin who's charged $110 worth of groceries to your account. Is that okay with you?

Synopsis. *At a nearby VA hospital, where he receives treatment for injuries he sustained in a car accident, Rockford witnesses a transaction between Dr. Lee Yost, who runs a organ donor service in conjunction with the hospital, and the parents of a male patient who has just died. Yost receives authorization to remove the dead man's cornea. A short while later, while looking for a telephone, Rockford stumbles past the surgical room and catches a glimpse of Yost performing the operation. To Rockford's surprise, he sees movement in the fingers of the allegedly deceased body! Despite assurances that what he witnessed is not an unusual medical phenome-non, Jim becomes curious about Yost — particularly after the doctor goes out of his way to befriend him. With the help of a hospital trustee, Rockford discovers that Yost is an amoral character who "collects donors," then arranges for their deaths so that he can sell their organs to his wealthy clientele.*

John Considine, who plays Dr. Yost, later co-starred with James Garner and Joanne Woodward in *Breathing Lessons*, a 1994 presentation of *The Hallmark Hall of Fame*.

Rockford Facts. A "deuce," in police lingo, refers to a person arrested for driving under the influence (DUI).

Rob Reiner and James Garner.

Sixth Season: 1979-1980

Sometime in the Summer of 1979, an accountant at Universal Studios provided James Garner with a profit-and-loss statement for the first five seasons of *The Rockford Files*. According to the statement, although the series grossed $52 million after the first five seasons, the production costs and other related expenditures amounted to over $61 million. In other words, the studio claimed that, after five seasons, *The Rockford Files* was over $9 million in the red.

Garner was dumbfounded, particularly since he had strived to produce the series on time and within budget every week. "It's pretty disheartening to know that you've done everything you could to bring a show in on schedule, and then find out it's all been a waste of time," he told *Playboy* in 1981. "We were no more than a total of seven days over on our shooting schedule [for the entire series]—and *nobody* had ever done that before. I also rented my company's semis and trucks and lights to the show for a lot less money than Universal would have charged in order to keep the show's costs down, to always keep it within our budget. I worked and scrimped and saved and pushed and cajoled and did everything I knew to make the show successful.... and then to find out it's all worthless, that'll punch a hole in your balloon." The news was particularly shocking in light of the fact that Garner had amended his contract in 1976, taking a cut in his per-episode salary in exchange for a personal percentage of the show's profits. Those negotiations were based on good faith that there would indeed be profits to share by the time the series was completed.

The news literally added insult to injury. Garner had planned to end *The Rockford Files* after five seasons, partially because his 51-year-old body was beginning to wear down from of the grueling demands of the series. By the end of the fifth season, Garner had undergone three knee operations; sustained a broken spinal bone; twice suffered broken kneecaps; and endured broken ribs, broken knuckles, a dislocated disk in his back and knee, as well as various dislocations, sprains, torn ligaments, and tendons—all of which occurred since the beginning of the series. Although Garner's contract with Universal had one more year to run, the studio's contract with NBC with regard to *Rockford Files* had expired at the end of the fifth season. Garner figured that if the series ended after five years, he could give his body a rest. However, NBC head of programming Fred Silverman elected to renew *The Rockford Files* for a sixth season.

Garner understood the situation from the network's point of view. Coming off a season in which it finished last among the three major networks for the first time in its history, NBC really couldn't afford to cancel *The Rockford Files*—one of the few established shows the network had. *Rockford* was still a Friday night staple—although its overall audience figures were 10% lower during its fifth season, that decrease was directly attributable to the show's temporary relocation to Saturday nights. NBC decided to make *Rockford* the anchor of the network's Friday schedule. Network president Mike Weinblatt explained the strategy to *Broadcasting Magazine* in September 1979: "We wanted to have every nine o'clock show on more solid structure—a returning show that had a built-in audience level—and let that show be the spine of the schedule. That's why we have *Rockford* back [at nine on Fridays]."

Garner tried to tough it out, frequently visiting the studio pharmacy for pain pills and muscle relaxants to keep him on his feet. But, one day in December 1979, "I was on the stage and I had such pains in my stomach and I didn't know what the trouble was," he told *Playboy* in 1981. "I just doubled up in pain, and I was bleeding rectally. I couldn't breathe because of one of my sinuses. It was not a wonderful moment. I said, 'Whoa, get me to a doctor,' so the studio doctor came out and discovered that my ulcer had come back with a vengeance."

For three days, Garner rehabilitated at the Scripps Medical Clinic in La Jolla, California, where his physicians advised him to take an immediate rest. As a result, Garner announced that *The Rockford Files* had shut down production for the year; a short time later, NBC announced that the series would leave the network's schedule following the January 10, 1980 telecast. *NOTE: At the time of his collapse, Garner had completed only 12 of the 22 episodes scheduled for the sixth season (the two-hour "Lions, Tigers, Monkeys and Dogs" was considered two episodes). Universal suspected that Garner faked his illness in order to shut down production — in retaliation against the studio's claim that the series had lost over $9 million. The matter soon found its way to court.*

In the meantime, the series went out on a few high notes. NBC announced that a number of "big names" would guest star on *The Rockford Files* during the 1979-1980 season, including Lauren Bacall; Rita Moreno (in her third appearance as Rita Capkovic); country-western recording artist Barbara Mandrell; and Mariette Hartley, who had co-starred with Garner in an award-winning series of television commercials for Polaroid cameras that were tremendously popular in the late 1970s.

Another highlight was "The Hawaiian Headache," an episode filmed entirely in Honolulu. "Universal wanted us to do a show in Hawaii," recalled Luis Delgado. "But, since there was nothing in Jim's contract addressing that, if they wanted to do a show out of state, they'd have to approach him first."

Garner agreed to make the special episode — on one condition. "Jim said that he'd do the show in Hawaii, only if he could take his whole crew over there," Delgado continued. "Universal didn't want to do that because that would have made the show even more expensive — because in addition to paying everyone's salaries, they'd have to fly everyone over and back, and pay for rooming, and per diem, and all of that. Jim said, 'Well then, I'm not going over there. If my crew doesn't go, then I'm not going.'"

Eventually, the studio gave in, and allowed Garner to take his entire staff and crew with him. While this may have been an exception as far as studio policy was concerned, there was nothing unusual about Garner's gesture. "Usually, when you go on location, the lowest man on the totem pole doesn't get to go any place," explained Delgado. "But, whenever we did *Rockford Files* out of state, the whole crew went. No one was left out — the cutters, the craftsmen, the stand-ins, the secretaries — everybody went, and then we stayed an extra day after we finished so we could have a party."

Stuart Margolin won his second consecutive Emmy for Best Supporting Actor in a Dramatic Series. *The Rockford Files* received several other nominations in its final season, including Best Dramatic Series, Best Dramatic Actor (James Garner), and Best Supporting Actor (Noah Beery Jr.).

* * *

In the fall of 1980, the sixth season episodes of *The Rockford Files* went into syndication, and the series has played continuously on local television stations across the United States and throughout the world ever since. In 1992, the Arts & Entertainment cable television network (A&E) obtained exclusive cable television rights to *The Rockford Files*. The series joined the network's daytime television lineup with a 12-hour Labor Day marathon. According to A&E spokesman Dave Charmatz, the reruns of *The Rockford Files* have consistently placed among the network's daytime Top Ten each week, and reaches over one million television cable households every day.

108. PARADISE COVE

Production Number: 53801

Original Airdate: September 28, 1979

Produced, Written and Directed by: *Stephen J. Cannell*

Guest Cast: Mariette Hartley (Althea Morgan), Leif Ericson (Carl Colton "C.C." Calloway), Byron Morrow (Don McLinton), Frederick Herrick (Cliff Calloway), Christine Avila (Nurse), Peter Brocco (Roscoe Ragland), John Davey (Rudy), Raymond O'Keefe (Jake Sands), Branscomb Richmond (Frankie Revy), Jerry Sommers (McJerrow), Tony Brubaker (Kermit Wilson)

Jim, this is Cal from the Leave The Whales Alone Club. Our protest leaves from the pier Saturday at 3:00 a.m. The whales need you, Jim!

Synopsis. *Jim's latest nemesis is his neighbor C.C. Calloway, a retired Malibu County sheriff who has been trying to incite the other members of the Paradise Cove Trailer Colony into drumming Rockford out of the neighborhood. In addition, Calloway won a $35,000 judgment against Rockford for a ruptured vertebrae that allegedly resulted from a car accident which Rockford caused. Rockford thinks that Calloway feigned the injury, particularly after he spots the old man maneuvering a metal detector around the beach with no apparent difficulty. With Angel's help, Rockford discovers why his neighbor wants him out of the way — Calloway thinks there's a fortune in gold bouillon buried underneath Rockford's trailer.*

When Rockford determines why Calloway wants him out of Paradise Cove, he agrees to move his trailer if Calloway signs an affidavit waiving the judgment and declaring that his back injury was caused prior to the accident. (In addition, Calloway must give Rockford 10% of whatever he finds underneath the trailer.) However, Rockford is able to trip up his neighbor. Calloway overlooked the fact that the gold was stolen from a U.S. military vault (and thus belongs to the government). Rockford swindled Calloway into surrendering his judgment for nothing.

Rockford Facts. Officer Billings (Luis Delgado) must been promoted to plainclothes detective in the sixth season, because he does not appear in uniform in any of his sixth-season appearances.

Mariette Hartley received an Emmy nomination for Best Actress in a Dramatic Series for her appearance in this episode.

109. LIONS, TIGERS, MONKEYS AND DOGS

(Two-hour episode)

Production Numbers: 53898/53899

Original Airdate: October 12, 1979

Produced and Written by: *Juanita Bartlett*
Directed by: *William Wiard*

Guest Cast: Lauren Bacall (Kendall Warren), Dana Wynter (Princess Irene Rachevsky), Ed Nelson (Blake Sternlight), Corinne Michaels (Linda Hassler), Michael Lombard (Gus Fairfield), Cristopher Thomas (Freddie Danzig), Carmine Caridi (Tommy Manett), Leo Gordon (Charles Martell), Robert Dunlap (Repairman Crane), Jon Cedar (Peter Pantazzi), Roger Til (Henri Tayir), Abel Franco (Max Rocorro), Shirley Anthony (Gwen Bagley), Michael DesBarres (Gordon Flack), Charles Picerni (Richard Soderling), Douglas Ryan (Second Partygoer), Julie Parrish (Donna Soderling), Ivan Barrick (Maitre D'), Melody Thomas (Sherry), Nicholas Worth (First Partygoer), Wally Taylor (Policeman), Paul Marin (Attorney), T. Maratti (Paul Juliano Jr.), Harold Ayer (Minister), Alfred Dennis (Paul Juliano Sr.)

This is Betty Furnell. I don't know who to call, but I can't reach my Foodaholics partner. I'm at Vito's, on my second pizza with sausage and mushroom — Jim, come and get me!

Jim, this is Jenelle. I'm flying tonight, so I can't make our date — and I've got to find a safe place for Daffy. He loves you, Jim, and you'll see — Great Danes are no problem.

Synopsis. *A chance meeting at a posh Beverly Hills restaurant brings Rockford to the attention of the elegant Princess Irene Rachevsky, who wants to hire the P.I. to probe a series of attacks targeted at her close friend Kendall Warren. Rockford rescues Kendall from a knife-wielding assailant at a costume party, then tracks down the hit man at a nearby hotel. When the hit man takes a fatal leap off the hotel balcony after trying to escape, Rockford becomes accused of his murder, but Kendall and the Princess have the charges dropped. At first, Jim believes that fashion news reporter Gus Fairfield, whom the Princess is suing for libel, is behind the attacks. As a precaution, Kendall stays with Rocky until Rockford can resolve the matter. But after Kendall is assaulted once again, Rockford suspects the Princess herself — the only other person who knew where he was sheltering Kendall.*

The dynamic onscreen rapport between James Garner and fellow screen legend Lauren Bacall highlights "Lions, Tigers, Monkeys and Dogs." It's fun watching them together, and it's clear that they both had fun filming the episode. "That show was definitely a star turn," added Juanita Bartlett.

Bacall, who received an Emmy nomination for this episode, later co-starred with Garner in *The Fan* (1981); earlier in 1979, they both appeared in *H.E.A.L.T.H.*, a 1979 feature directed by Robert Altman.

Rockford Facts. This episode is available as part of MCA/Universal's *Rockford Files* home video series.

110./111. ONLY ROCK 'N' ROLL WILL NEVER DIE

(Two-part episode)

Production Numbers: 53802/53806
Original Airdates: October 19 and 26, 1979

Written by: *David Chase*
Directed by: *William Wiard*

Guest Cast: Kristoffer Tabori (Tim Ritchie), Marcia Strassman (Whitney Cox), George Loros (Eddie), Lenny Baker (Ronny Martz), Stanley Brock (Bernie Seldon), Leigh Christian (Diane Bjornstrom), Jean Paul Vignon (Alain Florio), Fred Carney (Mitchell Robinson), Paul Champion (Dwight Deleau), Jan Marie Teague (Julie Immelman), Laurie Lea Schaefer (Linda Jones), Alan Chappius (Aonor Florio), Marion Yue (Chiyoko Takai), Jesse Dizon (Jerry Ito), Kathryn O'Neil (Secretary), Charles Rowe (Anchorman)

We're down at Hennesey'sBar, Jim, having a drink or two.

You'd better get down here quick, Jim—or we'll probably take up your stool!

[Drunken laughter ensues.]

Jimmy, this is Dora. I'm going to move in with the kids, but I'll sure miss you, dear. Thank you for taking out the garbage every week. I'll send you a card for your birthday.

Synopsis. *Pop music superstar Tim Ritchie, already facing a palimony lawsuit by his former live-in girlfriend Diane Bjornstrom, hires Rockford to locate his record producer and longtime friend Bryan Charles, who disappeared after they had a major dispute seven days earlier. Jim learns that Charles supplied Evergreen Management, a rival record label run by mobster Bernie Seldon, with bootlegged copies of Ritchie's latest LP Renegade Lotion — a move which has cost Ritchie's company $1.4 million in profits. The matter turns to murder when Rockford* *finds Charles buried in the back yard of his own home.*

Whitney Cox, the reporter from *Knickerbocker Magazine* who's writing a story on Tim Ritchie, tells Rockford that she thinks Ritchie is the most sensual rock star of his time. "It's my thesis that the 'macho man of action cowboy sex symbol' is not only over, it's history," she explains. "When you take Mick Jagger, Rod Stewart, even John Travolta, they've all proven that." The humor in that line—Whitney Cox is played by Marcia Strassman (*Honey, I Shrunk the Kids*), who co-starred with Travolta on ABC-TV's *Welcome Back, Kotter.*

Rockford Familiar Faces. George Loros, who played mobsters who were just a little too tightly-wound (such as Anthony Boy) in his previous appearances on *Rockford*, plays a good guy in this episode—Eddie, a former stir mate of Rockford's who was hired as Ritchie's bodyguard.

112. LOVE IS THE WORD

Production Number: 53815

Original Airdate: November 9, 1979

Produced and Written by: *David Chase*
Directed by: *John Patterson*

Guest Cast: Kathryn Harrold (Megan Dougherty), David-James Carroll (Randy Smith), Anthony Herrera (Jeffrey Smith), Van Williams (Lieutenant Duane Kiefer), Richard Cox (Kevin Spector), Rick Goldman (Lou Metzer), David Cadiente (Keith Keoloha), Lisa Figus (Mrs. Dougherty), Betty Kennedy (Patty Sevarisi), Eduardo Ricard (Waiter)

This is Marie at Liberty Bail Bonds. Your client Todd Lehman skipped, and his bail is forfeit. That's the pink slip on your '79 Firebird, I believe. Sorry, Jim—bring it on over.

Synopsis. On his way home from a trip to Houston, Jim pays an unexpected visit to Megan Dougherty (the blind psychologist with whom he began a "sometimes" love affair in "Black Mirror"), but the reunion becomes awkward when he learns that Megan has become engaged to architect Jeffrey Smith. However, after wrestling with his anger, hurt and disappointment, Rockford ultimately comes to Megan in a moment of need—when Smith mysteriously disappears, Jim volunteers his services (as "an early wedding present") to help her investigation. As they uncover a connection between Smith's departure, the architect's junkie brother, and the murder of a potential business partner, Rockford and Megan also discover that their feelings for each other are still very, very strong.

Country-western recording star Barbara Mandrell ("If Loving You is Wrong, I Don't Wanna Be Right"), who later headlined her own popular variety series on NBC from 1980-1982, makes a cameo appearance in this episode. Also featured: Van Williams (*Surfside Six, The Green Hornet*), who, like James Garner, began his acting career as a contract player at Warner Bros.

113. NICE GUYS FINISH DEAD

(a.k.a. "The Goodhues")

Production Number: 53809

Original Airdate: November 16, 1979

Written by: *Stephen J. Cannell*
Directed by: *John Patterson*

Guest Cast: James Whitmore Jr. (Fred Beamer), Tom Selleck (Lance White), Simon Oakland (Vern St. Cloud), Larry Manetti (Larry St. Cloud), Erica Hagen (Brandy Alexander), Joseph Bernard (Carmine DeAngelo), Fritzi Burr (Mrs. DeAngelo), Roscoe Born (TV Commentator), Fred Lerner (Carl Richman), Steve Jones (Newsman), Al Berry (Ed Fuller), Gregory Norman Cruz (Attendant), Larry Dunn (Norm Cross), John Lombardo (Police Clerk)

Jim? Dwight. I put a new outlet in the kitchen. I laid in the cable, then the box, then I pulled the breaker just like you said—and both of my TV sets started burning. What do I do now?

Synopsis. *The United Association of Licensed Investigators honors Rockford with the coveted Goodhue Award for his work in a case that set precedent in the field of accident insurance. But the ceremony is cut short when the keynote speaker—a state senator whose legislation banning the use of surveillance devices could adversely affect the P.I. industry if passed—is found dead in the men's bathroom. When Fred Beamer, who discovered the body, panics and runs away, he becomes the leading suspect. Rockford tries to clear Beamer, but he also must contend with Lance White, whose devil-may-care approach to the investigation may very well drive him straight to psychoanalysis.*

Larry Manetti, who co-starred with Simon Oakland on *Baa Baa Black Sheep* (created and produced by Stephen J. Cannell), later co-starred with Tom Selleck on *Magnum, P.I.* (which was produced by Charles Floyd Johnson). James Whitmore Jr., the son of Tony Award-winning actor James Whitmore, directed the 1994 *Rockford* movie, "I Still Love L.A."

Rockford Facts. This episode is available through MCA/Universal Home Video as part of its *Rockford Files* collection.

114. THE HAWAIIAN HEADACHE

Production Number: 53814

Original Airdate: November 23, 1979

Written by: *Stephen J. Cannell*
Directed by: *William Wiard*

Guest Cast: Ken Swofford (Colonel John "Howling Mad" Smith), W.K. Stratton (Agent Dwight Whipple), James Murtaugh (Agent Gordon Lyle), Christopher Cary (Dutch Ingram), Daniel Kamekona (Sergeant Okamoto), Jimmy Borges (Marshal Mingus), Esmond Chung (Shawn Kimotto), Paul Dennis Martin (Doorman), Jay Hoopai (Benny Kimotto), Elyssa Dulce Hoopai (Waitress), Carmella Ledman (Desk Clerk), Julie Blisett (Mrs. Ingram)

☎

Billings, L.A.P.D. You know, Thursday is Chapman's 20th year, and we're giving a little surprise party at the Captain's. I think you should come. By the way, we need five bucks for the present.

Synopsis. *The Rockfords think they've won an all-expenses-paid trip to Honolulu from Macy's Department Store. In truth, the trip was arranged by "Howling Mad" Smith, the military commander who once saved Rockford's life during the Korean War. Now a national intelligence agent, Smith recruits Rockford for "Operation Net Serve," which would lay the groundwork for sending a U.S. Ping Pong team to Vietnam. Smith wants Rockford to transport a suitcase with $100,000 in American money in exchange for $100,000 in Vietnamese money. But the apparently simple assignment brings Rockford nothing but trouble, as he is drugged, kidnapped and framed for murder — all in the same day.*

This episode was filmed entirely on location in Hawaii. "That show was really fun to make, because we had everybody over there, and it was just a marvelous, marvelous time," said Jack Garner. "We all enjoyed each other, and we worked well together. And it was directed by one of our favorite directors, Bill Wiard."

Jack Garner had known Wiard when the director was still a film editor. "One day, back when I first started acting, Bill told me that he had planned on becoming a director," Garner recalled. "So I said to him, 'When you become a director, use me.' And Bill said, 'Well, Jack, the first time I need a drunk blacksmith, you're it!' Some time later, my agent called me to see if I was available to do a segment of *Daniel Boone*—it was going to be directed by Bill Wiard, and he wanted me on the show.'"

Rockford Facts. According to this episode, Rocky has never been to Hawaii before; however, he had won a trip to the Islands a few years earlier (in the episode "Dirty Money, Black Light"). Hotel accommodations for this episode: Ilikai Hotel, Hawaii.

115. NO-FAULT AFFAIR

Production Number: 53811

Original Airdate: November 30, 1979

Produced and Written by: *Juanita Bartlett*
Directed by: *Corey Allen*

Guest Cast: Rita Moreno (Rita Capkovic), Pat Finley (Peggy Becker), Jerry Douglas (Al Halusca), Corinne Michaels (Linda Hassler), Ignatius Wolfington (Silky), Gloria Calomee (Hildy), William Beckley (Mr. Norman), Sandy Freeman (Mrs. Kramer), Karen Bercovici (Carla), Julian Kessler (Lily Showalter), Mavis Neal Palmer (Mrs. Stelmitz), Gregory Michaels (Doug), Michael Barker (Perry)

Oh, I thought this was Dial-a-Joke. I'm going to a party, and I need some ice-breakers. But, uh, I guess that's that.

Synopsis. *After advising a young girl to get out of prostitution while she can, Rita Capkovic decided to practice what she preached—she completed beauty school, and now wants to begin a new career as a hairdresser. But her brutal pimp, Al Halusca, won't let go of her, and to get his point across, he knocks Rita around and threatens to continue beating her unless she returns to the streets. Fearing for her life, and with nowhere else to go, Rita turns to Rockford, who nurses her back to health. After two weeks, however, the situation becomes a little complicated when Rockford realizes that Rita has fallen in love with him. In the meantime, a determined Halusca tracks down Rita and threatens to kill Rockford unless she abandons her plans for a new life.*

Both Rita and Angel save Rockford's life in this episode. Just as Halusca is about to shoot Rockford, Rita leaps into the line of fire and takes the bullet meant for Rockford in the shoulder (she is not wounded seriously). Meanwhile, Angel grabs a chair, lunges into Halusca and knocks him out. It's particularly nice to see Angel saving Rockford's life, after all the times when Rockford has bailed him out of trouble.

Rockford Funnies. This episode includes another reference to "Fannon's boat," which is named after prop master Bill Fannon.

116. THE BIG CHEESE

Production Number: 53810

Original Airdate: December 7, 1979

Written by: *Shel Willens*
Directed by: *Joseph Pevney*

Guest Cast: Constance Towers (Sally Sternhagen), Alan Manson (Chuck Ryan), Ben Andrews (Stamps), Mark Lonow (Coco), George Pentecost (George Neff), Mary Jackson (Postal Supervisor), Hank Brandt (Sergeant Roy Floyd), Eldon Quick (Willis Hoad), Bill McLean (Fred Barlow), Jimmy Weldon (John Rockfield), Frank McCarthy (Eddie Hellinger), Brian J. Pevney (Allen Calder), Anne Churchill (Clerk), Marie Denn (Newspaper-woman)

This is the Baron. Angel Martin tells me you buy information. Okay, meet me at 1:00 a.m. behind the bus depot, bring $500, and come alone — I'm serious.

Synopsis. *Rockford's only clue to linking the fatal stabbings of his longtime friend Eddie Hellinger and an accountant named Arnold Moe is a large parcel that Eddie had mailed to Rockford just before he was killed. Eddie, a reporter for the Globe newspaper, had been working on an exposé of union czar Chuck Ryan. Upon discovering that Moe was Ryan's accountant, Jim deduces that Moe had been supplying Eddie with information incriminating Ryan—and that Ryan had both men murdered in order to protect himself. Apparently, Eddie mailed the evidence to Rockford, but when the postal service inadvertently loses the package, the matter becomes a race between Rockford, Ryan and the police over who can retrieve it first. (Meanwhile, a desperate Lieutenant Chapman tries to doctor his taxes after the IRS informs him of a pending audit.)*

A well-paced, thoroughly entertaining caper, "The Big Cheese" features one of the best twists in the entire series—and a big laugh, at the expense of Lieutenant Chapman. First, when Rockford finally recovers the package, he finds that it contains nothing but a block of his favorite cheddar cheese — the key to the puzzle was really in the wrapping paper. Rockford's reaction when he opens the package is one of classic exasperation: "Oh, they're not gonna believe it. They're not gonna believe it, no matter what I tell them."

Then, after spending most of the episode scrambling to collect receipts (even for expenditures he didn't make), Chapman is confident he can beat the system (even though his accountant isn't so sure). "Those IRS guys never really check these things out," he brags to Rockford—at which point, Sally Sternhagen, the treasury agent who assisted Rockford in this episode, flashes her IRS identification badge ("You didn't give me a chance to introduce myself, lieutenant") and advises Chapman to keep his mouth shut before he gets himself in further trouble. The episode ends with a freeze-frame of Rockford enjoying a long-awaited last laugh at his longtime nemesis.

Rockford Family. Director Joseph Pevney, who had also directed James Garner in the 1959 film *Cash McCall*, cast his son Brian in a small role in this episode.

117. JUST A COUPLA GUYS

Production Number: 53812

Original Airdate: December 14, 1979

Produced and Written by: *David Chase*
Directed by: *Ivan Dixon*

Guest Cast: Greg Antonacci (Gene Conigliaro), Gene Davis (Mickey Long), Simon Oakland (Beppy Conigliaro), Gilbert Green (Joe Lombard), Antony Ponzini (Tony Martine), Arch Johnson (Cardinal Finnerty), Lisa Donaldson (Renee Lombard), Robin Riker (Kathleen O'Meara), Cliff Carnell (Albert Constantine), Eric Sinclair (Butler), Doug Tobey (Anthony Martine), Vincent Howard (Transit Cop), Joe Alfasa (Vito), Stephanie Hankinson (Car Rental Attendant), Jennifer Rhodes (Jean Martine), Ed Deemer (Delivery Man), Eric Taslitz (School Boy), Dean Wein (Detective), Frederick Rule (First Officer), Derek Thompson (Second Officer)

Mr. Rockford, this is Betty Jo Withers. I got four shirts of yours from the Bo-Peep Cleaners by mistake. I don't know why they gave me men's shirts, but they're going back!

Synopsis. *Renee Lombard flies Rockford to Newark, New Jersey, to help her father Joe, a prominent member of the Catholic Church (and, unbeknownst to Rockford, a former mobster). Tony Martine, the lord of New Jersey crime, wants Joe to convince the Archdiocese to reverse its decision barring Martine's late brother Vincent from receiving a full Catholic burial. (The Church will not allow Vincent, an unrepentant murderer, to be buried on consecrated grounds.) Meanwhile, Gene Conigliaro and Mickey Long, two inept hustlers who'll do anything to ingratiate themselves with the mob, set out to catch the vandal who has been torching Lombard's front lawn and littering it with animal carcasses, but they only exacerbate the situation—the vandal turns out to be the son of Tony Martine. An angry Martine first tries to kill Gene and Mickey, then later holds Renee captive unless the Church reverses its decision.*

"Just a Coupla Guys" was designed as a pilot for *The Jersey Bounce*, a possible *Rockford* spinoff series starring Greg Antonacci and Eugene Davis. The idea was not well received. "The show suffered a split personality," noted *Daily Variety*, "taking on the *Rockford* charm when Garner was on screen, lapsing into amateurish tedium when spinoff possibilities were being mined."

Perhaps this pilot fizzled because it confused the audience. "Just a Coupla Guys" were essentially the same "coupla guys" who had harassed Rocky, killed a man (and framed Rockford for the murder), and then tried to bump off each other in a fifth-season episode that was also entitled "The Jersey Bounce." Other than their sudden transmogrification into heroes, the inept hustlers in "Just a Coupla Guys" are indistinguishable from the dim-witted bad guys in "The Jersey Bounce"—they have the same names (Gene Conigliaro and Mickey Long), are played by the same actors (Antonacci and Davis), hail from the same town (Newark), and have the same dubious aspirations (ingratiating themselves with the mob). They're neither any more appealing from the first pair of characters, nor any less annoying.

118. DEADLOCK IN PARMA

(a.k.a. "How the Trout Became a Lox")

Production Number: 53807

Original Airdate: January 10, 1980

Teleplay by: *Donald L. Gold, Lester William Berke and Rudolph Borchert*
Story by: *Donald L. Gold and Lester William Berke*
Directed by: *Winrich Kolbe*

Guest Cast: Sandra Kerns (Carrie Osgood), Henry Beckman (Sheriff Neal), Jerry Hardin (Mayor Sindell), Joseph Sirola (Henry Gersh), Ben Piazza (Stan Belding), Michael Cavanaugh (John Traynor), J. Edward McKinley (Lee Melvin), Virgil Frye (Perry), Gary Grubbs (Deputy Murray), David Clover (Officer Chet), Ken Letner (Hy Newman), Al Dunlap (Councilman), John Davey (Mechanic), Paul Larson (Waiter), Mary Munday (City Hall Clerk), Janice Carroll (Doctor), Jim Scott (State Trooper), Frederick J. Flynn (Virgil), Diana Hale (Councilwoman)

Because of where you live says so much about you, your home has been selected by Royal Imperial Roofing and Siding as our neighborhood show-case. A bonded representative will call on you.

Synopsis. *Jim vacations in nearby Parma with his friend John Traynor, a member of the city council who is about to vote on an initiative that would legalize gambling in Parma — and allow for the development of a natural wilderness area into a vast hotel and casino complex. Traynor, who must cast the deciding vote on the issue, feigns illness, then cons Rockford into acting as his proxy. What Rockford doesn't realize: Traynor sold himself out to both the land developers (who have gangland ties) and the town mayor (who was bought off by a Las Vegas corporation that wants the measure defeated in order to stifle any competition). The matter becomes even more ugly when Rockford discovers Traynor dead in the woods.*

Keep your eyes peeled to the bright blue wall of the Parma Pharmacy during the scene with Belding and Sindell early in the third act. As Belding walks up to Sindell after removing all copies of *Tempo* (the magazine with his picture on the cover) from the newsrack, you can see the shadow of the camera operator, as well as the reflection of one of the spotlights used to light this scene.

Part 3:
The Real Rockford Files

In January 1980, Universal Studios filed a $1.5 million breach-of-contract lawsuit against James Garner, alleging that the actor failed to complete the 22-episode allotment for the 1979-1980 season. Universal claimed that Garner feigned his illness and in effect quit the show in retaliation against the studio's claims that *The Rockford Files* lost over $9 million through the end of the first five seasons.

Garner has always maintained that he had become physically worn out after subjecting his body to the grueling pace of series television. Judging from the evidence (the episodes themselves), it's extremely difficult to dispute his claim. Garner was the consummate pro, having never missed a show in five-and-a-half years. He was on-camera 90% of the time, which meant that he was required to be on the set (or at least, on site) every day—regardless of how long the day went. And although he was 51 years old at the time the series ended, he continued to meet the physical demands of the show, particularly with regard to performing his own stuntwork.

However, as far as the studio was concerned, although *The Rockford Files* had ceased production in December 1979, the series was never officially cancelled by NBC. That meant that the studio still had a commitment to produce 10 more shows for the network—and that Garner was still obligated to produce those episodes. (Garner, for his part, was ready to deliver. At the time of his collapse, the series was prepared to shoot two episodes—"Never Trust a Buss Boy" and "What Do They Want From Us?"—during December 1979. In addition, directors had already been lined up for eight additional episodes that were scheduled for production between January and March of 1980.)

The studio's argument was then dealt a major blow in early 1980, when NBC announced a pact between Garner, Warner Bros. and the network whereby Garner would star in and produce a new version of *Maverick* that would premiere in the Fall of 1981. That deal effectively killed any chance Universal had of forcing Garner to resume production of *The Rockford Files*. NBC's deal with Warners now meant that *Rockford* actually *was* cancelled, which not only severed the network's contract with Universal regarding *Rockford*, but also freed Garner from having to produce the remaining 10 episodes.

"We thought it was a tremendous breach of ethics on NBC's part," recalled Frank Price, now the chairman of Price Entertainment, an independent motion picture company. "Without telling us, NBC made a deal with Jim Garner, and in essence, cancelled *Rockford Files*. The minute the network made that deal directly with Jim, we were no longer in the position where we could influence anything—because not only was *Rockford* cancelled, but Jim already had his next series. It was a better deal for Jim, because he now had control over everything."

The focus of the dispute eventually shifted away from the breach of contract allegations against Garner and toward the matter of the profit participation. Garner believed that the studio failed to live up to its promise to provide him with his share of the *Rockford Files* profits. He also accused the studio of "creative bookkeeping" — i.e., doctoring the books by including false expenditures (or by inflating the amount of actual expenditures), either to create the impression that no profits existed, or to understate the actual amount of profits available.

Garner was not the first in the film industry to challenge a major studio on the issue of creative bookkeeping. Actors Fess Parker, Robert Wagner and Natalie Wood and Universal Studios producer Harve Bennett had all filed similar lawsuits; in fact, the Bennett and Wagner/Wood litigations were settled shortly before Garner commenced his action against

Universal. Garner's dispute, however, was one of the first to attract national attention, first in an item televised on *60 Minutes* in the Fall of 1980, and later in an interview published in *Playboy* in early 1981.

Sidney Sheinberg, president of Universal's parent company MCA, also appeared on the *60 Minutes* segment. Sheinberg suggested that Garner had nothing to complain about because he'd already been "adequately compensated" for his work on the series (to the tune of $5 million total salary), then punctuated his remarks by calling the actor "worse than a crybaby." The studio's thinking: while the matter of profit participation may have been written into the contract, the matter of whether the series made any profit was not guaranteed. "I don't think your audience (those who are employed and those who are unemployed) are going to lose a great deal of sleep out of the fact that Jim Garner only is going to make $5-6 million out of *The Rockford Files*," Sheinberg told *60 Minutes*.

However, the issue didn't concern how much money Garner earned in salary. The issue concerned what happened to all the revenue generated from the phenomenal success of *The Rockford Files*. "If you work that hard," said Garner on *60 Minutes*, "and you do it right, and it is a tremendously successful series, you've got to believe that there's going to be profit at the end."

Given the "creative bookkeeping" charges, Garner anticipated that it would be a lengthy battle just to get a look at the studio's books. "It would be like trying to open the books at any major company," he acknowledged. "I'll be ten years in the courts trying to get a good look at their books, but that's all right. I'm not going anywhere." Garner's remarks proved to be very prophetic — nearly ten years would pass between the time the matter first surfaced (Summer 1979) and the time it was finally settled (Spring 1989).

On several occasions between June 1980 and July 1982, Universal asked Garner to refrain from taking any action against the studio in order to allow the studio the opportunity "to furnish complete accountings and complete financial information concerning the series and its profitability," according to Garner's complaint. At one point, the studio even stated in writing that it would provide such information to Garner no later than August 31, 1982. Although Garner agreed to wait and see, apparently the studio never provided him with any information throughout that two-year period.

In the meantime, Garner broached Roy Huggins about the possibility of joining him in his lawsuit against the studio. Although Huggins had been entitled to 25% of the profits of all seven series he'd created for Universal — *Run for Your Life*, *The Outsider*, *The Bold Ones: The Lawyers*, *Cool Million*, *Toma/Baretta*, *The Rockford Files*, *City of Angels* — he had yet to see a dime of profit from any of those series.

"Jim wanted me to join him — and, in fact, I probably should have," Huggins said. "But at the time I didn't want to, because I thought my case was different from Jim's. I felt that if I ever had to take Universal to court over the matter of profit participation, I would sue them over the profits for all seven series."

While Huggins may have felt his case was different than Garner's, the issues he faced were certainly similar. The complaint Huggins eventually filed in 1990 eloquently addressed one such obstacle that he and Garner would have to face:

"When and if any such profit participants are able to overcome the obstacles created by this conduct and demonstrate the computation of the overall profits is understated, and that they are consequently entitled to greater amounts than contended by defendants, defendants attempt to 'negotiate' settlements which enable them to retain a portion of their wrongful gain as well as avoid paying interest for the use of the profit participants' money, upon the threat, expressed or implied, that otherwise the profit participants must face the prospect of a long, arduous and expensive litigation."

Garner had discussed the same problem in the *Playboy* interview. "We will try to go over their books, and then we will sue them," he said. "They will say, 'Well, let's not do it that way. Let's see if we can settle it amicably.' They'll offer to give me about ten cents on the dollar, but I won't take it."

In July 1983, Garner finally filed a $22.5 million breach-of-contract lawsuit against Universal, alleging that the studio failed "to properly account to Garner the true and correct accountings of the revenues, costs and other charges in connection with the series." The complaint also accused the studio of providing Garner with "substantially erroneous and deliberately improper statements of costs, income, revenues and profits" in order to create the impression "that no amounts were payable to Garner on account of his profit participation for the series."

In 1986, a court order consolidated Garner's action with the lawsuit Universal had filed in 1980. In the meantime, while the litigation took its natural course, *The Rockford Files* continued to generate revenue. In January 1988, Garner finally won the right to examine the studio's books — by that time, although *Rockford* had generated $119.3 million, the studio still claimed that the show was $1.6 million in the red.

Garner conducted two separate audits (one examining the *Rockford* books through June 1980, the other through June 1985). The first audit estimated that the studio either overstated costs or underestimated revenue by approximately $10.9 million. The second audit raised even more questions. "The largest and most debatable charges raised by the auditors was a $7.9 million interest expense," reported *Barron's* in February 1989. "What Garner's suit claims, in short, is that Universal recorded expenses immediately, but deferred recording revenues and profits until cash was in hand. It would be as if you added up all your anticipated living expenses for the next ten years, and charged 6% interest against the amount, but at the same time, you added up your income only through yesterday, when you got paid. Of course, most businesses like to keep their books in exactly the opposite way — put off expenses as long as possible, and record income as quickly as possible."

From the time the action commenced through the present time, MCA/Universal has never commented on Garner's allegations. However, MCA president Sheinberg did reveal a key facet of Universal's defense during the *60 Minutes* interview telecast in 1980. "We all live by our contracts," Sheinberg said. "When you are a big company called Cherokee Productions, and a big star called Jim Garner, and you've got big lawyers and big accountants, and big agents, you can't play the role of being the fella who just wandered in from Nashville."

In other words, Universal contended that Garner did not enter into any negotiations by himself — he had been well represented by parties who should have informed him of any loopholes or any other questionable conditions of the agreement. While that may have been true, it still doesn't address the issue of what happened to all the revenue.

The stress of the protracted legal battle had an effect on Garner's health — the actor underwent two heart operations (including a quadruple bypass surgery) between April and June 1988. While Garner recuperated, Universal issued a new financial statement in late 1988 indicating for the first time that *The Rockford Files* had turned a profit (after generating nearly $123 million to that point). According to *Barron's*, Garner received an initial payment of $243,313, plus additional payments totalling $363,687 over the next few months.

Meanwhile, Roy Huggins, who had been entitled to 25% of the show's profits under his contract, also received a payment in December 1988 ($99,542.39) — a development which led Huggins to reevaluate his own situation with the studio. "I now had evidence that they were making a profit on *The Rockford Files*," he explained. "Although the amount that they paid me was by no means small, [my wife] Adele and I felt that it was nowhere near what they actually owed me. So at that point, I changed my line of thinking. I decided that, if I had to, I would take them to court on *Rockford* alone."

Although the long-awaited trial between Garner and Universal was set to begin on March

15, 1989, the parties resumed settlement talks and reached a tentative agreement at the 11th hour. The matter finally ended two weeks later, when both sides signed the settlement agreement on March 31, 1989. The exact terms of the settlement agreement are confidential.

According to *Barron's*, Garner elected to settle rather than risk having the entire case thrown out of court, while Universal chose to settle in lieu of having to explain its accounting practices in open court. "Some entertainment lawyers questioned whether Garner's case would hold up in court, opining that Universal's accounting, fair or not, was nevertheless consistent with industry practices," reported *Barron's* in 1989. "[However], it was expected that Universal would likely have had to defend itself against such charges of unfair practices as 'block booking,' whereby a distributor of television shows forces a TV station to buy a series it didn't want in order to acquire a popular show... If proved, block booking would have the effect of reducing syndication receipts from *The Rockford Files*, one way of postponing the point at which the series began making a profit and thus delaying the time at which Garner [and Huggins] were entitled to begin sharing in those profits."

A lawsuit is a long and incredibly draining process, particularly for the litigants. Not only had Garner gone through that experience before, he had also previously taken a major studio to court (he defeated Warner Bros. in 1960 after proving that the studio had breached his contract by unlawfully suspending his salary). Despite the toll it had taken on his health, Garner hung in there, and never questioned that he would ultimately prevail. "I never had one doubt," he said. "When I commit myself to something, I commit myself — and I committed myself to that matter the first day I decided to do it. There was never, ever any question of backing out."

The circumstances in both cases, however, were quite different. Although both cases were ostensibly about money, they also concerned issues much deeper than that. In the Warners lawsuit, Garner fought for the right to become a "free agent" in the film industry, but he did so at great risk. Because the Warners lawsuit took place in 1960 (at the start of his career), Garner faced the possibility of never working in the industry again had he lost the case; whereas in 1980, Garner was an established star who had the resources to take on a major studio like Universal and withstand a long, arduous fight. "These cases require an unusual plaintiff," said Michael R. White (Garner's attorney) in 1989. "He has to have a lot of money, but not be so flush that the outcome isn't important to him. Plus, he needs a property that's been successful and makes a lot a money. Few TV shows or movies ever achieve the success of *The Rockford Files*."

Although White had predicted at the time of the settlement that there wouldn't be the likes of *Universal v. Garner* for a long time, series co-creator Roy Huggins filed a $25 million breach-of-contract lawsuit of his own in July 1990. Although Huggins had been entitled to 25% of the net profits of all seven series he produced for Universal between 1965 and 1980, he concentrated his lawsuit on *The Rockford Files* because "I was afraid that I'd waited too long on the others," he said. "I was concerned that there may have been a statute of limitations problem that would have prohibited me from taking action on the other shows. And, also, the other shows hadn't gone that magic number of years [five years, or approximately 100 episodes] that guaranteed a profit. By the time Jim's suit was settled, I now had evidence that *Rockford* had turned a profit, so I decided to sue them on that show alone."

Huggins' matter was settled in far less time than Garner's lawsuit, due in part to a factor that wasn't present in the Garner case — Huggins' age. The writer/producer was 76 at the time the action commenced; under California law, that entitled him to preference in getting a trial. In March 1993, Huggins won the right to examine the *Rockford* books for the first time. Although Universal succeeded in having several of Huggins' allegations thrown out of the case two months later, the crux of the complaint — failure to provide Huggins with his rightful share of all profits, and failure to render a proper accounting of all expenses pertaining to the series — remained at issue. This, in turn, meant that had the matter proceeded to trial, Universal faced the likelihood of explaining its accounting practices. Rather than face that prospect, Universal elected to settle with Huggins in early 1994 (just as the studio has done with Garner in 1989). The terms of this settlement are also confidential.

James Garner as Jim Rockford and Joanna Cassidy as his ex-wife in "I Love L. A." the first of the new *Rockford Files*.

Part 4:
Six More of a Good Thing

It was only a matter of time before *The Rockford Files* came back; after all, the series ended just as network television embarked on a wave of nostalgia. In the 15 years since *Rockford* left NBC, nearly 100 popular series of the 60s and 70s have been exhumed and returned to prime time, either as "reunion specials" or as full-fledged series. In fact, James Garner himself resurrected *Maverick* in *Bret Maverick* (NBC, 1981-1982), an updated series of adventures featuring the gentle grafter that first made him a star in the late 1950s. In some cases (such as *The Perry Mason Mysteries* and *Columbo*), the revivals are as popular and as successful as the original series.

In the years following the settlement of his lawsuit with Universal, Garner had been approached on several occasions about reviving *The Rockford Files*. As much as he loved playing the character, Garner steadfastly refused as a matter of principle. After all, because Universal maintained majority ownership of the series, any revival of the series would have to be done through the studio. As far as Garner was concerned, too many bad memories lingered from the long, bitter legal battle, and it was too soon for the two sides to go back to work with each other. But the talks persisted, and finally, in the Spring of 1994, the studio announced that Garner had agreed to produce and star in a series of six two-hour *Rockford* episodes that would air on CBS-TV over the course of the 1994-95 and 1995-96 seasons. (Ironically, the announcement of the new *Rockford*s was made shortly before the release of Garner's latest feature — a big screen version of *Maverick*.)

"I finally thought, Well, if I'm going to do it, now is the time, as far as my availability and my health are concerned," Garner told *TV Guide* in 1994. "Four years from now, it's too late. And it's a marvelous character. It's a shame we haven't been doing it before, but I just couldn't bring myself to do it."

While Garner agreed to make the films for the studio, he made it very clear that he wouldn't shoot them *at* the studio. That would be asking too much. "I told this to the Universal people when we were negotiating: 'As soon as I got to that gate, it would be like sticking in a knife in my ribs and reminding me of a very bad circumstance before.' I could not do that to myself. It's too late in life to be miserable."

Interior footage for the CBS *Rockford* episodes is filmed at a small studio in Hollywood, where Garner's offices are also located. Garner serves as co-executive producer of the new series, along with Juanita Bartlett and Charles Floyd Johnson (two of the producers from the original series). Also aboard: Stephen J. Cannell and David Chase, who (along with Bartlett) will write the teleplays for the new shows; music composers Mike Post and Pete Carpenter; executive assistant Luis Delgado; cast members Stuart Margolin, Joe Santos and Jack Garner; and many of the series' original crew members, including assistant directors Cliff Coleman and Les Berke, cinematographer Steve Yaconelli, stunt coordinator Roydon Clark, and property masters Bill Fannon and Greg Brinkley.

The first episode, "I Still Love L.A.," brought the series up to date by showing how Rockford contended with some of the major events that have occurred in Los Angeles in recent years: the riots following the Rodney King verdict in 1992; the fires in Malibu during the Fall of 1993; and the Northridge earthquake of early 1994. Rockford still has his old Pontiac Firebird (although it's in repairs for most of the film). He also has a new trailer — out of necessity. The original trailer had been destroyed years before, although apparently little was left of it to begin with. "We'd have to tow the trailer, from the studio to Paradise

Cove and back again, on the original show," Garner told CNN in 1994. "One night, they took it out on the Ventura freeway, and the trailer just fell in half! It fell right out and blocked four lanes of the freeway for hours."

Joining the series is Joanna Cassidy as a new character, Halley "Kit" Kittredge, Rockford's attorney (and former wife). Although Gretchen Corbett, who played attorney Beth Davenport in the original series, did not appear in the first CBS movie ("I Still Love L.A."), it's possible that she may return to *Rockford* in the future. "Gretchen called me and said that if there was anything that she could do, she'd like to do it," Garner said. "We weren't able to work her into the first show, but we're going to keep her in mind." *(Note: Corbett will appear as Beth in one of the movies that will air during the 1995-96 season.)*

Also missing from the original cast: Noah Beery Jr. ("Rocky"), who had been in poor health since he suffered a stroke in the mid-1980s. Beery died on November 1, 1994 (less than one month before "I Still Love L.A." premiered on CBS), but the entire *Rockford* family paid tribute to the actor and the character in a heartfelt sequence that occurs near the end of the film. Following a phone conversation between Rockford and his father, the camera cuts to the photo of Rocky that Jim keeps on his desk. Rockford then picks up the photo and smiles warmly.

"That was filmed before Pidge [Beery] died," Garner explained. "We knew that we wouldn't be able to have him on the show, so we put the picture on the table, and then I did that conversation on the phone. That was our little tribute to Pidge." The film also ends with the following dedication: "To Noah Beery Jr. — We love you and we miss you, Pidge."

"I Still Love L.A." was telecast on November 27, 1994, and benefitted from three factors: (1) a built-in audience familiar with the show; (2) a widespread publicity campaign that included televised segments on *CNN Showbiz Today, CBS This Morning, Extra!, The Tonight Show,* and *CBS Sneak Peek*, as well as detailed features in *TV Guide* and *The Los Angeles Times*; and (3) a strategically placed time slot, following the perennial Top Ten favorite, *Murder, She Wrote.* "As I understand it, that was something that Jim and Universal negotiated with the network," said Charles Floyd Johnson. "Jim wanted a network that would appreciate the show, and a guarantee that the films would be shown in a good time slot. The first thing was easy — all three networks wanted *The Rockford Files*, so it wasn't a matter of having to sell the idea. All Universal had to do was say, 'We want to do *Rockford* again,' and they all came running.

"We went with CBS because they offered us Sunday night at nine, after *Murder, She Wrote.* Jim thought that was not only one of the best time slots in television, but also the best time slot for the show."

Apparently ABC and NBC were willing to rearrange their programming schedules in order to accommodate *The Rockford Files*. There was even talk that ABC might offer Garner a Wednesday night time slot (with *Roseanne* as a lead-in) or that NBC would air the TV-movies on Thursday nights (following *Seinfeld*). Because *Roseanne* and *Seinfeld* are also Top Ten shows, a scenario with either of those shows as a lead-in would have also offered the prospect of a huge audience. However, Garner felt that *Murder, She Wrote*'s demographics were much more compatible with *Rockford*'s core audience. Whereas *Roseanne* and *Seinfeld* are highly popular with "younger viewers" [ages 21-49], *Murder, She Wrote* is particularly strong among viewers 50-and-older — the same age bracket from which *Rockford* has always drawn its greatest audience. In other words, Garner chose CBS because he believed *Murder, She Wrote*'s audience was more likely to stay tuned to watch *Rockford* than either *Roseanne*'s or *Seinfeld*'s.

That proved to be shrewd thinking on Garner's part. "I Still Love L.A." was the No. 1 show on the West Coast that night (and placed No. 4 in the overall Nielsen ratings for that week), with an 18.6 rating, and a 27 share. It was the highest-rated made-for-TV movie of the entire 1994-95 season. An estimated 17,649,000 television households tuned in that night, an audience figure comparable to what the series was drawing at the peak of its popularity in 1975. The film scored particularly well with older viewers.

The most inspired scene of the movie occurs in the first act, when Rockford watches live television footage of the looting caused by the riots in Los Angeles. The TV camera zooms in and catches Angel red-handed as he is removing merchandise from an electronics store. Then we cut to Rockford, whose look says it all — on the one hand, he can't believe what he's seeing; but on the other hand, he can, because nothing Angel does ever really surprises him. "Stuart came up with something when we first filmed that scene that made me laugh out loud," said Bartlett, who wrote "I Still Love L.A." "[Director] Jimmy Whitmore shot that sequence from a high angle, because it's supposed to be footage taken from a helicopter camera. Angel looks up, sees the camera, and panics, so he reaches out and takes a trash bag and puts it over his head — only it's a see-through trash bag. Stuart does things like that all the time. He has all those wonderful, off-the-wall ideas that are just marvelous."

"I Still Love L.A." has much of the flavor of the original series, such as colorful characters (including a Hollywood agent who's subpoenaed by the police while waiting outside Oliver Stone's office), as well as Angel's crazy antics (he plans to hawk stolen merchandise on the Home Shopping Network). There is not as much "action" (in terms of car chases and fist fights) in the film as we might expect from *Rockford*, but that's because of the nature of the story. "For the most part, Rockford was up against natural disasters in that first show — earthquakes, fires, and the like," said Bartlett. "There wasn't anybody who was actively trying to do him hard — other than, apparently, God. Now, you talk about your big time heavies...."

Another reason why Rockford is not quite as physical as he was before: Garner is 15 years older. Given the many injuries he sustained while making the original series, that would be asking too much of the 67-year-old star. "Jim likes to do some stunts himself, but we don't allow him to do any of them on these new shows," said Luis Delgado. "What he did do, however, was his own driving."

One item that still needs to be worked out is the matter of Rockford's daily rate in 1995. "I would hope he'd get a little raise," joked Garner. "There wasn't a scene in the first film where we got into that, but I'm sure that Steve or Juanita will bring it up for him. We'll establish another price — probably around $350 a day."

The key, says Garner, is not to overprice him. "You want to underprice him," he said. "You don't want to go over, but it's okay to go a little under."

Garner earned a nomination from the Screen Actors Guild for Best Actor in a TV-Movie or Miniseries for his performance in "I Still Love L.A."

* * *

Jo Swerling paid a visit to the set of "A Blessing in Disguise," the second *Rockford Files* movie (written by Stephen J. Cannell), which was filmed in December 1994. "They happened to be shooting down in the marina where I live," he said. "On my way home, I dropped in (they were shooting at night), and I visited the guys on the set. Nearly everybody from the old show was there — Joe Santos; Stu Margolin; Jimmy; Jimmy's stunt double, Roy Clark; the director of photography (Steve Yaconelli) was the camera operator on the old show; and the prop man (Bill Fannon) was the same on the old show. Charles Johnson and the other producers did a remarkable job of gathering as many of the key people as they did. As a matter of fact, the guy who was the production manager on the original show (Les Berke) was back, only he was working as a second assistant director — *just to be on the show*. And the first assistant director, Cliff Coleman, was one of our first A.D.s on the original show. I also go back a long ways with the director (Jeannot Szwarc). It was an eerie feeling — it was almost as if I had stepped back in time, and it was old home week. It was a lot of fun."

James Garner and Stuart Margolin in " A Blessing in Disguise", the
second in the new *Rockford Files* series.

James Garner as Jim Rockford with Renee O'Connor, who plays a movie
actress who hires Rockford for protection in "A Blessing in Disguise".

James Garner with Dionne Warwick in a 1978 *Rockford Files*.

From a 1979 *Rockford Files*, James Garner and Rita Moreno.

JAMES GARNER

in

THE ROCKFORD FILES:

I Still Love L.A.

A CBS Sunday Night Movie

Original Airdate: November 27, 1994

Written by: *Juanita Bartlett*
Directed by: *James Whitmore, Jr.*

Additional Cast: Joanna Cassidy (Halley "Kit" Kittredge), Joe Santos (Dennis Becker), Stuart Margolin (Angel Martin), Joseph Campanella (Mickey Ryder), Geoffrey Nauffts (Josh Lansing), Shannon Kenny (Dorie Lansing), Lawrence Pressman (Sidney Kornblum), Daniel Benzali (Paco), Sherry Hursey (Maddie), David Purdham (Dr. Izo), Hoke Howell (Ed Emmenthaler), Lesley Woods (Myrna Emmenthaler), Sam Scarber (Lloyd Sanders), Lori Alan (Karen Kupfer), James A. Watson Jr. (Pete McCool), Jack Garner (Captain McEnroe), Eddie Mekka (Gus), Michael Bailey Smith (Philip Warsche), Bob Minor (Duty Officer), Shirley Anthony (Sally), Eliana Alexander (Officer No. 1), Diana Tanaka (Kornblum's Secretary), Jean Bartel (Lila Lansing)

Jim, it's Benny. I know your sewer's backed up, but I can't get out there today. Maybe your buyers won't notice....

Synopsis. *As a favor to his ex-wife, attorney Halley "Kit" Kittredge, Rockford agrees to meet Josh and Dorie Lansing, the adult children of slain film star Lila Lansing. Josh claims that two masked assailants killed Lila and stole her car, but Rockford doesn't believe him (neither he nor Dorie seemed particularly distraught over their mother's death). After discovering a surveillance camera situated across the street from the Lansing estate, Rockford notifies the police — and is not entirely surprised to learn that the tape contains evidence incriminating the Lansing children. Josh and Dorie are arraigned on charges of first-degree murder. Eighteen months later, unbeknownst to Kit, the Lansings concoct a bizarre defense strategy — they claim their stepfather, baseball great Mickey Ryder, was a Satanist who sexually abused them with their mother's consent. Rockford, who'd never liked Josh to begin with, becomes so infuriated that he quits the case and decides to warn Ryder. The baseball star vehemently denies the charges — but, to Jim's surprise, he later confirms them in a televised press conference. However, two months later, Ryder tells Rockford that he was coerced into confessing "as a favor" to his attorney, Sidney Kornblum. Rockford and Kit soon find Ryder dead, an apparent suicide. The police believe Ryder killed himself out of shame, but Jim suspects that Kornblum, who has ties to Las Vegas mobster "Big Al" Manett, had his client murdered. Rockford endangers his own life in order to entrap Kornblum — and exonerate the good names of Mickey Ryder and Lila Lansing.*

JAMES GARNER

in

THE ROCKFORD FILES

A BLESSING IN DISGUISE

A CBS Sunday Night Movie
Original Airdate May 14, 1995

Executive Producers: *James Garner, Charles Floyd Johnson, Juanita Bartlett*
Written by: *Stephen J. Cannell*
Directed by: *Jeannot Szwarc*

Additional Cast: Stuart Margolin (Angel Martin), Joe Santos (Dennis Becker), Renee O'Connor (Laura Sue Dean), Richard Romanus (Vincent Penguinetti), Ahron Ipale (Branka Decosta), Reuven Bar-Yotam (Milovan D'Sant), Eric Lutes (Danny Barkley), Morton Downey Jr. (Himself), Robert Desiderio (Jerry Michaels), Stuart Fratkin (Jerry Jamison), Mark Davenport (Marty Martinson), Vince Melocchi (Kyle Wendell), Bari K. Willerford (Zachery "Zack" Irons), Joel McKinnon Miller (Brian "Mackie" MacDonald), Niles Allen Stewart (Stevie), Elsa Raven (Sarah Lanka), Christine Romeo (Sister Eve), Carl Ciarfalio (Brother Bob), Shane Sweet (Little "Zeke" Ezekial), Joey Hamilton (Man #1), Sparkle (Woman #1), Merciful Angels Choir (Themselves).

Jim, it's Paul. Hey, I've been waiting two months for that invitation, buddy. Are you gonna get that new sportschannel before the Rams leave L. A. ?

Synopsis. *Angel Martin's latest entrepreneurial scheme has transformed him into a televangelist. Rockford discovers that not only is "Reverend" Martin living the lifestyle of the rich and famous, he has also appropriated half of Jim's wardrobe. After confronting the "Reverend" at the Temple of Holy Light, Jim is unceremoniously ejected, landing in the middle of a church-supported demonstration which becomes nasty when the star of the ultra-low budget film Little Ezekial is set upon by the angry crowd. Jim rescues actress Laura Sue Dean, who reveals that she has been getting anonymous threats which she believes are linked to Angel's congregation. Rockford agrees to guard Laura Sue until the producers of her film can arrange for celebrity security. Meanwhile, ever in pursuit of fame and fortune, "Reverend" Angel Martin manages to parlay his film boycott scam into a near-death experience for Rockford and Laura Sue.*

Appendix

PRODUCTION CREDITS

1974-1980

JAMES GARNER
in
THE ROCKFORD FILES

Also Starring
Noah Beery as Joseph "Rocky" Rockford
Joe Santos as Dennis Becker
Gretchen Corbett as Beth Davenport
  (1974-1978)
and Stuart Margolin as Angel Martin

Co-Starring
Tom Atkins as Lieutenant Diel
  (1974-1976, 1977-1978)
James Luisi as Lieutenant Chapman
  (1976-1980)
Luis Delgado in various roles (1974-1976)
  and as Officer Billings (1976-1980)
Jack Garner in various roles (1974-1979)
  and as Captain McEnroe (1979-1980)

Executive Producer
Meta Rosenberg

Supervising Producers
Jo Swerling Jr. (1974-1975)
Stephen J. Cannell (1975-1980)
Juanita Bartlett (1979-1980)

Produced by
Stephen J. Cannell (1974-1975)
Chas. Floyd Johnson (1976-1980)
David Chase (1976-1980)

Created by
Roy Huggins and Stephen J. Cannell

Associate Producers
Chas. Floyd Johnson (1974-1976)
William F. Phillips (1974)
J. Rickley Dumm (1978-1979)
John David (1978-1980)

Creative Consultant/
  Executive Story Editor
Juanita Bartlett (1974-1979)

Musical Score
Mike Post and Pete Carpenter

Additional Music
Dick DeBenedictis and Artie Kane
  (1974-1975)

Musical Supervision
Hal Mooney (1974-1975)
Morrie McNaughton (1976-1980)

Directors of Photography
Lamar Boren (1974-1976)
Andrew Jackson (1976-1980)
Leonard J. South (1974)

Art Directors
Robert Crawley Sr.
Robert Luthardt (1974)

Set Decorators
Gary Moreno (1974-1975)
Robert L. Zilliox (1975-1980)
Ed Baer (1975)

Assistant Directors
Robert Jones (1974-1979)
Cliff Coleman (1974-1977, 1979-1980)
Dave Menteer (1976-1979)
Leonard R. Garner (1978-1979)
Jan Lloyd (1978-1979)
Pat Duffy (1978-1979)
Reuben Watt (1979-1980)
David Beanes (1979-1980)
Cal Naylor (1979-1980)
Robert J. Doherty (1979-1980)
Michael Kane (1979-1980)

Unit Production Managers
Les Berke (1974-1978)
Rowe Wallerstein (1976-1977)
Zane Radney (1978-1979)
Sam Freedle (1979-1980)
Bill Carroll (1979-1980)

Casting
Dodie McLean

Film Editors
George R. Rohrs
Buford F. Hayes (1974-1977)
Diane Adler (1976-1980)
Roderic Stephens (1977-1979)
Edward A. Biery (1974-1975)
Frederic Baratta (1974-1975)
John Dumas (1974-1975)
John Kaufman (1974-1975)
John Kaufman Jr. (1974-1975)
Robert Leeds (1975-1976)
I. Robert Levy (1975-1976)
Robert L. Kimball (1976-1977)
Lawrence J. Vallario (1976-1977)
Jerry Dronsky (1977-1978)

Sound Mixers
John Carter
John Kean (1974-1975)
Vic Carpenter (1974-1975)
Albert D. Cuesta (1974-1975)
Jack F. Lilly (1976-1977)

Sound Effects Editors
Walter Jenevein
Dave Schonleber (1976-1977)

Editorial Supervision
Richard Belding

Stunt Coordinator
Roydon Clark

Assistant to Mr. Garner
MaryAnn Rea

Costume Designer
Charles Waldo (1974-1978)
Kent Warner (1978-1980)

Make-Up Artists
Dick Blair
Jack Wilson (1974-1975)

Property Master
William Fannon

Main Title Design
Jack Cole

Color by Technicolor

Titles and Optical Effects
Universal Title

A Public Arts/Roy Huggins
Production in Association with
Cherokee Productions and
Universal — an MCA Company

PRODUCTION CREDITS
for first new *Rockford Files*

Executive Producers: James Garner, Charles Floyd Johnson, Juanita Bartlett

Supervising Producers: Stephen J. Cannell, David Chase

Produced by: Mark Horowitz, David L. Beanes

Created by: Roy Huggins and Stephen J. Cannell

Written by: Juanita Bartlett

Directed by: James Whitmore Jr.

Music by: Mike Post and Pete Carpenter

Film Editor: Pam Malouf-Cundy

Production Designer: Anthony Cowley

Director of Photography: Steve Yaconelli

Associate Producer: MaryAnn Rea

Unit Production Manage: David L. Beanes

Assistant Directors: Cliff Coleman, Les Burke, David L. D'Ovidio

Casting: Reuben Cannon & Associate David Giella, CSA

Costume Designer: April Ferry

Art Director: Sandy Getzler

Set Decorator: Robert L. Zilliox

Property Master: Bill Fannon

Makeup: Charlene Roberson

Hair Stylist: Don Sheldon

Stunt Coordinator: Roydon Clark

Special Effects Coordinator: Tom Love

Sound Mixer: Darin Knight

Gaffer: Thomas Barone

Key Grip: Ron Stafford

Location Manager: Karlene Gallegly

Transportation Coordinator: Steve Hellerstein

Script Supervisor: Suzanne Gundlach

Assistant to Executive Producer: Luis Delgado

Panaflex Camera and Lenses by: Panavision

Sound Editor: Ron Horwitz

Music Editor: Patty McGettighan

Post-Production Coordinator: Carrie Smith-Ludwig

Assistant Film Editor: Michael Carlich

Bibliography

Most of the information in this book was derived from personal interviews with the following: Juanita Bartlett, Howard Browne, Stephen J. Cannell, Gretchen Corbett, Luis Delgado, Jack Garner, James Garner, Roy Huggins, Charles Floyd Johnson, Frank Price, Jo Swerling, and Jack Wilson.

The items listed below were also of tremendous value:

Books

Brooks, Tim, *The Complete Directory to Prime Time TV Stars, 1946-Present*. New York: Ballantine Books, 1987.

Brooks, Tim and Earle Marsh, *The Complete Directory to Prime Time Network TV Shows, 1946-Present*. New York: Ballantine Books, 1988. Fourth edition. First published in 1979.

Broughton, Irv, *Producers on Producing: The Making of Film and Television*. Jefferson, N.C.: McFarland & Company, Inc., 1986.

Castleman, Harry, and Walter J. Podriziak, *Harry and Wally's Favorite TV Shows*. New York: Prentice Hall Press, 1989.

—*Watching TV: Four Decades of American Television*. New York: McGraw-Hill Book Company, 1982.

Christensen, Mark, and Cameron Stauth, *The Sweeps: Behind the Scenes in Network TV*, New York: William Morrow and Company, Inc., 1984.

Gianakos, Larry James, *Television Drama Series Programming: A Comprehensive Chronicle*, Vols. I-III, VI. Meutchen, NJ: The Scarecrow Press, Inc.

Levinson, Richard, and William Link, *Stay Tuned: An Inside Look at the Making of Prime Time Television*, New York: St. Martin's Press, 1981.

Marc, David, and Robert Thompson. *Prime Time, Prime Movers*. Boston: Little, Brown. 1992.

Martindale, David, *The Rockford Phile*. Las Vegas: Pioneer Books, Inc., 1991.

Meyers, Ric, *Murder on the Air*. New York: Mysterious Press, 1989.

McNeil, Alex, *Total Television*. New York: Penguin Books, 1991. Third edition. First published in 1980.

Parish, James Robert and Vincent Terrace, *The Complete Actors' Television Credits, 1948-1988, Volume I: Actors*. Metuchen: The Scarecrow Press, Inc. 1989. Second edition.

Stempel, Tom, *Storytellers to the Nation: A History of American Television Writing*. New York: Continuum Publishing Company, 1992.

Strait, Raymond, *James Garner: A Biography*. New York: St. Martin's Press, 1985.

Terrace, Vincent, *Encyclopedia of Television: Series, Pilots and Specials. Volumes I and III*. New York: New York Zoetrope, 1986.

Variety Television Reviews, 1923-1988, in 15 volumes. New York: Garland Publishing Company, 1988.

Magazine and Newspaper Articles

Amory, Cleveland, "Review: *The Rockford Files*," *TV Guide*, December 21, 1974.

"Annals of Law: Taking the Fifth," *The New Yorker*, April 1976.

Beck, Marilyn, "James Garner Never Fails to Thank His Lucky Star," Special Features/New York Times Syndicate, August 24, 1974.

Benson, Ray, "Garner in *Rockford* is First Non-Western," *Columbia Record*, March 23, 1974.

Boyer, Peter J., "Rockford Opens His Last File," Associated Press, January 10, 1980.

Carman, John, "James Garner to Reprise *Rockford*," *San Francisco Chronicle*, July 25, 1994.

Deeb, Gary, "Can Jim Work *Maverick* Magic Again?" *Dallas Times-Herald*, January 1980.

Dyer, Bob, "Man Behind the Badge Still Roams the Tube Next Season," *Phoenix Gazette*, July 27, 1974.

Foster, Bob, "Jim Garner to Try TV Series Again," *San Mateo Times*, August 1, 1974.

Hano, Arnold, "The Incredible Shrinking Actor," *TV Guide*, February 1, 1975.

Hawkes, Ellen, "Gentle Heart, Tough Guy," *Parade*, July 12, 1992.

King, Susan, "Reactivating *Rockford*: James Garner Gets Back in the P.I. Business with Movies for CBS," *Los Angeles Times*, November 27, 1994.

Lewis, Dan, "Garner Recalls *Maverick* Fondly," *San Diego Union*, November 10, 1974.

Linderman, Lawrence, "James Garner: A Candid Conversation with the Easygoing Star about *Maverick*, *Rockford*, Funny Commercials, His Bizarre Childhood, and Corruption in Hollywood," *Playboy*, March 1981.

Moss, Morton, "Noah Beery Jr.: Long Career Recipe," *Los Angeles Herald-Examiner*," August 20, 1974.

"New Housewife Blues, The," *Time*, March 14, 1977.

O'Flaherty, Terence, "Oh, My Aching Back," *San Francisco Chronicle*, September 16, 1974.

Pond, Steve, "The Garner Files: Jim Garner's Back, with Plenty to Say About *Rockford* and the Ups and Downs of Life," *TV Guide*, November 26, 1994.

Prelutsky, Burt, "Q. What Strange Twists of Fortune Brought Joe Santos from Construction Work to His Role in *The Rockford Files*? A. He Failed at Everything Else," *TV Guide*, August 26, 1977.

Raddatz, Leslie, "Old Pidge," *TV Guide*, March 6, 1976.

Roth, Arnold, "A *Rockford Files* Sketchbook," *TV Guide*, March 5, 1977.

Ryan, Barbara Haddad, "James Garner to Try Again in *The Rockford Files*," *Denver Post*, June 26, 1974.

Scholl, Jaye, "The *Rockford* File; or, James Garner Learns Accounting the Hollywood Style," *Barron's*, February 6, 1989.

——"No *Rockford* Trials: MCA Unit Settles with James Garner," *Barron's*, April 3, 1989.

Swertlow, Frank, "As We See It: Garner Expected to File Suit Against Universal," *TV Guide*, January 30, 1982.

——"As We See It: Garner Sues to Collect *Rockford* Money," *TV Guide*, July 23, 1983.

Thomas, Bob, "James Garner: Alive and Well," Associated Press, November 14, 1974.

Torgerson, Ellen, "James Garner Believes in Good Coffee — and a Mean Punch," *TV Guide*, June 2, 1979.

Utterback, Betty, "Meta Rosenberg: How This Female TV Producer Got to the Top," *Rochester Democrat-Chronicle*, September 24, 1974.

Vallely, Jean, "The James Garner Files," *Esquire*, July 3-19, 1979.

Voorhees, John, "NBC Betting on Garner for *Files*," *Seattle Times*, August 30, 1974.

Walker, Wendy Heinz, "James Garner: Getting to the Heart of the Matter," *Vim & Vigor*, Summer 1992.

Weinstein, Steve, "James Garner: A Weight Off His Broad Shoulders," *Los Angeles Times*, April 3, 1989.

Witbeck, Charles, "Jim Garner's New Series," King Features Syndicate, August 14, 1974.

Zuanich, Barbra, "Joseph Cotten: Limitations Led to Stardom," *Los Angeles Herald-Examiner*, August 14, 1974.

Other Sources

"*Jim Rockford, Private Investigator*: Episode Titles and Numbers, Stars and Guest Stars, Log Lines for TV Listings, Cast and Credits." Program kit distributed by MCA-TV, 1979.

James Garner v. Universal City Studios, Inc., Los Angeles County Superior Court No. C-459-716. First Amended Complaint for Damages, filed October 11, 1983. (Action later consolidated with *Universal City Studios, Inc. v. James Garner*, Los Angeles County Superior Court No. C-310-140, originally filed January 1980.)

Roy Huggins v. Universal City Studios, Inc., Los Angeles County Superior Court No. BC007038. Complaint for Damages, filed July 31, 1990.

NOTE: *All other documents pertaining to the above litigations cited in this text were obtained via the Los Angeles County Archives Center.*

Memoranda and other documents pertaining to the creation of *The Rockford Files* cited herein are from the personal files of Roy Huggins.

Television programs cited herein are from the personal collection of the author.

Ed Robertson

About the Author

Ed Robertson was born and raised in San Francisco, and earned his B.A. degree in English and Drama at Saint Mary's College of California. He is the author of two other television histories—*The Fugitive Recaptured* (1993) and *Maverick: Legend of the West* (1994). Ed lives and writes in San Francisco.